T0268012

What's the Worst That Could Happen?

What's the Worst
That Could Happen?

Existential Risk and Extreme Politics

Andrew Leigh

The MIT Press

Cambridge, Massachusetts | London, England

The MIT Press would like to thank the anonymous peer reviewers who provided comments on drafts of this book. The generous work of academic experts is essential for establishing the authority and quality of our publications. We acknowledge with gratitude the contributions of these otherwise uncredited readers.

This book was set in Stone Serif and Stone Sans by Jen Jackowitz. Printed and bound in the United States of America.

Library of Congress Cataloging-in-Publication Data

Names: Leigh, Andrew, 1972- author.
Title: What's the worst that could happen? : existential risk and extreme
    politics / Andrew Leigh.
Description: Cambridge, Massachusetts : The MIT Press, 2021. | Includes
    bibliographical references and index. | Summary: "An analysis of the ways in
    which populist politics place our long-term well-being at risk, exploring pan-
    demics, climate change, nuclear war and other issues"-- Provided by publisher.
Identifiers: LCCN 2021000480 | ISBN 9780262046077 (hardcover)
Subjects: LCSH: Populism. | Radicalism. | Democracy. | Existentialism.
Classification: LCC JC423 .L455 2021 | DDC 320.56/62--dc23
LC record available at https://lccn.loc.gov/2021000480

10 9 8 7 6 5 4 3 2 1

Contents

1 Why the Future Matters   1

2 Bad Bugs   17

3 A Second Venus   35

4 First We Got the Bomb   57

5 The Last Invention   73

6 What Are the Odds?   89

7 The Populist Risk   103

8 The Death of Democracy   129

9 Fixing Politics   145

10 The End   157

Acknowledgments   169

Notes   171

Index   211

1
Why the Future Matters

Imagine a world in which each person's days are filled with beauty, meaning, and commitment—doing deep work, spending plenty of time with friends and family, savoring delicious food, and enjoying exotic holidays. Suppose that everyone can live in perfect health for more than a century. In this world, people are secure in their neighborhoods, without the need to fear for their property or safety.

Now imagine that humanity uses this opportunity to expand our knowledge and wisdom—exploring the frontiers of science and the humanities. Suppose we reshaped careers so that everyone could experience a sense of flow in their job and take a break from work when they wished. Imagine that we solve the problem of commuting—effectively stretching the day so that people can enjoy more leisure, work, or sleep. Think how much better the world would be if we could make a lasting impact on mental illness through better treatments for depression, anxiety, and addiction. Suppose that cancer has been cured, obesity has a simple treatment, and even the common cold has been vanquished.

Think how much more beautiful we could make the spaces around us. To live in an apartment designed by Antoni Gaudí, stroll in a park designed by Martha Schwartz, or enjoy the sculptures of Teresita Fernández is a pleasure reserved for a fortunate few in today's world. But imagine how much joy it would bring us to live in a world where all our living spaces were conceived by extraordinary designers and constructed by master craftspeople.

Such a world may seem closer to the heavenly paradise offered by the world's great religions than to our lives on earth. Attaining it is a pipe dream for our generation. Indeed, there is little chance we could attain it in the twenty-first or even twenty-second century. Yet this future is *probable* if humans can survive for another thousand years. And it is *almost certain* if humans can survive for ten thousand years. After all, the past ten thousand years has seen humans progress from foraging nomads to digitally connected urbanites, and the pace of change is accelerating, with each century more innovative than the previous one.[1]

But we have to get there first.

In 1947, a group of concerned scientists created the "Doomsday Clock"—symbolizing how close humans are to Armageddon. Initially, the clock was arbitrarily set at seven minutes to midnight.[2] Two years later, when the Soviet Union tested its first nuclear bomb, the clock was moved to three minutes to midnight. With the signing of the partial atomic test ban treaty in 1963, it was moved back to twelve minutes to midnight. Over the years, the Doomsday Clock has been moved forward and backward twenty-four times. In January 2020, it was moved to one minute and twenty seconds to midnight. These scientists estimate that the world is closer to destruction now than at any other time.

The catastrophic risks that threaten our species have been the focus of so many movies that you could run a disaster film festival. We've seen movies featuring natural pandemics (*Outbreak*, *Carriers*, and *Contagion*), bioterrorism (*12 Monkeys*, *V for Vendetta*, and *28 Days Later*), asteroid strikes (*Deep Impact*, *Armageddon*, and *Judgment Day*), nuclear war (*Dr. Strangelove*, *On the Beach*, and *The Day After*), artificial intelligence (*Avengers: The Age of Ultron*, *The Matrix*, and *Terminator*), and climate change (*Waterworld*, *Mad Max: Fury Road*, and *Blade Runner 2049*). These dangers have had us on the edge of our movie seats, but they haven't gotten most people off the couch to act. You're more likely to get robbed if you leave your wallet on a park bench than if you leave your home unlocked. But it doesn't follow that an unattended wallet is a bigger risk than an unlocked house. Losing everything of value in your house is unlikely to occur, but horribly upsetting if it does.

The same psychological mistake applies to public policy. Policy makers sweat the details of programs to regulate stock markets or build stadiums. But we rarely devote as much attention to reducing long-term risks. Policy deals largely in the world of immediate certainties, not distant hazards.

How likely is it that humanity could end? Experts working on catastrophic risk have estimated the chances of disaster for a wide range of the hazards that our species faces. Adding up the threats, philosopher Toby Ord estimates the odds that humanity could become extinct over the next century at one in six, with an out-of-control superintelligence, bioterrorism, and totalitarianism among the largest risks. He argues that most of the risks have arisen because technology has advanced more rapidly than safeguards to keep it in check. To encapsulate the situation facing humanity, Ord titled his book *The Precipice*.

A one in six chance of going the way of dodos and dinosaurs effectively means we are playing a game of Russian roulette with humanity's future. Six chambers. One bullet. Even the most foolhardy soldier usually finds an excuse not to play Russian roulette. And that's when just their own life is at stake. In considering extinction risk, we're contemplating not one fatality but the death of billions or possibly trillions of people—not to mention countless animals.

It can seem impossible to imagine our species becoming extinct due to a catastrophe such as nuclear war, asteroids, or a pandemic. But in reality, the danger surpasses plenty of perils we already worry about. One way to put catastrophic risk into perspective is to compare it with more familiar risks. If extinction risk poses a one in six risk to our species over the next century, then it means that it is far more hazardous than many everyday risks. Specifically, it suggests that the typical US resident is fifteen times more likely to die from a catastrophic risk—such as nuclear war or bioterrorism—than in car crash.[3]

Extinction risk outstrips other dangers too. Ask people about their greatest fears, and you'll get answers like "street violence," "snakes," "heights," and "terrorism."[4] But in reality, these are much less hazardous than catastrophic risks. People in the United States are 31 times more likely to die from a catastrophic risk than from homicide. Catastrophic risk is 3,519 times likelier to kill than falls from a height, and 6,194 times more likely to kill than venomous plants and animals. If you have ever worried about any of these threats, you should be more fearful about catastrophic risk. Extinction risks aren't just more dangerous than any of them; they are more hazardous than all of them put together. Catastrophic risk poses a greater danger to the life of the typical US resident than car accidents, murder, drowning, high falls, electrocution, and rattlesnakes put together.

A one in six risk is just the danger in a single century. Suppose that the risk of extinction remains at one in six for each century. That means there's a five in six chance humanity makes it to the end of the twenty-first century, but less than an even chance we survive to the end of the twenty-fourth century. The odds that we survive all the way to the year 3000 are just one in six. In other words, if we continue playing Russian roulette once a century, it's probable that we blow our brains out before the millennium is halfway through, and there's only a small chance that we make it to the end of the millennium.

Part of the reason humans undervalue the future is that it's hard to get our heads around the idea that our genetic code could live on for millions of years. At present, the best estimates are that our species, Homo sapiens, evolved around three hundred thousand years ago.[5] That means we have existed for about ten thousand generations. But we have another one billion years before the increasing heat of our sun brings most plant life to an end.[6] That's plenty of time to figure out how to become an interstellar species and move to a more suitable solar system. Humans could live to enjoy another thirty million generations on earth.

Thinking about the mind-boggling scale of these numbers, I'm reminded of the Total Perspective Vortex machine, created by Douglas Adams in *The Restaurant at the End of the Universe*. Anyone brave enough to enter sees a scale model of the entire universe, with an arrow indicating their current position. As a result, their brain explodes. As Adams reflects, the machine proves that "if life is going to exist in a universe of this size, then the one thing it cannot afford to have is a sense of proportion."

Still, let's try. Imagine your ancestors a hundred generations ago. They are your great-grandparents. These people lived around 1000 BCE, at the start of the Iron Age. They might have been part of Homeric

Greece, ancient Egypt, Vedic age India, the preclassic Maya, or Zhou Dynasty China.

Contemplate for a moment about what the hundred generations between our Iron Age ancestors and today have achieved. They built the Taj Mahal and Sistine Chapel, the Angkor Wat and Empire State Building. Thanks to them, we can relish the poetry of Maya Angelou, novels of Leo Tolstoy, and music of Ludwig van Beethoven. An abundance of inventions has delivered us delicious food, homes that are comfortable year-round, and technology that provides online access to a bottomless well of entertainment. If time machines existed, we might pop in to visit our great[100] grandparents, but few would volunteer to stay in the Iron Age.

Yet humanity is really just getting started. If things go well, it's ten thousand generations down, thirty million to go. Imagine what those future generations could do, and how much time they have to enjoy. Here's one way to think about what it means to have thirty million generations ahead. Suppose humanity's potential time on the planet was shrunk down to a single eighty-year life span. In that event, we would now be a newborn baby—just nine days old. Homo sapiens is a mere 0.03 percent through all we could experience on earth.

We won't meet most of those who follow us on the planet, but we should cherish future generations all the same. If you value humanity's past achievements—the Aztec and Roman civilizations, art of the Renaissance, and breakthroughs of the Industrial Revolution— then the generations to come are just as worthy. This is what political philosopher Edmund Burke meant when he described society as "a partnership not only between those who are living, but between those who are living, those who are dead, and those who are to be born."[7] To appreciate the past is akin to admiring the achievements of distant places. Like geography, history helps us better understand the way of the world.

Politicians like me like to speak fondly about looking after "our children and our grandchildren." But it usually stops after a generation or two. Policy pays little heed to the many generations that will follow. For my own part, it took a coronavirus-induced shutdown to have the time to spend reflecting deeply about the long term. This book had been rattling around in my head for years, but it was only when all my meetings, events, and travel were canceled that I had the time to write it. Pandemics are one of the threats to humanity that I'll discuss in this book, but in this instance, it provided a chance to reflect on the long term.

It's tempting to ignore the distant future. It's easier to love the grandchildren whom we hug than the great-great-great-grandchildren whom we'll never get to smile on. But that doesn't make those far-flung generations any less important. Via my wife, our children can trace their lineage to Benjamin Franklin, but I'm more excited about the potential achievements of the generations yet to be born.

For companies and governments, a major impediment to long-term thinking is the idea of discounting the future. When investing money, this is a reasonable approach. A dollar in a decade's time is less valuable than a dollar today for the simple reason that a dollar today could be invested and earn a real return. Share markets have good and bad years, but based on returns from the past 120 years, someone who put $1,000 into the US stock market for an average year could expect it to be worth $1,065 after twelve months (accounting for dividends and inflation).[8] Approximating these returns, when governments contemplate making investments, they often apply a discount rate of around 5 percent, while companies use rates that are higher still.[9]

When it comes to growing your greenbacks, this makes perfect sense. If Kanesha offered you $1,000 today, and Jane offered you

$1,000 in a year's time, most of us would think that Kanesha was making the more generous offer. Kanesha's cash can be put to productive use and would be worth more than Jane's when the year is out.

But what if we're talking about Kanesha and Jane themselves? Suppose Kanesha is alive today, and Jane is yet to be born. When discounting is applied to lives, it suggests that Kanesha's life today is worth twice as much as Jane's life in fifteen years' time. It implies that Kanesha today is worth 132 times as much as Jane in a century's time. So if we're spending money to keep them safe, a 5 percent discount rate indicates that we should spend more than a hundred times as much to protect Kanesha today than to protect Jane in a century's time.

The further we stretch the time period, the more ridiculous the results become. Discounting at a rate of 5 percent implies that Christopher Columbus is worth more than all eight billion people on the planet today.[10] Naturally, it also implies that your life is worth more than eight billion lives in five hundred years' time. Even if you value the hug of a loved one over the unseen successes of next century's generations, is it fair to ruthlessly dismiss the distant future? Discounting is the enemy of the long term.

As philosopher Will MacAskill points out, there is something morally repugnant about concluding that the happiness of those who will be alive in the 2100s is inconsequential simply because they live in the future. MacAskill coined the term "presentism" to refer to prejudice against people who are yet unborn.[11] Just like racism, sexism, or other forms of bigotry, he argues that mistreating those who live a long way in the future is unfair. To discriminate in favor of Kanesha against unborn Jane is a form of presentism. If you traveled back in time to the 1500s and met someone who claimed that they were worth more than everyone alive in the 2000s, you'd rightly regard them as an egomaniac. Isn't it equally narcissistic to ignore the happiness of people in the 2500s?

Some have contended that we should favor the living over the unborn for the same reason that philanthropy favors the downtrodden over the wealthy. If incomes rise over time, the argument goes, then asking today's citizens to help those in the future is like taking from the poor to give to the rich.[12] But this reasoning ignores the fact that we are talking about the *survival* of future generations. Theoretical riches won't do them any good if they are practically dead—or if planetary apocalypse snuffs out their chance to be born. Similarly, it misses the possibility that future pandemics, wars, or climate disasters could make coming generations significantly poorer.[13]

Insights from behavioral science help explain why humans aren't good at understanding extinction risk.[14] Our thinking about dangers is skewed by an "availability bias": a tendency to focus on familiar risks. Like the traders who failed to forecast the collapse of the securitized housing debt market, we are lousy at judging the probability of rare but catastrophic events. Most important, our instincts fail us as the magnitudes grow larger. In research titled "The More Who Die, the Less We Care," psychologists Paul Slovic and Daniel Västfjäll argue that we become numb to suffering as the body count grows.[15] Humans' compassionate instincts are aroused by stories, not statistics. Indeed, one study found that people were more likely to donate to help a single victim than they were to assist eight victims. This may help explain why the international community has been so slow to respond to genocide, including recent incidents in Rwanda, Darfur, and Myanmar. As artificial intelligence researcher Eliezer Yudkowsky notes, human neurotransmitters are unable to feel sorrow that is thousands of times stronger than a single funeral.[16] The problem is starker still when it comes to extinction risk. Our emotional brains cannot multiply by billions.

Add to this a media cycle that has become a media cyclone, in which stories explode in a matter of minutes, and "outrage porn" seems to drive the news choices of many outlets. In the 2016 US election, researchers found that for every piece of professional news shared on Twitter, there was one piece of "junk news."[17] Conflict fueled by social media keeps us in a primal state of rage and retaliation. And this isn't the only force that makes politics myopic. Campaign contributions tend to come from donors who have an immediate interest in a "today" issue rather than from people aiming to solve long-term problems. This kind of "instant noodle" politics prioritizes quick results and sidelines fundamental challenges.

In this environment, a special style of politics has thrived: populism. The term "populist" gets thrown around a lot—typically as an insult—so it's worth taking a moment to define it precisely.[18]

Populists see politics as a conflict between crooked elites and the pure mass of people. Many candidates trying to defeat an incumbent will criticize "insiders," but populists make a stronger attack on elites, claiming that they are dishonest or corrupt. Populists then claim that they—and only they—represent the "real people." Populists combine a fierce critique of elites and personal appeal to the "silent majority."

The political strategy of populists involves critiquing intellectuals, institutions, and internationalism. The political style of populists tends to be fierce. They do not strive for unity and calm consensus. Populists share with revolutionaries a desire for sudden and dramatic change. They have little respect for experts and the systems of government. Populists' priorities tend to be immediate issues such as crime, migration, jobs, and taxes. Consequently, the electoral success of populists has served to sideline work on long-term dangers such as climate change and nuclear war.

Donald Trump may have lost his presidential reelection bid, but he has transformed the Republican Party, which has jettisoned its longstanding commitment to free trade, immigration, and global alliances. Many moderate Republicans, who might have served comfortably under Ronald Reagan or George H. W. Bush, have quit the party or been defeated by Trump-supporting populists.

The Republican Party, which holds nearly half the seats in Congress and controls a majority of state legislatures, has embraced populism to a degree that was unimaginable when it was led by George W. Bush, John McCain, or Mitt Romney. After four years under President Trump, the Republican Party is now more cynical and isolationist, focused on immediate grievances rather than long-term challenges.

Yet while the strength of populism threatened to sideline issues of catastrophic risk, coronavirus did the opposite. The worst pandemic in a century led to the most severe economic crisis since the Great Depression. Churches and concert halls fell silent. International travel collapsed. The Summer Olympics were postponed. Stocks plunged, and for a brief moment, the price of a barrel of oil went negative. Globally, millions lost their jobs, and millions more faced famine.

COVID-19 never threatened to extinguish humanity, but it highlighted our vulnerability to infectious diseases. More than at any time in living memory, people focused on the dangers of pandemics. The popularity of Geraldine Brooks's *Year of Wonders*, Stephen King's *The Stand*, Emily St. John Mandel's *Station Eleven*, and Albert Camus's *The Plague* vividly illustrates the way in which fear of pandemics has become more acute.

We know that disasters can remake society. The black death helped usher in the Renaissance.[19] The Great Depression made a generation of investors more risk averse.[20] World War II spawned the United Nations and formed the modern welfare state. In autocracies, droughts and floods can topple dictators.[21]

Coronavirus is reshaping the world in numerous ways.[22] Handwashing is in. Cheek kissing is out. The rise of big cities is slowing as people consider the downsides of density. Firms that automated their production systems to deal with physical distancing requirements and stay-at-home orders are discovering that they can get by permanently with fewer staff. More teleworking and less business travel is leading to a drop in demand for receptionists, bus drivers, office cleaners, and security guards. When it comes to our use of technology, coronavirus suddenly accelerated the world to 2030. When it comes to globalization, the pandemic took us back to 2010.

But it's still an open question as to how COVID-19 will affect humanity's ability to think about the long term. Most of the examples I've listed are instances in which crises affected societies organically: the shock came, and it changed our behavior. But accentuating the long term requires taking risk more seriously and placing greater emphasis on saving our species. Linebackers are swift to respond when an offensive player suddenly takes a step to the right. But it takes longer to recognize that a team's offensive plays are skewed to the right and modify the defensive formation accordingly.

Like a football team that adapts its tactics, this book argues that we should lengthen our thinking. At minimal cost, society can massively reduce the odds of catastrophe. By ensuring that the big threats get the attention and resources they need, we can safeguard the future of our species. As insurance policies go, this one is a bargain.

In the chapters that follow, I'll outline the biggest risks facing humanity. I'll begin in chapter 2 with pandemics, such as the possibility that the next virus might combine the infectiousness of COVID-19 with the deadliness of Ebola. What can we do to shut down exotic animal markets, speed up vaccine development, and create surge capacity in hospitals? I'll then delve into bioterrorism, and the danger of extremists developing their own versions of smallpox or the bubonic plague. How difficult is it for them to create these devilish diseases, and what can we do to prevent it?

In chapter 3, I'll then explore climate change—perhaps the intergenerational issue that has received the most public attention in recent years. While much of the modeling looks at how global warming could be bad, my focus is on the chances that it's catastrophic. This isn't about climate change shortening the ski season; it's about the possibility of temperatures rising by 18°F (10°C), rendering large sections of the planet uninhabitable. What does the risk of cataclysmic climate change mean for energy policy?

Next, I'll turn to nukes. As a child in the 1980s, I vividly remember watching *The Day After*. My classmates and I agreed that a nuclear war was inevitable. When the Cold War ended, the world seemed safer, but in the three decades since, the threat from new nuclear powers has made the problem less predictable. As I discuss in chapter 4, what we used to call an arms race now looks more like a bar fight, with hazards coming from unexpected directions, including terrorist groups. Yet just as there are practical ways to avoid pub brawls (don't drink past midnight, avoid the stairs, look out for the glass), so too are there sensible strategies that can reduce the odds of nuclear catastrophe (adopt a "no first use" policy, reduce the stockpiles, control loose nukes).

A superintelligence has been dubbed the "last invention" we'll ever make. An artificial intelligence machine whose abilities exceed our own could turbocharge productivity and living standards. But it could also spell disaster. If we program our artificial intelligence to maximize human happiness, it could fulfill our wishes literally by immobilizing everyone and attaching electrodes to the pleasure centers of our brains. As chapter 5 notes, what makes artificial intelligence different from every other risky technology is its runaway potential. Once a superintelligence can improve itself, it is unstoppable. So we need to build the guardrails before the highway.

What are the odds? In chapter 6, I complete the discussion of catastrophic danger by examining less risky risks, including asteroids and supervolcanoes. I also consider the prospect of "unknown unknowns." For example, prior to the first atomic bomb test, some scientists thought there was a chance it could set the atmosphere on fire, destroying the planet. When the Large Hadron Collider was being built, critics warned that the particle collisions inside it could create micro black holes. Although neither situation eventuated, they raise the question of what other doomsday scenarios could be lurking around the corner. How should the prospect of these unexpected risks change our approach to cutting-edge science? Drawing together these dangers with the major hazards, I report the likely probability of each, benchmarking existential risks such as nuclear war and pandemics against individual risks such as being struck by lightning or dying on the battlefield.

Ultimately, tackling existential risks is a political problem. Private citizens can achieve many things, but preventing nuclear war, averting bioterrorism, and curbing greenhouse emissions are fundamentally problems of government. Governments control the military, levy taxes, and provide public goods. So the values of those who run the country will determine how much of a priority the nation places on averting catastrophe.

That's why the rise of populists is crucial to humanity's long-term survival. In chapter 7, I discuss the factors that have led to the electoral success of populists during recent decades, and why populists tend to be uninterested in dealing with long-term threats. Populists' focus on the short term means that—like a driver distracted by a back seat squabble—we're in danger of missing the threats that could kill us. I'll explore why populists around the world struggled to respond to COVID-19, and what this says about the dangers that populism poses to our species. Most critics of populism have concentrated on the present day. They're missing the bigger picture. Populists are primarily endangering the unborn.

Bad politics doesn't just exacerbate other dangers; it represents a risk factor in itself through the possibility of a totalitarian turn—in which democracy is replaced by an enduring autocracy. The road to democracy is not a one-way street. Over the centuries, dozens of countries have backslid from democracy into autocracy—abandoning the institutions of fair elections, protection for minorities, and free expression. Such an outcome could be deadly for dissenters and miserable for the multitudes. Chapter 8 explores why democracy dies and identifies the signs that institutions are being undermined. Chapter 9 suggests how we might strengthen democracies to allow citizens to have a greater say, and lower the chances of the few taking over from the many. Chapter 10 concludes the book.

When COVID-19 hit, many rushed out to buy life insurance.[23] In our personal lives, we know that spending a small amount on insurance can guard against financial ruin. Societies can take a similar approach: implementing modest measures today to safeguard the immense future of our species. For each of the existential risks we face, there are sensible approaches that could curtail the dangers. For all the risks we face, a better politics will lead to a safer world.

Because of its focus on the urgent over the important, populist politics should perhaps bear the label, "Warning: populism can harm your children." But what is the alternative? In the conclusion, I argue that the answer lies in the ancient philosophy of stoicism. A stoic approach to politics isn't about favoring one side of the ideological fence over another. Instead, it's about the temperament of good political leadership. Stoicism emphasizes that character matters and holds that virtue is the only good. Decisions are based on empirical evidence, not emotion. Anger has no place in effective leadership. Strength comes from civility, courage, and endurance. Stoics make a sharp distinction between the things they can change and those they cannot.

Stoics are cosmopolitan, not xenophobic. As philosopher Martha Nussbaum points out, this can lead to a politics based on "the humanity that we share rather than the marks of local origin, status, class, and gender that divide us."[24] Cosmopolitans still cherish their own country. As writer George Orwell put it, there's a difference between thinking that your nation is superior and being devoted to your country and its traditions.[25] A philosophy of national superiority can be inspired by hate. Devotion to national traditions starts with love.

In the traditions of Cicero, Adam Smith, and Nelson Mandela, the cosmopolitan approach focuses on the commonalities between people and shared challenges humanity confronts. I turn now to those challenges, beginning with the most microscopic of all: diseases.

2
Bad Bugs

Clade X was the product of an extremist environmental movement dubbed "A Brighter Dawn," whose goal was to dramatically reduce the world's population. Eventually, a split occurred within the movement. A terrorist group of about thirty members, many with bioscience training, decided to take direct action to reduce the world's population to preindustrial levels. Masquerading as a biotechnology start-up, the group established a laboratory outside the Swiss city of Zurich and altered the Nipah virus to create Clade X, a virus that spread like influenza and killed one-tenth of those who contracted it. Self-sacrificing volunteers from A Brighter Dawn traveled around the world and used aerosolizers to disperse the virus in crowded public places. Within a year, 150 million people worldwide had been killed, including 15 million in the United States.

As you may have guessed, Clade X wasn't real. The scenario was a one-day pandemic preparedness exercise conducted in 2018 by the Johns Hopkins Center for Health Security. In total, the center has conducted four "germ games," two of which have had an eerie prescience. In June 2001, Hopkins ran the Dark Winter scenario, simulating a bioterrorist attack in which residents of Oklahoma City were deliberately infected with smallpox, which quickly spread across the country. Just a few months after the simulated attack took place, a real bioterrorist attack occurred: envelopes containing anthrax were mailed to media outlets and politicians' offices, killing five people.

In October 2019, the Hopkins center ran Event 201, simulating an outbreak of a novel coronavirus transmitted from bats to pigs to people. Originating in Brazil, the fictional CAPS virus went on to kill sixty-five million people. Within two months, the not-at-all-fictional COVID-19 virus made its way from bats to humans—perhaps via civets or pangolins—and swept from Wuhan, China, to every other country in the world.

Indeed, the timing of Event 201 was so close to the COVID-19 outbreak that some people found it hard to believe that Event 201 was a coincidence. The fact that the Bill and Melinda Gates Foundation had partly funded the exercise helped fuel the conspiracy that Bill Gates had deliberately engineered COVID-19.[1] There is no evidence for this, nor for other coronavirus conspiracy theories, such as the claim that the virus was developed by the Chinese in the Wuhan Institute of Virology or deliberately released by the US Army at the Military World Games, held in Wuhan in October 2019.

Germs have taken a brutal toll on humanity. In 1347, the black death swept across Europe. Giovanni Boccaccio wrote about its impact on the Italian city of Florence, where

> the plague began to show its sorrowful effects in an extraordinary manner . . . by means of swellings either in the groin or under the armpits, some of which grew to the size of an ordinary apple and others to the size of an egg. . . . Neither a doctor's advice nor the strength of medicine could do anything to cure this illness . . . and almost all died after the third day. . . . This pestilence was so powerful that it was transmitted to the healthy by contact with the sick, the way a fire close to dry or oily things will set them aflame. And the evil of the plague went even further: not only did talking to or being around the sick bring infection and a common death, but also touching the clothes of the sick or anything touched or used

by them seemed to communicate this very disease to the person involved. . . . The city was full of corpses.[2]

Spread by rat-borne fleas, the black death killed three-quarters of Florence's population, and more than half the population of Europe. In just five years, from 1346 to 1351, Europe's population fell from eighty to thirty million people.[3]

An even higher death rate was visited on Native Americans after the arrival of Columbus in 1492. In the century after Europeans arrival in the Americas, measles, smallpox, cholera, influenza, and other diseases killed at least four-fifths of Native Americans.[4] In some cases, entire communities were wiped out by the "Columbian Exchange." From 1707 to 1709, smallpox swept through Iceland, killing one-quarter of the population.[5] At the end of that century, English settlers arrived in Australia, bringing the same cocktail of diseases with which Europeans had infected Native Americans, and reduced the Indigenous population on that continent by at least four-fifths as well.[6]

Diseases have been called "our deadliest enemy," often posing a greater danger than combat. A century ago, the 1918 influenza pandemic infected one-third of the world's population, killing one in fifty people.[7] Twice as many people died from that pandemic as were slaughtered in combat in World War I. Over the full twentieth century, infectious diseases—what some scientists dubbed the "oldie moldies"—killed twenty times as many US citizens as wars.[8]

Yet the twentieth century also marked a turning point in the war against disease. In 1900, infectious diseases were the leading killers in the United States, with pneumonia, influenza, tuberculosis, and gastrointestinal infections ranking as the top causes of death.[9] By the start of the twenty-first century, following a hundred years of advances in vaccines, antibiotics, and sanitation, infectious diseases were not among the top five causes of death in the United States. Only in the poorest nations were people more likely to die from infectious disease than anything else. From 1970 to 2016, worldwide mortality from infectious diseases dropped from fifteen million (35 percent of all deaths) to eight million (15 percent of all deaths).[10] Consequently, people began to think of public health less as a matter of collective action, and more as a function of personal decisions such as diet and exercise.

Then, at the end of 2019, a new infectious disease threw the world into chaos. COVID-19 is a coronavirus—a specific kind of RNA virus that has proven especially virulent. SARS and MERS are forms of coronaviruses. Many coronaviruses are mild. When you catch a cold, there's about a one in six chance it's a coronavirus (the rest of our colds are rhinoviruses, which are also RNA viruses, but lacking some of the features of coronaviruses such as a viral envelope). Designing a vaccine against a coronavirus is tricky. Coronaviruses infect the upper respiratory tract, an area that we think of as being inside our body, but that our immune system regards as almost external. As one expert remarked, "It's a bit like trying to get a vaccine to kill a virus on the surface of your skin."[11]

COVID-19 is also highly infectious. Doctors measure disease transmission by calculating the reproduction ratio, or R_0. This measures how many people each patient can be expected to infect. If the R_0 is above one, then the disease will spread. If it is below one, the disease will die out because it cannot infect enough people. Seasonal flu has an R_0 of one to two, meaning that each person who gets it infects one or two others. Common colds have an R_0 of two to three. Smallpox has an R_0 of five to seven.[12] Without physical distancing, COVID-19 has an R_0 of between two and six, meaning that each person can be expected to infect two to six others.[13] Some who contract COVID-19, especially younger patients, may be infectious despite having no symptoms. In February 2020, COVID-19 was spreading so rapidly through Italy that the number of cases was doubling daily. Vaccines, mask-wearing, social distancing, and enforced lockdown measures help slow the spread, but more infectious virus strains (such as variant B.1.1.7) have a higher R_0, making them harder to control.

In 2020, COVID-19 claimed 1.8 million lives, and the death toll in 2021 is likely to be higher still. These huge numbers are of a similar magnitude to tuberculosis, which kills 1.3 million people annually. The economic cost of avoiding the virus has been massive. Globally, hundreds of millions of people have lost their jobs, and as much as $9 trillion of economic activity may be destroyed.[14] For the first time in the twenty-first century, world poverty rates are expected to rise.[15] The Great Lockdown led to the worst economic slump since the Great Depression.

COVID-19 has also been a reminder of how modern living has affected the ability of viruses to jump the species barrier. The spread of human settlements and livestock farms next to natural forests raise the odds of animal viruses infecting humans.[16] Three-quarters of new human diseases—including HIV/AIDS and Ebola—have their source in other animals.[17] Each year, five new diseases emerge.[18] When researchers took blood samples from bats in twenty countries, they estimated that there are over three thousand potential coronaviruses, most of which are yet to be described.[19] Transmission to humans is commonplace. Every year, more than a million people are infected by bat coronaviruses.[20]

With their mind-boggling numbers and ability to replicate speedily, viruses mutate more rapidly than any other organism.[21] Over the past eight million years, humans have evolved by 1 percent.[22] Many viruses can evolve by more than this in just a few days. As COVID-19 has shown, the factors that have driven prosperity—urbanization, busy workplaces, and global travel—also allow viruses and bacteria to spread further and faster than they could in the era of the black death.

The coronavirus pandemic has prompted an unprecedented surge of research into how the virus emerged, and how to treat it. "Wet markets"—wild animal markets, in which dozens of different species are caged close together and sold for human consumption—have been described as "the perfect place" for viruses or bacteria to jump the species barrier.[23] As Laurence Fishburne's character says in the film *Contagion*, "Someone doesn't have to weaponize the bird flu—the birds are already doing that." China's wet markets were partially shut down after the 2003 SARS, 2013–2014 bird flu, and 2019–2020 coronavirus outbreaks. Many have pushed for a permanent end to the trade, though experts note that a full ban would also require a strategy for curtailing the unregulated black market that would inevitably emerge in response.[24]

Put enough monkeys in a room with enough typewriters, and it's a sure bet that one monkey will eventually murder another with a typewriter. Likewise, the mathematics of viral replication is guaranteed to keep creating new diseases. As molecular biologist Joshua Lederberg ruefully observed of new infectious diseases, "It's our wits versus their genes."[25] Viruses are not alive; they are virtual organisms, running on the hardware of plants or animals, and reproducing by infecting cells. Viruses outnumber all living things by a factor of ten. A gallon of seawater or pound of dried soil contains around four hundred billion virus particles.[26] So pure chance will invariably lead to new diseases, and close-knit societies risk spreading them quicker than ever.

But bad luck isn't all we have to worry about. Bad actors are looking to create and weaponize biological agents too. Biological warfare dates back more than two thousand years.[27] In the Trojan War, archers dipped their arrows into poison. Roman commanders poisoned the wells of besieged towns. Mongol attackers catapulted the bodies of plague victims over castle walls. In the Ohio River valley, British soldiers gave smallpox-infected blankets to Native Americans. During World War I, Germany attempted to infect Allied horses with anthrax.

In World War II, advances in microbiology led the Soviet Union, Germany, Britain, and the United States to develop bioweapons programs. Japan created plague epidemics by dropping infected fleas from aircraft into Chinese cities. During the 1950s and 1960s, the United States carried out an active bioweapons program, investigating yellow fever, typhus, and the plague.[28] The program also experimented with how to disperse the germs, using pseudo biological weapons. In 1965, government agents at what is now Reagan National Airport secretly sprayed harmless bacteria onto passengers. In New York the following year, agents smashed bacteria-filled light bulbs in the subway. The government sprayed chemicals from aircraft onto north central Texas and from ships into the San Francisco Bay. By the time it was shut down in 1969, the program had mass-produced a half-dozen biological weapons, including anthrax, tularemia, and botulism. These weapons were destroyed over the next few years, as the United States signed onto the Biological Weapons Convention, banning all biological weapons.

The Soviet Union signed the Biological Weapons Convention as well, but continued to secretly develop biological weapons through the 1970s and 1980s. Employing thirty thousand people across eighteen laboratories and production centers, the Soviet Biopreparat program created "veepox," a hybrid of Venezuelan equine encephalitis with smallpox, and "ebolapox," a hybrid of Ebola with smallpox.[29] It stockpiled twenty tons of smallpox, twenty tons of bubonic plague, and hundreds of tons of anthrax.[30] Only when leading scientists defected and exposed the program did the Russian leadership admit its existence and begin closing it down.

The Soviets weren't the only ones skirting the law. During the 1980s, Saddam Hussein produced over a hundred million gallons of biological weapons, including botulinum toxin, anthrax, and aflatoxin.[31] So lax were the international controls that Hussein's scientists were able to source much of their equipment and materials from Germany, France, and the United States. Adhering to guidelines that encouraged the free exchange of samples among researchers, the American Type Culture Collection in Virginia mailed strains of the bubonic plague, West Nile virus, and dengue fever to Basra and Baghdad, where they were used to develop Iraqi germ weapons.[32] In the twenty-first century, most government-run biological weapons programs seem to have ceased, though the Syrian regime, aided by the Russian government, appears to have used chemical weapons (chlorine and sarin) to attack dissidents.[33]

Beyond governments, terrorist groups have recruited scientists to work on germ warfare. In 1984, the worst biological terror attack in US history took place in the Dalles, a farming town of about 10,000 people situated an hour and a half's drive west of Portland, Oregon. Thousands of members of a religious cult run by Bhagwan Shree Rajneesh had established a commune and won political control of the nearest town, Antelope (which they renamed "Rajneesh"). They planned to win county elections in Wasco County by deterring other residents from voting. To achieve their goal, they sprinkled salmonella into the salad bars of ten restaurants, poisoning 751 people, all of whom eventually recovered. The decision to use a nonlethal bacteria came only after cult members had considered deadlier alternatives. As part of their planning, they obtained samples that would have caused typhoid fever, tularemia, and shigellosis. They also tried to culture HIV/AIDS, drawing blood from a homeless man who was infected with the virus.[34]

Among the most advanced terrorist biological weapons program was that of the Japanese Aum Shinrikyo doomsday cult, which aimed to bring about the end of the world so its followers could attain salvation. In the early 1990s, cult members attempted to obtain Ebola virus in Zaire and carried out three unsuccessful biological attacks. Later interviews with cult members revealed how close they came to unleashing botulism and anthrax, failing in one case merely because they used a vaccine strain of anthrax rather than a lethal one.[35] In 1995, cult members released sarin gas into the Tokyo subway system during rush hour, injuring six thousand people and killing fourteen.[36] When officials later raided the cult's headquarters at the foot of Mount Fuji, they found enough sarin to kill over four million people.[37]

The leading danger today arises from synthetic biology—techniques that blend physical and genetic engineering to create new life-forms. Many applications of the technology can have enormous benefits, such as helping create higher-yielding crops, novel health treatments, and new biofuels. But the same technology can be misused to alter existing bacteria or viruses in order to make them more dangerous. This might involve creating superbugs by adapting bacteria so that they are resistant to antibiotics, making vaccine-resistant diseases, changing bugs so that they produce harmful toxins, or combining multiple diseases into dangerous hybrids.

So far, this is merely the stuff of fiction. In Richard Preston's 1998 thriller *The Cobra Event*, an attacker engineers a disease called "brainpox" from smallpox and the common cold. But fiction has a way of influencing policy making. Preston's novel was reportedly influential on President Bill Clinton, who read it on the recommendation of genetic researcher Craig Venter and subsequently commissioned work from his national security advisers on the risks of recombinant biotechnology.[38]

In the two decades since, synthetic biology has advanced considerably. As Ord has underscored, the cost has also fallen dramatically. The project that led to sequencing the first human genome cost taxpayers $3.4 billion.[39] Today, a range of US laboratories will speedily sequence your genome for less than $1,000. A Chinese company recently claimed that it can do the task for just $100.[40] Gene editing technology has now become so simple that high schoolers are being taught to create proteins containing genes that make them resistant to antibiotics.[41]

Intelligence agencies are concerned. A leading review of the health security implications of gene editing pointed out that the techniques are likely to be valuable in identifying, diagnosing, and treating outbreaks of infectious diseases. Yet it also acknowledged that "CRISPR gene editors could be used bluntly as a bioweapon if a delivery mechanism could be devised."[42] Similarly, the US intelligence community's *Worldwide Threat Assessment* names bioterrorism as one of the threats to national security, noting that "these technologies hold great promise for advances in precision medicine, agriculture, and manufacturing, but they also introduce risks, such as the potential for adversaries to develop novel biological warfare agents, threaten food security, and enhance or degrade human performance."[43]

The practical risks of gene editing were highlighted when two researchers at the University of Alberta in Canada showed that it was possible to make horsepox, a disease cousin of smallpox, by ordering parts of DNA on the internet and reassembling them. The project cost $100,000 and took about six months. Although the researchers claimed that their work could lead to a better smallpox vaccine, critics noted that an effective vaccine already exists. The research demonstrated the tension between academics' instinctive desire for openness and the risk that malevolent actors might misuse the findings (what security researchers call a "dual use"). When the researchers submitted their findings to the journal *Science*, the editors replied, "While recognizing the technical achievement, ultimately we have decided that your paper would not offer *Science* readers a sufficient gain of novel biological knowledge to offset the significant administrative burden the manuscript represents in terms of dual-use research of concern." But the researchers simply sent their findings to another journal, which published the study. Some scientists were outraged, with one critic arguing, "If anyone wants to recreate another poxvirus, they now have the instructions to do that in one place."[44]

When it comes to bioengineered bugs, two factors determine how dangerous they are to a population: deadliness and contagiousness. These are simple concepts, but they can be tricky to measure. Do we measure the deadliness of the bubonic plague in medieval Europe or a world with antibiotics? Do we estimate the contagiousness of COVID-19 with or without vaccines?

In figure 2.1, I rely on the work of data journalist David McCand-less, who has reviewed the scientific literature to estimate the dead-liness and contagiousness of more than a dozen diseases. Where possible, deadliness estimates are for a patient who is untreated, and contagiousness estimates are in the absence of a concerted community response.[45]

Some diseases are natural-born killers. Ebola and bird flu (H5N1) kill about half of those who contract them. Other diseases are extremely contagious, spreading like a new internet meme. Mumps has an R_0 of around seven. Measles has an R_0 of around nine.[46] But thankfully the most dangerous diseases don't tend be as infectious. Ebola and bird flu lack the supercontagion of mumps and measles. Conversely, over 99 percent of those infected with mumps and measles will make a full recovery. Few diseases are both extremely deadly and ultracontagious. Pathogens that kill their host quickly don't allow much time to infect others.

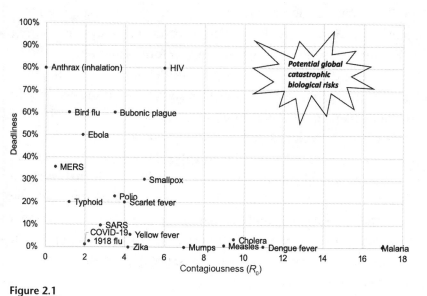

Figure 2.1

Contagiousness and deadliness of various diseases. *Source*: Adapted from David McCandless, informationisbeautiful.net. Deadliness estimates are without treatment.

Yet while germs are rarely fast spreading *and* fatal, such a disease is not impossible. The greatest risk to humanity comes from a bioengineered bug that would fit in the top right corner of figure 2.1. This would mean that the disease had both a high mortality rate and high R_0. In 2011, a researcher at the Erasmus Medical Center in Rotterdam reported that he had "mutated the hell out of H5N1," and created a virus that would attach to nose and trachea cells—a contagious bird flu.[47] Another example was raised in a 2018 report from the Bipartisan Commission on Biodefense: a hypothetical scenario in which terrorists released a version of the plague that had been aerosolized and genetically engineered to make it resistant to antibiotics.[48]

*   *   *

If Spock were president, argues business professor Scott Galloway, he would respond to the fact that more people have died from pathogens than war by boosting the budget for the Centers for Disease Control and Prevention (CDC) from $7 billion (its current level) to $700 billion (the level of the national defense budget). The problem, he maintains, is that "fighting pathogens makes for boring half-time flyovers (vs. F-15s) and dull uniforms (think hazmat)."[49]

There's little prospect of disease control budgets exceeding military spending, but they will hopefully increase in future decades. To prevent pandemics, these additional resources should be devoted to science, surveillance, surge capacity, and stockpiles. As Oxford's Cassidy Nelson points out, scientific breakthroughs that would be especially valuable include broad-spectrum antivirals that could be deployed in a manner similar to generic antibiotics, and genetic sequencing tests for multiple pathogens. As well as traditional research grants, these could be funded through innovation prizes in which national or international bodies specify the goal, and pay the first team to achieve it.

COVID-19 saw nations scrambling to track the disease as it spread from Wuhan across the world. But what if pandemic detection was automated? Ideally, surveillance systems should be designed to detect pathogens in hospitals, train stations, and airports. Other innovative approaches could be used. For example, researchers found that COVID-19 traces in sewage almost perfectly predicted hospital admissions three days later.[50] Internet data can also reveal symptoms, such as the finding that web searches for "loss of smell" closely matched coronavirus outbreaks.[51] One study of Fitbit users found that the devices could identify one-fifth of coronavirus cases the day *before* symptoms emerged—suggesting that wearables might help with early detection.[52]

Another valuable initiative is the Program for Monitoring Emerging Diseases (ProMED), a global network of health professionals who share information about disease outbreaks. In the case of SARS, MERS, and COVID-19, ProMED was alerting doctors worldwide about the disease before it had been officially acknowledged.[53] Yet ProMED's global budget is only $1 million a year, or roughly the cost of building a single suburban playground.[54] Given ProMED's proven record of early detection, it would make sense to provide it with more resources to identify new outbreaks and share knowledge about how to bring them under control.

Surge capacity requires that governments develop a strategy to rapidly increase health care personnel and build hospital facilities. This may involve creating a system of "health care reserves," as the military does when preparing for war. It could also entail plans to use actual military resources to quickly construct health care facilities. Military assets have great potential to be used in a pandemic, but as New York City's experience with naval floating hospitals demonstrated, civilian and military protocols do not mesh smoothly. The coronavirus outbreak showed the inadequacies of the existing stockpiles too, with states forced to bid against one another for masks, ventilators, and test kits. Centralizing these procurement processes in future pandemics would allow states to focus on other pressing issues.

Guarding against bioterrorism involves many of the same approaches as reducing pandemic risk: science, surveillance, surge capacity, and stockpiles. Whether a disease emerges by chance in nature or by design in a laboratory, the development of effective tests, treatments, and preventive measures will be essential. But there are also particular measures that can be taken to reduce the danger of bioterrorism.

One solution would be to strengthen the Biological Weapons Convention. A key reason that the Nixon administration renounced the nation's biological weapons program was the recognition that such weapons have limited tactical value on the battlefield, but could readily be turned against the United States by a weaker adversary. It is in the interests of the dominant power, the Nixon administration realized, to curtail the use of biological weapons across the globe. They are "a poor man's atomic bomb."[55]

Given this reality, it makes sense for the United States, along with China and other dominant powers that do not condone biological weapons, to ensure that the Biological Weapons Convention is working as effectively as possible. A major problem with the Biological Weapons Convention is that unlike conventions on chemical or nuclear weapons, there is no effective means to verify compliance. In improving monitoring, funding for the convention should also be increased. At present, it has just three employees and a budget of $1.4 million (smaller than the average McDonald's restaurant, Toby Ord notes).[56] Giving the Biological Weapons Convention some teeth—and some bread—would be a valuable investment in securing the future of humanity.

We should also improve safety procedures in laboratories that conduct biological research. US laboratories have mistakenly mailed out live anthrax bacteria and Ebola virus samples. A British laboratory erroneously contaminated nearby farms with foot-and-mouth disease. In a Chinese laboratory, researchers were accidentally exposed to SARS, leading to one person's death.[57] The last person in the world to die from smallpox caught it from a laboratory outbreak.[58] A succession of reports have found instances of inadequate protective equipment, safety procedures, and security systems in these laboratories.[59] Since the start of the twenty-first century, the number of US BSL-4 facilities—the highest-containment laboratories—has more than doubled. One analysis estimated that if a lab works on a highly pathogenic avian influenza virus, there is about a 1 percent chance per decade that the lab will release it into the community and seed a pandemic.[60] With fourteen laboratories currently conducting this kind of work, this clearly points to the need to raise safety standards at such laboratories.

One kind of research is particularly risky. A small group of disease specialists practice what is known as gain-of-function research, in which they attempt to make pathogens deadlier and more transmissible—like the Rotterdam researchers who created a more lethal bird flu. Those who favor gain-of-function research argue that it helps prepare for the worst. But given the trillions of possible mutations that nature could produce, it is unlikely that scientists will discover a particular disease before it emerges in the wild. Given the risk that bioengineered pathogens could escape the laboratory, it would be safer to implement a global moratorium on gain-of-function research, at least until we are confident that these megabugs can never be released.[61]

It is also vital to improve the security of DNA synthesis, a technology that allows researchers to cheaply "print" DNA for insertion into a cell. At a cost of around eight cents per base pair, researchers can upload a sequence to a firm such as GenScript, Blue Heron, or Biomatik, and have the DNA shipped to them within days. This process is vital for medical and crop researchers, but malign actors must not be allowed to order the DNA for the 1918 influenza.[62] Most laboratories presently run background checks on clients and screen orders against a list of known pathogens.[63] But screening should be made universal while keeping secret the list of dangerous pathogens. MIT's Kevin Esvelt proposes that the system be revamped using a one-way encryption approach common in cryptography so that it checks "essential segments" of risky sequences.[64] This could then be extended to benchtop DNA synthesis machines, ensuring that the 1918 influenza strain is as hard to synthesize as to buy.

Finally, we need to ensure that research cannot be readily weaponized by terrorists. Academics say that if they want to keep their jobs, they must "publish or perish." But when it comes to dangerous research, we need to ensure society doesn't publish *and* perish. Since the Enlightenment, publication and the dissemination of peer reviewed research have served the world enormously well. Yet when it comes to dual-use research—with high potential to be misused—greater thought should be given to whether it makes sense to publish the findings or even conduct the analysis in the first place. Aspects of biological research are as dangerous to humanity as nuclear research, and their costs and benefits should be judged just as rigorously. For most problems, communication helps. But occasionally silence is safer.

Humanity's achievements in controlling and curing disease over the past century represent a triumph of evidence over folk wisdom. For centuries, people believed that diseases were a form of divine punishment, that they were caused by imbalances between our four "humors" (yellow bile, black bile, phlegm, and blood), or that they were the result of miasmas—poisonous emanations from dead bodies and molds. Doctors confidently employed quack cures such as mercury, leeches, bloodletting, and trepanning (boring a hole in the skull). Treatments were tightly guarded and not tested in randomized clinical trials. As the saying goes, before there was evidence-based medicine, there was eminence-based medicine.

Devastating as COVID-19 has been, the final death toll will be considerably smaller than the 1918 influenza pandemic. That's thanks to science. Yet the risks of naturally occurring pandemics and bioterrorism remain unacceptably high. Surveying the danger, the Future of Humanity Institute's Gregory Lewis concludes that for those who care about the survival of our species, it is "among the most pressing problems to work on"—a challenge that is "both neglected and tractable."[65] Just as individuals mask up, there are plenty of protective measures society can take to ward off the baddest bugs of all.

3

A Second Venus

At 130°F, Furnace Creek in Death Valley holds the record for the hottest place on earth.[1] On a typical July day, you can expect a daily high temperature of 116°F. Longtime residents say they can adjust to air temperatures of 100°F, but when the mercury soars above 120°F, it feels like being in an oven. The fluid in your eyes starts to dry out. The heat scorches the inside of your nasal passages. The highest ground temperature ever recorded is 201°F, just 11°F short of the boiling point. You can literally fry an egg on the sidewalk of Furnace Creek.

There's a limit to what the human body can do in the world's hottest places. Asuncion Valdivia, a fifty-three-year-old farmworker, suffered a fatal stroke after picking grapes on a California farm for ten hours in 105°F temperatures. Peggy Frank, a sixty-three-year-old postal worker, was found dead in her mail truck on a 117°F day. Brent Robinson, a fifty-five-year-old technician for Verizon, perished after installing a telephone line in an attic where the temperatures exceeded 100°F.

Humans are two-legged radiators, creating as much warmth at rest as a hundred-watt light bulb. To stay alive, we need somewhere for this heat to go. Our body's natural temperature is 98°F, so we're most comfortable when the outside temperature is below that level.[2] When the air is hotter than our body, we survive by sweating. But sweat only cools us down if it evaporates. When the humidity is 100 percent, an outside temperature of 95°F can be fatal—even to a healthy person, and even if there is plenty of water to drink. Heat index temperatures suggest that 95°F at 100 percent humidity feels like dry heat of over 160°F: more dangerous than the hottest day in Death Valley. When the humidity is at 50 percent, the lethal threshold is 114°F (an environment that feels like dry heat above 160°F).

Our bodies evolved to operate in a narrow temperature range. When body temperatures rise above 104°F, heatstroke begins. Its onset can be marked by seizures and vomiting. Cells begin to break down, with damage often concentrated in the liver and kidneys. At 105°F, the body responds by increasing its metabolism, generating heat at a more rapid rate and compounding the problem. At this point, muscle tissues can break down and internal hemorrhaging occurs. By this time, the person has frequently stopped sweating and may be unconscious. Death can occur through a heart attack, kidney failure, or clotting cascade in which the body reacts to internal damage by clotting blood throughout the system.[3]

Heatstroke is not the only risk from catastrophic climate change, but it is among the most potent. A heat wave in Europe in 2003 cost seventy thousand lives—a death toll that would have been regarded as a calamity if it had been caused by a cyclone, flood, or earthquake.[4] In the 2010 Moscow heat wave, ten thousand people died. India's 2015 heat wave killed more than two thousand.

Just as our bodies have evolved to function in a narrow temperature band, so too human societies have adapted to live in a narrow band of the planet. This temperature niche isn't just where we've built our cities, it's also the climatic zone for which we've bred our crops and livestock. Yet over the next fifty years, one team of scientists reports that unchecked climate change is expected to shift the location of humanity's temperature sweet spot further than it has moved in the past six thousand years.[5] Without migration, one billion people will live in insufferable heat within half a century. Asked whether his research group was surprised by these findings, coauthor Marten Scheffer candidly responded, "We were blown away by the magnitude."[6]

How bad could global warming get? The earliest reports suggesting that carbon emissions might warm the planet emerged at the start of the twentieth century. For a time, scientists thought that carbon dioxide might be absorbed by plants and oceans. But by the 1950s and 1960s, it was recognized that transferring billions of tons of carbon from the earth's crust to the atmosphere would lead to global warming. Reports for the "Club of Rome" in the early 1970s flagged the greenhouse effect. In 1988, scientist James Hansen testified to the US Congress that climate change was already underway. That year, the World Meteorological Organization established the Intergovernmental Panel on Climate Change (IPCC), which has since produced five reports summarizing the state of the science on climate change. These consensus reports suggest that global warming has already increased average temperatures by about 2°F (1°C), with each of the past three decades clocking in as the hottest on record.

Projections indicate that if carbon emissions continue to rise at their current rate, temperatures are likely to increase by 6–8°F (3–4°C) above their preindustrial levels by the end of 2100. This in itself could produce disastrous outcomes. The scale of the warming as well as other human-driven changes in the earth's ecosystem has even led to some scientists proposing that the current age should be regarded as a new geologic epoch, "the Anthropocene." Geologically, this would be a big deal. The last time we began a new epoch was 11,650 years ago.

But what makes climate change a true existential risk is the possibility of even greater warming.

Dubbed by one journalist "the man who got economists to take climate nightmares seriously," economist Martin Weitzman was a brilliant though reclusive researcher who worried that the greatest risk of climate change is not in the most probable outcomes but rather in the extremes.[7] Working from Harvard University and a cabin on an island he bought off the Massachusetts coast, Weitzman pointed out there is massive uncertainty about the likely temperature rises. Nor can we be sure of the societal cost if temperatures soar. These uncertainties mean that there is a real possibility of a disastrous collapse in planetary well-being. In *Climate Shock,* a book coauthored with fellow economist Gernot Wagner, Weitzman argued, "Most everything we know tells us climate change is bad. Most everything we don't know tells us it's probably much worse."[8]

Where does the uncertainty come from? Scientific models tend to be skewed toward what is known, which can lead them to underpredict the rate at which warming occurs. In 1995, the IPCC anticipated "little change in the extent of the Greenland and Antarctic ice sheets . . . over the next 50–100 years." In 2007, it acknowledged "that losses from the ice sheets of Greenland and Antarctica have very likely contributed to sea level rise over 1993 to 2003." This error led the earlier modelers to drastically underestimate the extent to which oceans would rise.[9]

It's possible that we may still be underestimating the risks of ice sheet melting. According to one recent study, the Amundsen Sea embayment of West Antarctica might have passed a tipping point at which it will inevitably collapse, destabilizing the rest of that West Antarctica ice sheet "like toppling dominoes," and resulting in sea levels rising by ten feet.[10]

Another potential climate tipping point relates to the Amazon as we know it, where 17 percent of the forest cover has been lost since 1970. Air that has passed over deforested areas in the preceding few days produces only half as much rain as if it had passed over extensive vegetation.[11] So fewer trees means less rainfall. This creates the risk that the Amazon could fall into a death spiral, with extended dry spells transforming the rainforest into a savanna or dry forest. Estimates of this tipping point range from 20 to 40 percent deforestation—frighteningly close to the 17 percent already lost.[12] Forests are also vulnerable to extreme heat, which slows tree growth, reducing their ability to store carbon.[13]

In the Arctic, thawing permafrost is already releasing carbon dioxide and methane, a greenhouse gas that is thirty times more potent than carbon dioxide over a century-long period. Arctic peat fires, moving across the ground at the speed of a few feet a week, are exacerbating the problem. Contained beneath the permafrost are massive stores of methane and carbon dioxide, accumulated over millions of years as bacteria digest organic matter. Most of this 1.5 trillion ton "carbon bomb" sits within ten feet of the surface and is equivalent to twice as much carbon dioxide as is in the atmosphere today.[14] With the Arctic currently warming twice as fast as the planetary average, a dangerously accelerating feedback loop could occur.

Predicting the path of a volatile and accelerating system is made even more difficult because of uncertainties around how much greenhouse gases will be emitted, how emissions will translate into atmospheric concentrations, how those concentrations will affect global temperatures, how temperature rises will affect the planet, and how those planetary changes will affect humanity.[15] For example, suppose that we emit more carbon than expected, and that each ton of emissions leads to higher atmospheric concentrations than anticipated. Now suppose that global temperatures turn out to be increasingly responsive to carbon concentrations, and that the effects on humanity—such as through extreme weather events—are harsher than we thought. In that hypothetical, the chances of catastrophe are suddenly much higher than current models predict.

What are the odds that climate change could render the planet unlivable? Higher than you might think, Weitzman contended. To pin down the risk, he extracted nearly two dozen studies cited by the IPCC and examined their temperature predictions.[16] On average, the studies estimated that a doubling of atmospheric carbon concentrations would likely lead to temperature increases in the range of 1.5 to 4.5°C (2.7 to 8°F), with a best estimate of 3°C (5.4°F). To be precise, there's a two in three chance that warming will be in that range.

But the studies also reported *unlikely* outcomes—the one in three chance that warming is outside the band between 1.5 and 4.5°C. These estimates are shown in figure 3.1. On the low end, the IPCC studies indicated that warming below 1.5°C is extremely unlikely; the world has already warmed by about 1°C already, and emissions already in the atmosphere will drive continued warming. So the unlikely outcomes are mostly in the "too hot" category: warming that exceeds 4.5°C. These outcomes are shaped by what Weitzman dubbed a "climate sensitivity factor": the possibility of feedback loops caused by ice sheet melting, deforestation, or permafrost melting.

Wagner and Weitzman point out that the IPCC's estimates often assume that humanity stops at a doubling of atmospheric carbon concentrations, but this is looking increasingly optimistic. Before the Industrial Revolution, atmospheric carbon concentrations stood at 280 parts per million. They now exceed 400 parts per million. Counting other greenhouse gases, carbon dioxide equivalent levels exceed 500 parts per million, or close to double their preindustrial levels.[17]

If emissions hit 700 parts per million—which is where the International Energy Agency projects the world will end up in 2100 even if all governments keep all their current climate change mitigation commitments—then Wagner and Weitzman argue that there is a 10 percent chance of warming beyond 6°C. In more speculative work, based on figures he admits to be "wildly uncertain, unbelievably crude ballpark estimates," Weitzman went further, estimating what would happen if the probability distributions are "fat tailed"—meaning that extreme outcomes are more likely than standard approaches suggest. Such calculations imply a 5 percent chance of warming above 10°C (18°F) and a 1 percent chance of warming above 20°C (36°F).[18] These temperatures would not occur in the twenty-first century, which is why they are not depicted in figure 3.1.[19] But if we hit 6°C by 2100, cascading feedback loops could send temperatures soaring further still. In other words, once we warm the planet by 6°C, all bets are off.[20]

No one argues that warming of 6°C is probable. But neither is it so unlikely that it can be safely ignored. A one in ten chance of 6°C warming, one in twenty chance of 10°C warming, and one in a hundred chance of 20°C warming cannot be dismissed as trivial odds. To put them into perspective, many people fear aircraft crashes. Yet flying is so safe that if you took a flight *every day of your life*, then the chances of ever dying in a plane crash are still just one

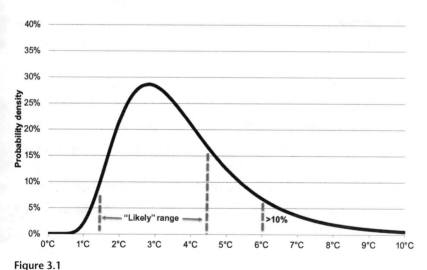

Figure 3.1
Eventual global average warming based on passing 700 parts per million CO2e. *Source*: Gernot Wagner and Martin Weitzman, *Climate Shock: The Economic Consequences of a Hotter Planet* (Princeton, NJ: Princeton University Press, 2016).

in fifteen hundred.[21] By contrast, when we're talking about catastrophic climate change, we're talking about chances of one in ten, one in twenty, or one in a hundred. Would you board a plane with a one in a hundred chance of crashing?

In his book *Six Degrees*, environmental journalist Mark Lynas devotes six chapters to outlining what would happen if the world warmed by 1°C, 2°C, and so on. The final chapter, describing life in a 6°C world, begins with a reference to Dante's sixth circle of hell.[22] As Wagner and Weitzman put it, a 6°C temperature change represents "the end of human adventure on this planet as we now know it."[23]

An understanding of the full possibilities of the effects of climate change is hampered by two conventions in global climate modeling: few studies analyze the impact of 6°C or more of warming, and most fail to discuss outcomes beyond 2100. This is problematic given that a recent analysis suggests that there is a one in three chance that emissions will exceed the IPCC's most extreme climate change scenario—a scenario known as RCP 8.5.[24] Guided by the existing literature, most of the discussion in this chapter will focus on the consequences of warming to 4°C by 2100. It should be regarded as just a curtain opener for what a 6°C or warmer world could deliver.

I've already looked at one impact: extreme heat. A global analysis of documented lethal heat events identified a threshold beyond which the temperature and humidity become deadly. It estimates that 30 percent of the world's population is currently exposed to lethal heat conditions for at least twenty days a year. This figure would grow to 74 percent of the world's population under a "business-as-usual" scenario in which average temperatures increase by 4°C by 2100. In humid tropical areas such as Indonesia, Panama, and Cameroon, the heat index would be at a dangerous level almost year-round.[25]

If temperatures rise by 4°C, one billion people could live in conditions that make strenuous outdoor activity hazardous. People living in parts of the southeastern United States could endure more than three months a year with heat indexes above the current once-a-year peak.[26] Focusing on New York, researchers estimate that 1°C of global warming could lead to a tenfold increase in the number of days on which the temperature exceeds 100°F.[27] The increase in heat deaths will more than offset the reduction in cold deaths.[28] Rising temperatures exacerbate other problems too. Across the United States, unhealthy ozone pollution is rising.[29] Ozone is formed in the atmosphere by pollutants, and heat waves speed up the process. While emissions from tailpipes and power plants are falling, this is more than offset by the increased number of hot days.[30]

Our bodies evolved over millennia to the current climate, and they won't adapt within a century or two. But societal adaptation will be difficult too. Air-conditioning will become more common, but it only solves the problem indoors—not much help for construction workers, delivery workers, or anyone who exercises outdoors. And unless electricity is fully sourced from renewables, air-conditioning only adds to the climate problem.

In response to unlivable temperatures, people will attempt to move, but mass migration will press up against international borders. Even within nations, people may opt to swelter in place rather than move to an unfamiliar part of the country. In the case of mountain-dwelling animals, scientists have described an "escalator to extinction" in which climate change causes each species to move a little farther up the mountain in order to stay in a comfortable environment.[31] Each step of the escalator means the species at the mountaintop has nowhere to go and dies out. In the case of humans, we will eventually struggle to fit a growing population into a shrinking set of habitable spaces as we press up against deserts and shorelines.

Extreme temperatures will also bring extreme weather events. Because hot air holds more water than cool air, a rise in global temperatures will increase the amount of rain dumped in storms. More rainfall means bigger floods and worse hailstorms, like the baseball-size hailstones that struck Colorado Springs in 2018. Lightning strikes, wildfires, and droughts will become more frequent. As Journalist David Wallace-Wells puts it, we may stop calling them "natural disasters" and start calling extreme events simply "weather."

Overall, we know that global warming is contributing to increased climatic volatility.[32] Each year, the American Meteorological Society analyses extreme weather events to look for the fingerprints of climate change. Its latest reports identify climate change as a culprit in a spate of recent hurricanes, snowstorms, and flooding events.[33] Since 1980, the number of catastrophic weather events worldwide has more than tripled.[34]

In 2018, Northern California was hit by the Camp Fire, the most destructive wildfire the state had ever seen. Ignited by a faulty electric line, the fire burned swiftly through the dry oaks and pines. By that time of year, the region would have typically received around five inches of autumn rain. In 2018, only one-seventh of an inch had fallen. When the fire reached Paradise, a town with more than twenty thousand residents, it incinerated 95 percent of the buildings. Eighty-five people died, and the Camp Fire became the year's most expensive natural disaster in the world in terms of insurance losses. Even moguls and celebrities have been affected by California's blazes, with Rupert Murdoch's Bel Air estate scorched, and Kim Kardashian calling in private firefighters to save her $50 million mansion.

Climate change has already doubled the number of large fires in the western United States.[35] California's fire season used to peak in September and October, but August 2020 saw over one million acres burned in less than a fortnight.[36] Looking to the future, a recent study projected that each degree Celsius of warming would quadruple the area burned in California.[37] In 2019, Siberian wildfires burned an area larger than Belgium, disrupting air travel. In summer 2019–2020, wildfires burned across 1 percent of the Australian landmass, sending smoke as far away as Chile.[38] Australian firefighters are now encountering "pyroconvective" events, in which fires are so intense that they create their own thunderstorms, with lightning and strong winds exacerbating the fires.

Severe hurricanes are often referred to as 1-in-500-year events—because we once estimated their annual probability at 0.2 percent. Referring to the hurricanes that hit Houston in 2015, 2016, and 2017, Ed Emmett, the chief executive of the county that encompasses Houston, quipped, "Three 500-year floods in three years means either we're free and clear for the next 1,500 years, or something has seriously changed."[39] One study predicts that the twenty-first century will see thirteen million US inhabitants forced to migrate away from submerged coastlines.[40] That would be the largest migration in US history—surpassing the twentieth-century Great Migration that saw six million African Americans move northward.[41]

Hurricane Harvey, which dumped over fifteen trillion gallons of water on Houston in 2017, tied with 2005's Hurricane Katrina as the costliest tropical cyclone to hit the United States. It was followed a month later by Hurricane Maria, which killed nearly three thousand people in Puerto Rico. In 2018, Hurricane Michael hit the Florida panhandle, recording a maximum wind speed of 139 miles per hour before it broke the wind gauge. Between 1980 and 2015, there was an average of five billion-dollar disasters annually. From 2016 to 2018, there was an average of fifteen each year.[42]

As the planet warms, storms will worsen. Globally, 4°C of warming will increase the damage from flooding by a factor of four and raise flooding risk sixfold.[43] In New York City, floods that occurred once every five hundred years in preindustrial times now happen once every twenty-five years and are projected to occur once every five years by 2045.[44] Nashville's 2010 floods were described as "biblical." It's doubly apt: an inundation of that scale should literally only happen a couple of times every two thousand years. And these floods led to the spectacle of a forty-foot-long portable building from Lighthouse Christian School floating down Interstate 24.[45] The IPCC's 2019 report on climate change and the oceans vividly describes the trend: storms that used to occur once a century will happen once a year by midcentury.[46] If the planet continues to warm, "once a century" events will happen once a month.

Because hurricanes get their destructive power from ocean heat, warmer waters increase the impact of extreme storms.[47] North America, serving as a channel between the polar regions and Gulf of Mexico, is especially vulnerable. Meteorologists theorize about future megastorms that could materialize. Rice University researchers have modeled a fictional "Hurricane Isaiah" that crashes through oil refineries in coastal Texas, sending a hundred million gallons of petrochemicals flooding into schools, homes, and offices.[48] The ARkStorm, a hypothetical scenario developed by the US Geological Survey, would see ten feet of water dumped into California's Central Valley, resulting in hundreds of landslides and the evacuation of 1.5 million people. Hypercanes are hurricanes that could theoretically develop as a result of extreme ocean warming—reaching twenty miles into the upper stratosphere, producing winds over five hundred miles per hour, and damaging the ozone layer.

In 2017, a 150-foot-tall iceberg—nearly twice as high as the one that sunk the *Titanic*—floated past Canada's east coast. That area of the North Atlantic Ocean is known as "iceberg alley" because of the icebergs that float past each spring, but this block of ice turned the heads of longtime residents, and brought tourists flocking to photograph an iceberg so large that it towered over the clapboard houses in the small coastal town of Ferryland. These icebergs are the debris from the breakup of Arctic sea ice, and they're becoming more common. According to the US Coast Guard, six hundred icebergs appeared that year in North Atlantic shipping lanes, or seven times more than usual.[49] Recent research predicts that the North Pole, which is currently covered by sea ice year-round, could become ice free in summer by 2050.[50] Each metric ton of carbon emissions—what the typical person in the United States emits every three weeks—is responsible for the loss of 3 square meters of Arctic sea ice.[51]

As glaciers and polar ice caps melt, sea levels will inevitably rise. Already, sea levels have risen by 8 inches (20 centimeters), and the rate of sea level rise is accelerating. This is an immediate existential threat for Tuvalu, most of which sits a mere 6 feet above the Pacific Ocean. As former Tuvalu prime minister Enele Sopoaga puts it, "Tuvalu's future at current warming is already bleak. Any further temperature increase will spell the total demise of Tuvalu." In the Maldives, government ministers donned scuba gear to hold the world's first underwater cabinet meeting. Sea level rise will render such countries uninhabitable and is already prompting emigration.

But it's not just those living on atolls who need to worry about sea level rises. One billion of the world's eight billion people presently live within 33 feet (10 meters) above current high tide lines. Raise the water level by 4 inches (10 centimeters) and 10 million people's homes become uninhabitable. With 4°C of warming, the most likely increase in water levels is between 24 inches (61 centimeters) and 43 inches (110 centimeters) by 2100.[52] Projected forward to the year 2300, the anticipated sea level rise is 7.5 feet (2.3 meters) to 17.7 feet (5.4 meters). With 6°C of warming, the chances of finding ourselves in that worst-case world are higher still.

What does it mean when water levels rise 6 feet or more? In *The Water Will Come*, US writer Jeff Goodell spells it out: "Gone will be the beach where you first kissed your boyfriend; the mangrove forests in Bangladesh where Bengal tigers thrive; the crocodile nests in Florida Bay; Facebook headquarters in Silicon Valley; St. Mark's Basilica in Venice. Fort Sumter in Charleston, South Carolina; America's biggest naval base in Norfolk, Virginia; NASA's Kennedy Space Center; graves on the Isle of the Dead in Tasmania; the slums of Jakarta, Indonesia [a city with a population of ten million]."[53] Some regions may be protected by massive sea walls, but the costs could run into hundreds of billions of dollars annually.[54] Moreover, the higher the wall, the greater the danger if it is breached. Would you buy a house at the bottom of a dam wall?[55] Eventually, inland migration is more likely, and Atlantis-like underwater cities would dot the coastlines—sunken memorials to a time before the great sea level rise.

For crops, more carbon emissions might sound like good news. Indeed, climate skeptics have derided global warming by calling carbon dioxide "plant food." But scientific analysis suggests that in most regions of the world, hotter temperatures and more volatile rainfall will overwhelm any benefit of increased carbon dioxide concentrations. Aggregating the studies across crops and regions, the IPCC concludes that most research points to reduced crop yields, with the effects being worst in the tropics.[56] Increased carbon dioxide is also likely to lower the nutritional content of food. If emissions rise 4°C by 2100, the IPCC forecasts "large risks to food security globally."[57] Fish and livestock will be directly affected too, with many struggling to survive at hotter temperatures. Poor city dwellers will suffer the most from this aspect of climate change. A foretaste of these impacts occurred in the synchronized crop failures of 2007–2008 and 2010–2012, when food prices spiked—partly due to weather effects—to more than twice their usual levels. Forty-four million people were thrown into extreme poverty, and riots broke out from Bangladesh to Yemen.[58] In a warmer world, crops would fail on a larger scale, inflicting a higher human toll.

A hotter temperature, food shortages, and land loss sound like the conditions a Hollywood producer would dream up to create a global fight club. As with extreme weather events, experts are often reluctant to blame climate change for any specific violent conflict. But we know that hotter temperatures increase the incidence of crimes, including homicide, rape, robbery, assault, burglary, and car theft. One study estimates that a further 1°C of warming would lead to an additional hundred thousand crimes across the United

States.[59] Heat waves lead to more fatal traffic accidents.[60] On hotter days, drivers are quicker to honk their horns, baseball pitchers are more likely to intentionally hit batters, and school students do worse on standardized tests.[61]

This holds true globally. Civil conflicts are more common in hotter months, with researchers finding that conflicts in tropical areas are twice as likely in warmer El Niño years than in cooler La Niña years.[62] A database of water-related conflicts maintained by the California-based Pacific Institute lists 686 twenty-first-century water conflicts, including deadly clashes between farmers and herders in Sudan, battles over water wells in Yemen, and violence over water access in Mexico.[63] Another study concluded that 4°C of warming would increase climate-induced violence by a factor of five.[64]

Despite heat waves, hurricanes, wildfires, rising sea levels, crop failures and conflict, a reasonable person might concede that global warming will be bad, yet decide that there's zero chance it could lead to extinction. But such a conclusion may be too sanguine, since most scientific analysis of the effect of climate change stops at the artificial borders of a world warmed by 4°C in 2100. Push the temperature up or the time frame out, and a climate catastrophe no longer looks impossible.

As Wallace-Wells notes, another reason to be concerned about calamitous climate change is that we're running an unprecedented experiment with the earth's atmosphere. Humans are putting carbon into the atmosphere at a rate one hundred times faster than at any point before the Industrial Revolution.[65] The last time atmospheric carbon levels were as high as they are now was in the Pliocene epoch, three to five million years ago. Back then, there were no humans. North and South America had just joined up. Rhinos lived in North America. Crocodiles and alligators lived in Europe. Trees grew in the Arctic. Temperatures were 4–6°F (2–3°C) hotter, while ocean levels were seventy-five feet (twenty-five meters) higher.[66] To put it into context, a seventy-five-foot increase in sea levels puts many of the world's major cities underwater, including London, Miami, Tokyo, Manila, New York, Amsterdam, Stockholm, Jakarta, Dhaka, and Shanghai.

In the past five hundred million years, the planet has experienced five mass extinction events.[67] The Ordovician-Silurian extinction killed over 60 percent of all species. The Late Devonian extinction killed at least 70 percent of all species. The Permian-Triassic extinction (the "Great Dying") killed over 90 percent of all species. The Triassic-Jurassic extinction killed over 70 percent of all species. And the Cretaceous-Paleogene extinction killed 75 percent of all species. All were related to the carbon cycle, and only one was caused by an asteroid, with the other four being driven by greenhouse gases. Studying the carbon cycle changes that led to these extinction events, geophysicist Daniel Rothman concludes that the threshold for a sixth extinction event is when more than 310 gigatons of carbon are added to the oceans.[68] On a business-as-usual trajectory, human carbon emissions are currently on track to add 500 gigatons by 2100.

Another instructive comparison is with Venus, a planet sometimes called our "sister planet" because it is about the same size as Earth, and was formed around the same time. In the planet's early years, it probably had about as much water as Earth and was likely habitable. Venus is closer to the sun than we are, but in the first billion years, it was probably cool enough to allow some forms of life. Three and a half billion years ago, Venus suffered a runaway greenhouse effect. Evaporating water served as a steam blanket, warming the planet further. In the upper atmosphere, solar radiation broke the water vapor into hydrogen and oxygen, and the hydrogen was swept away by solar winds. In as little as ten million years, the water was virtually gone. Venus today has a surface temperature of 863°F (462°C), making it the hottest planet in the solar system. Its atmospheric pressure is equivalent to the pressure found three thousand feet under the Earth's ocean. Clouds of sulfuric acid envelop the planet. Writer Mark Lynas asks, Could the combination of unchecked carbon emissions and feedback loops trigger a greenhouse effect that would "turn Earth into a second Venus"?[69]

*   *   *

We often hear people distinguishing the slow-moving climate from the fast-changing weather. But scientists recently showed that if you took the global weather readings on any single day in the past decade, you could detect the fingerprint of externally driven climate change and conclude that the planet was warming.[70] Global warming can now be detected in just one day's weather data.

Extreme meteorological events are bumping up against the limits of existing weather scales. Following record-breaking heat in 2013, the Australian Bureau of Meteorology added two new colors to its temperature maps, raising the top temperature from 122°F (50°C) to 129°F (54°C). After Hurricane Harvey, the US National Weather Service added two new shades of purple to its rainfall maps, raising the upper limit from fifteen to thirty inches. After Australia's "Black Saturday" fires, roadside fire danger signs were updated to add another category: "catastrophic," or code red. Meteorologist Jeff Masters proposes that the existing five-category hurricane scale be expanded by including a category six hurricane—what he described as a "black swan" storm.

When I became a politician in 2010, there were conspiracy theorists who argued that global warming ceased in 1998, that a past "little ice age" proved that temperatures were not rising, or that El Niño explained temperature changes. Since then, the climate skeptics have shifted tack, no longer deriding mainstream climate change researchers as "warmists." Today, most climate skeptics accept that the planet is getting hotter, but nonetheless deny the need for action. As the climate scientist Katharine Hayhoe writes, "The six stages of climate denial are: It's not real. It's not us. It's not that bad. It's too expensive to fix. Aha, here's a great solution (that actually does nothing). And—oh no! Now it's too late. You really should have warned us earlier."[71]

Under the 1997 Kyoto Protocol and 2015 Paris Agreement, most nations have signed up to reduce their greenhouse gas emissions. Through these international agreements, nations commit to shrinking their carbon footprint, but it is up to each country to determine how it will achieve its goals. Nations are changing their energy mix—producing more electricity from renewables and less from coal-fired power plants. Carbon-intensive industries such as steel and cement are becoming more efficient. New cars use less fuel, with hybrids and electric vehicles constituting a growing share of the fleet. Builders are erecting homes and offices that are more energy efficient. An increasing number of countries are halting logging and financing reforestation efforts.

Nations are using a variety of approaches to foster emissions reduction. Green financing initiatives—both private and public sector—are proliferating as a means of boosting the uptake of clean technologies. Carbon offset markets have gained credibility through better monitoring, allowing the sale of carbon credits across borders. Carbon pricing schemes now cover about 20 percent of global emissions. These include the European Union's emissions trading scheme (the world's largest, launched in 2005), national schemes in South Korea, South Africa, Canada, and Mexico, and regional carbon pricing markets in California, Guangdong, and Hubei.[72] Globally, these measures will not come close to meeting the Paris climate targets. According to an assessment by the nongovernmental organization Climate Action Tracker, only a handful of nations have implemented climate policies that are consistent with 2°C of warming, while a few (such as the European Union) would come close.[73] Most countries' policies, the body says, are "insufficient," "highly insufficient," or "critically insufficient."

Under President Trump, the United States was rated "critically insufficient," with Climate Action Tracker noting that his administration had rolled back over sixty domestic environmental measures, including vehicle emissions standards and limits on carbon emissions from coal plants.[74] Trump once claimed that climate change is a "hoax," and asserted that "global warming was created by and for the Chinese in order to make US manufacturing noncompetitive." President Biden's decision to rejoin the Paris climate accord and develop a unified national response to the climate crisis mark a U-turn in the United States' approach to climate change. Yet precious time has been lost, and the United States has yet to adopt the sorts of rapid decarbonization measures that are being pursued by the European Union.

In Brazil, President Jair Bolsonaro took office in 2018, and quickly set about loosening controls over land clearing in the Amazon. This has led farmers to accelerate deforestation by logging and burning. In mid-2019, satellite analysis of major fires in the Amazon showed that an area the size of Yellowstone National Park had been burned.[75] Researchers estimate that by 2030, this could lead to the loss of an area equivalent in size to the United Kingdom.[76] The impact would be to release thirteen gigatons of carbon dioxide equivalent—a quantity larger than China's annual emissions.[77] This additional deforestation could push the Amazon rainforest toward a tipping point.

*   *   *

What's the best way of persuading people that climate change matters? Extinction risk is a powerful argument—but it is not a necessary one. Even ignoring "tail risks," the cost of inaction is far greater than the cost of action. These economic costs include the risks detailed above: heat waves that cause premature deaths and restrict outdoor work, hurricanes and wildfires that take lives and damage property, destruction of coastal property, and reduced agricultural yields. It also includes impacts that are costly but not cataclysmic: premature deaths from worsened air quality, increased maintenance costs for roads, bridges, and railways, and the collapse of tourism to ski fields and coral reefs. Across the United States, the cost of unchecked climate change is largest in the southeast, where it is estimated to reach $190,000 per person by 2090. No region of the country escapes some mix of adverse impacts.[78]

There are also considerable benefits from shifting energy production to renewables. A study conducted by researchers at the National Oceanic and Atmospheric Administration and the University of Colorado Boulder found that investment in wind and solar power, along with moving from a regionally divided electricity sector to a national grid, could reduce carbon emissions from the electricity sector by up to 80 percent, while cutting electricity bills by 10 percent.[79] Both wind and solar benefit from a "learning curve" effect in which costs fall as production rises. In the case of wind, a doubling in take-up leads to a one-fifth price drop. For solar photovoltaic, a doubling in take-up leads to a one-quarter price reduction.[80] Once installed, these technologies produce electricity at essentially zero cost. With more renewables in the system, the average US coal plant ran at less than half its capacity in 2019. In early 2020, renewables produced more energy than coal in the United States. Britain now goes for weeks at a time without using any coal power.[81]

If these benefits appear tempting, they should sound doubly attractive when the prospect of averting a global catastrophe is added to the picture. If future lives matter as much as ours, it is callous not to reduce carbon emissions. The case for decisive action is strengthened still further by recognizing that much of the problem has been created relatively recently. As Wallace-Wells observes, "The majority of the burning has come since the premiere of *Seinfeld.*"[82] Climate change is not solely a problem bequeathed to us by our ancestors. Many of those responsible for the carbon emissions that are causing the planet to warm are still alive today.

What should be done? A starting point is to recognize that when it comes to avoiding extinction, any action is helpful. Eventual global temperatures scale linearly with carbon emissions, so cutting emissions puts the world on a flatter temperature trajectory. Remember Wagner and Weitzman's estimate that 6°C of warming has a 10 percent chance of occurring if humanity's emissions take us to seven hundred parts per million by 2100? Those odds drop to a more reassuring 2 percent if emissions are kept at five hundred parts per million. Conversely, they rise to 17 percent if emissions hit eight hundred parts per million in 2100. All emissions reductions are good emissions reductions.

It also helps to start early. Greenhouse gas emissions do not cause an instantaneous increase in planetary temperatures, and cutting them does not immediately fix the problem. It can take decades before the effect of reducing carbon pollution shows up in climate data.[83] In a lagging system, delay is not your friend.

In terms of global action, investment in renewables will be helpful in moving the planet along the learning curve. Research can improve the efficiency of photovoltaic cells, the optimal design of windmills, and the operation of batteries. Consumers can also benefit from incremental improvements in manufacturing processes and deployment as well as economies of scale.[84] A similar process applies to electric vehicles, which currently comprise just 0.5 percent of the global vehicle fleet. An analysis by BloombergNEF forecasts that electric vehicles will reach price parity with internal combustion vehicles in the mid-2020s.[85] The sooner this crossover point arrives, the faster emissions will fall.

Subsidizing clean technology is all well and good, but it is important to encourage the phase out of polluting technologies too. The Biden administration aims to reach net zero emissions in the power sector by 2035 and the entire economy by 2050. To achieve significant emissions reductions, the administration proposes to invest $2 trillion in renewable energy innovation, battery systems, public transit, and energy efficiency. Nor will everything in the plan necessarily become the victim of partisan gridlock. Although there is a significant partisan split in voters' attitudes toward climate change, some measures—tree planting, restricting power plant carbon emissions, and tightening fuel efficiency standards for cars—enjoy bipartisan support.[86]

Finally, reducing carbon emissions will involve working with developing countries—especially China and India—to ensure that they shift their energy mix toward renewables. This will require a change in approach. In the lead-up to the 1992 Rio Earth Summit, President George H. W. Bush proclaimed that "the American way of life is not up for negotiation." But to sustain the American way of life, it will be necessary to negotiate respectfully with nations that reasonably ask why they should take a cleaner development path than today's developed nations.

With 6°C of warming, summer in Las Vegas, Phoenix, and Palm Springs will become as hot as Death Valley is today. Boston will be as hot as Miami is today. Chicago will be as hot as Houston is today. Philadelphia will become as hot as Dallas. And once warming reaches that level, the mercury is almost certain to keep rising. Tackling climate change is a worthy career goal for budding scientists, economists, and policy advocates. Its sheer complexity can be daunting, but the payoff is enormous. Curbing emissions will not only help avert the catastrophic outcomes that Weitzman warned about; it will make life a good deal more comfortable for our generation and those to come.

4
First We Got the Bomb

At 9:28 a.m. in Moscow on January 25, 1995, a military aide to Boris Yeltsin saw a light flash on the Russian president's nuclear briefcase. Interrupting the president, the aide opened the briefcase and told Yeltsin that four minutes earlier, a rocket had been launched.[1] At the press of a button, Yeltsin could authorize a nuclear strike. If he did not, much of his arsenal could be wiped out.

Across Russia, nuclear commanders were readied. Every missile commander, every nuclear-armed submarine, and every air base with nuclear bombers was told to await President Yeltsin's decision. The Russian military officers knew the awesome damage their weapons could unleash, but they also knew that they were prime targets. In an all-out war, the first attacks would seek out Russia's nuclear weapons. Why not launch a retaliatory strike before you die?

Consulting with Russian radar officers, Yeltsin and Mikhail Kolesnikov, chief of the general staff, discussed the possibilities. They had detected only a single rocket, launched from the vicinity of the Norwegian Sea, and could not yet determine its trajectory. But if it was headed to Moscow, it would take only five or six more minutes to arrive. There was a possibility that its purpose was to deliver a massive electromagnetic pulse—destroying electronic systems and confusing radars—in advance of a full-scale attack.

The briefcase containing Yeltsin's nuclear controls was open—the first time this had ever occurred. With the press of a button, he could deploy forty-seven hundred nuclear missiles toward Europe and the United States. He waited. A few minutes later, it became clear that the rocket was not heading toward Russia. At 9:48 a.m. Moscow time, it landed in Svalbard, an icy Norwegian archipelago between mainland Norway and the North Pole.

The rocket that Russian radar had detected was a Black Brant XII research rocket. Launched by Norway, its purpose was to study the aurora borealis, or northern lights. The Russian government had been informed of the launch some weeks prior, but the message had been lost. To the Russian military, Black Brant looked nothing like the small single-stage scientific rockets the Norwegians had previously launched. It was forty-nine feet long, had four stages, and bore a frightening resemblance to the Trident missile, a submarine-launched nuclear weapon. In the months before the incident, US submarines had been increasing their activity in the seas around Norway, so the Russian military was suspicious of such an attack.

The instant when Yeltsin opened his nuclear briefcase might have been the most dangerous moment of the nuclear age. But it is just one of dozens that have occurred since the invention of the atomic bomb in 1945.

During the 1962 Cuban missile crisis, a Soviet B-59 submarine dived to avoid detection by US destroyers and lost contact with Moscow for days. A US ship began dropping practice depth charges to make the submarine surface, but the submarine's captain mistook them for real depth charges. Concluding that war had begun, the captain ordered the use of a nuclear torpedo—nearly as powerful as the one exploded in Hiroshima. But by chance, the Soviet flotilla commander, Vasili Arkhipov, was aboard the submarine. He countermanded the order to fire. Without Arkhipov, the nuclear torpedo would have obliterated the USS *Randolph*, an aircraft carrier with a crew of over three thousand. The United States might well have retaliated against Moscow, prompting a full-scale Soviet counterattack against European and North American targets.[2]

Another incident occurred at around 11:00 a.m. on November 9, 1979, when computer screens at both the Pentagon and North American Aerospace Defense Command showed that the United States was under attack. Soviet missiles had been launched from submarines and land. Immediately, fighter planes took off to look for signs of the strike. Across the dozens of Strategic Air Command bases, klaxons sounded. Air traffic controllers were warned that they may have to immediately ground all commercial flights, clearing the skies for the military. As military leaders prepared to respond, someone discovered that a technician had put a training tape into a computer from a war game exercise that simulated a Soviet attack.[3] It was fortunate that the incident had occurred at a time of relatively low tensions between the Cold War powers, otherwise the duty officers might not have double checked what their screens were telling them.

Four years later, tensions were higher. The United States had adopted a provocative practice of sending a squadron of bombers screaming across Europe toward the Soviet Union, peeling off just before they reached Russian airspace. Reagan had called the Soviet Union "the Evil Empire." Russia was led by hard-liner Yuri Andropov, whose military had just shot down a Korean passenger jet that had mistakenly flown over the Soviet Union, killing all 269 people on board. In September 1983, screens in an air defense bunker south of Moscow showed five incoming US missiles. The Soviet general staff was alerted. The officer on duty, Stanislav Petrov, was asked whether the attack was real. Reasoning that a first strike would involve more missiles, he told them it was not. It later turned out that sunlight flashing off high-altitude clouds had aligned in an unusual way with the satellite: giving the illusion of incoming missiles.[4] Although geopolitics made an attack plausible, the cool-headed response of the duty officer averted the crisis.

In the Stanley Kubrick comedy *Dr. Strangelove*, the Soviet Union builds a Doomsday Machine, which will irreversibly obliterate the world if a single nuclear weapon strikes Russia. But a week before the Soviets plan to reveal its existence, an insane US general launches a rogue strike, which triggers the machine. While *Dr. Strangelove* was fiction, nightmares about a rogue launch were real, even prior to the film's release. In response to fears of such an accident, US defense secretary Robert McNamara ordered that all nuclear weapons be secured with unique codes, equivalent to a safety catch on a gun. These Permissive Action Links were supposed to guarantee that nuclear weapons were not under the independent control of local commanders, and ensure that those stationed in Germany and Turkey could not fall into foreign control. According to one account, though, the Strategic Air Command feared that this could unnecessarily slow its ability to respond to an attack. So it set many of the codes to 00000000.[5]

The logic of nuclear deterrence has its roots in game theory. If two nuclear adversaries both know that they cannot win a nuclear war, then they have no incentive to strike first. The notion of "mutually assured destruction" (MAD) keeps both from pressing the button, no matter how much they dislike one another. The idea goes back well before the atomic bomb. Writing in 1863, science fiction writer Jules Verne imagined a world in which "the engines of warfare were perfected to such a degree" that they brought peace to the world.[6] So long as no one could win a nuclear war, the theory went, no one would have an incentive to start one.

During the 1960s, MAD led to the expansion of nuclear-armed submarines by both Cold War adversaries. Unlike land-based missiles, which could be targeted in a first strike, sea-based missiles were always moving and hard to detect—raising the chance that they could be used to retaliate.

But MAD lacked the perfection that Verne envisioned. One threat came from missile interceptor systems. If it was possible to shoot down all incoming missiles, then a nuclear war could be winnable. When the Soviet Union installed antimissile systems in the 1960s, the United States saw this as destabilizing MAD. It responded by building missiles that carried multiple warheads, each capable of targeting a different missile launcher. Here the aim was to avoid antimissile interceptors, maintaining the strategic balance that would make a successful first strike impossible. A more serious threat to MAD came with President Reagan's announcement in 1983 that the United States would create a missile defense system— the Strategic Defense Initiative—that would use weapons such as satellite-mounted lasers to shoot down incoming missiles. Until this system, dubbed "Star Wars," ended a decade later, many feared that it would have made a nuclear war more likely by undermining nuclear deterrence.

Another limitation of MAD is that it assumes both sides are coolly calculating the implications of their actions, perfectly informed by the available information. But leaders who are enraged, delusional, or uninformed might launch a first strike because they don't understand the consequences, or don't care about them. If you've ever tried to reason with a hungry toddler, you'll have seen the limits of rational negotiation. Ironically, MAD doesn't work if one of the leaders is mad.

It gets worse. Knowing that the other side is led by a maniac changes the incentives for the sensible party. If there is a small advantage to be gained by striking first, then the best tactic may be to fire before the psychopath on the other side does. In a study titled "War with Crazy Types," game theorists Avidit Acharya and Edoardo Grillo argue that the rational response to a crazy adversary is to pretend to be crazy.[7] This in turn increases the chances of war.

There's another problem with the theory that MAD lets us sleep safely at night: it's based on a theory of just two adversaries. Yet as

I've noted, what we used to call an arms race now looks more like a bar fight, with hazards coming from unexpected directions. In his jaunty song "Who's Next?" Tom Lehrer recounts how nuclear proliferation began: "First we got the bomb and that was good, / 'Cause we love peace and motherhood. / Then Russia got the bomb, but that's O.K., / 'Cause the balance of power's maintained that way!"[8]

The period in which the world had just two nuclear powers lasted less than a decade. By 1965, when Lehrer's song came out, the other three permanent members of the UN Security Council—China, Britain, and France—had tested nuclear weapons.

Since then, more nations have joined the nuclear club. Israel probably developed a deliverable nuclear weapon in the late 1960s, though its nuclear program was only exposed by whistleblower Mordechai Vanunu two decades later. Although Israel refuses to reveal whether it is a nuclear power, some clues can be gleaned from the treatment of Vanunu. A female Israeli intelligence operative lured him from London to Rome, where he was drugged, taken to Israel, tried in secret, and sentenced to eighteen years in prison.[9] Israel's nuclear program is periodically cited by Iraq and Iran as a justification for their own attempts to build an atomic bomb.

In South Asia, relations between India and Pakistan have been tense since partition in 1947, when up to a million Hindus and Muslims were killed. Since then, the countries have fought multiple wars and engaged in numerous border skirmishes. India accuses Pakistan of sponsoring terrorist attacks on the Indian Parliament in 2001 and Mumbai in 2008. Nearly five hundred miles of the border between the two nations is disputed.[10] Yet since the 1980s, both nations have possessed nuclear weapons. The hostility between Indian and Pakistani leaders is underpinned by the mutual loathing of their populations for one another. According to one poll, 62 percent of Pakistanis have a negative view of India, while 85 percent of Indians have a negative view of Pakistan.[11]

In recent decades, a plethora of other countries—including Argentina, Brazil, Taiwan, Egypt, Iraq, North Korea, Libya, and Iran—have attempted to build nuclear weapons. Of these, only North Korea has succeeded. As a brutal military dictatorship that tortures, imprisons, and murders its critics, North Korean leader Kim Jong-un and his predecessors sought nuclear weapons as part of the country's program of "all-fortressization." The program began around the 1980s, at a time when US nuclear weapons were stationed in South Korea. In the 1990s, Pakistan's top scientist, A. Q. Khan, gave North Korea information on uranium enrichment in exchange for North Korea sharing its knowledge of missile technology with Pakistan. In 2006, North Korea announced that it had conducted its first nuclear test. The following year, the country confirmed that it had nuclear weapons. Self-indulgent, vicious, and egotistical, Kim is the epitome of a "crazy type" dictator.

The road to nuclear weapons tends to be a one-way street. In the nuclear age, only South Africa has voluntarily given up nuclear weapons, dismantling its stockpile of six nuclear weapons in the 1990s. To this we might add Ukraine, Kazakhstan, and Belarus, which transferred nuclear weapons to Russia after the breakup of the Soviet Union. But typically, once countries have nuclear weapons, Rick Astley's words ring true: "Never Gonna Give You Up." This is also true of nuclear aspirants, who might look at the example of former Libyan dictator Mu'ammar Gaddhafi. In 2003, Gaddhafi decommissioned his country's nuclear weapons program. Eight years later, a popular uprising against Gaddhafi was supported by North Atlantic Treaty Organization (NATO) air strikes, and he was publicly murdered. While the uprising was a response to Gaddhafi's human rights abuses, it is highly unlikely that NATO would have ordered air strikes against a nuclear-armed adversary.

Across the world's nine nuclear powers, there are around fourteen thousand nuclear weapons.[12] Of these, about thirteen thousand are held by the United States and Russia. Among the remaining powers, Britain, France, China, India, and Pakistan have a few hundred nuclear weapons apiece, while North Korea and Israel are suspected to have less than one hundred each. But in the case of nuclear weapons, it doesn't take thousands of missiles to cause calamitous outcomes. A single nuclear weapon can devastate a city. One hundred nuclear weapons could kill more people than died in World War II.

A world with nine nuclear powers is considerably more volatile than a world with two powers. If MAD was problematic when applied to a pair of adversaries, it becomes even more fragile when several players are involved. When multiple people are pointing their guns at one another, one trigger pull can cause a chain reaction where everyone dies.

Mathematically, the number of relationships that can go sour increases rapidly as the number of nuclear powers grows. With two nuclear powers, there's only one relationship to worry about. With three powers, there's three bilateral relationships. With five powers, there's ten relationships. Between the current nine nuclear powers, there's thirty-six possible relationships that could go bad.

Add more actors, and the combinations rapidly explode. Mathematicians like to point out that if you have a group of more than twenty-three people, the odds are better than even that two of them will share a birthday. When it comes to conflict, the same math means that as the number of nuclear states increases, the chances grow that two of them will have a territorial dispute or an ethnoreligious conflict. A world with twenty-three nuclear powers could mean many fewer happy birthdays.

It's not just Iran that covets nuclear weapons. The Institute for Science and International Security, based in Washington, DC, suspects that Syria had intentions to produce nuclear weapons before Israel destroyed a key facility in 2007. Analyzing countries' civilian nuclear facilities, external threats and domestic politics, the institute lists Saudi Arabia, the United Arab Emirates, Turkey, Algeria,

Egypt, South Korea, and Taiwan as among the nations that could seek nuclear weapons in the future.[13]

The world's stockpile of nuclear weapons has been reduced from seventy thousand at the height of the Cold War to around fourteen thousand today. Yet the current arsenal still has devastating power. The bombs that were dropped on Hiroshima and Nagasaki were atomic bombs, based on fission reactions. But the world's leading nuclear powers now have stockpiles of hydrogen bombs, in which the fission explosion detonates a fusion reaction. In a modern nuclear weapon, the atomic explosion is just the percussion cap. Consequently, the B83, the United States' most powerful nuclear weapon, is seventy times as powerful as the bomb that killed a hundred thousand Hiroshima residents. Russia is reportedly investigating weapons that would be almost a hundred times more powerful than the B83.

Watching the awesome power of the first nuclear test, scientist Robert Oppenheimer was reminded of a line from the Hindu scripture, the Bhagavad Gita: "Now I am become Death, the destroyer of worlds." But the risk to humanity goes beyond the ability of these weapons to annihilate entire cities. In 1983, physicist Richard Turco coined the phrase "nuclear winter" to describe what might happen to the climate if hundreds—or even thousands—of weapons were detonated, sending dust and smoke into the upper atmosphere. Would the debris simply be rained out, or might it have an ongoing impact on the climate? According to a 2007 study, an all-out nuclear war would reduce temperatures in large areas of North America by 36°F (20°C) and much of Eurasia by 54°F (30°C).[14] Another study found that even a regional nuclear war, involving fewer than a hundred weapons being detonated, could cause a global nuclear famine.[15] As we have seen, climate change models indicate that raising global temperatures by a handful of degrees Celsius could be devastating for agriculture—so imagine what a drop of 20°C or 30°C could do to crop yields.

It's not just nation-states that are looking to obtain nuclear weapons. In 2001, Al Qaeda leader Osama bin Laden met with a retired Pakistani nuclear scientist, who drew him a rough sketch of a simple nuclear weapon. Two years later, bin Laden requested a religious ruling on the use of nuclear weapons under Islamic law. A radical Saudi cleric obliged, stating, "If a bomb that killed 10 million of them and burned as much of their land as they have burned Muslims' land were dropped on them, it would be permissible."[16] The terrorist group attempted to buy stolen nuclear material, recruit nuclear scientists, and break into nuclear facilities, particularly in Pakistan. Raids on Al Qaeda training camps revealed extensive materials on nuclear weapons, including bomb designs. When it took control of the city of Mosul, the terrorist group Daesh (ISIS) gained access to dangerous nuclear material inside machines at a local hospital.[17] The group apparently never realized its potential to be weaponized.

"The single most important national security threat that we face," President Barack Obama once said, "is nuclear weapons falling into the hands of terrorists."[18] This might happen in several ways. Terror groups could build an improvised nuclear device using highly enriched uranium or plutonium. Developing weapons-grade material is difficult, but the International Atomic Energy Agency has documented over twenty cases in which such material has been lost or stolen. Alternatively, terrorists could steal an existing weapon. Since advanced country launch sites are heavily fortified, they could target a mobile intercontinental ballistic missile, or raid nuclear stockpiles in India or Pakistan (which are seen as especially vulnerable). Another possibility is that a rogue group could buy a weapon from a government. When he was spreading nuclear technology and materials to Iran, North Korea, and Libya in the 1980s and 1990s, rogue Pakistani scientist A. Q. Khan dealt only with governments. But what if North Korea now established its own "A. Q. Kim" network, supplying terrorists with nuclear weapons?[19]

In 2004, nuclear terrorism expert Graham Allison bet some of his colleagues that terrorists would explode a nuclear bomb somewhere in the world by 2014. As he wrote afterward, "I was happy to lose those bets."[20] But he doesn't believe that he was wrong about the underlying probabilities. Instead, he thinks the world just got lucky. Indeed, Allison argues that the risk of nuclear terrorism is on the rise. Nuclear security cooperation between the United States and Russia has broken down. North Korea's successful nuclear program has emboldened other rogue regimes. Daesh and its affiliates seek nuclear weapons. More information than ever before is available to scientists about how to enrich nuclear materials and build a weapon.

Nuclear terrorism is terrifying, but probably not world ending. Its biggest risk to our species would be if terrorists could trick a nuclear state into thinking that it was under attack from a rival nuclear power—causing it to launch a retaliatory strike.

*   *   *

Half a century after atomic bombs razed Hiroshima and Nagasaki, former military analyst Daniel Ellsberg proposed a "Manhattan Project II."[21] Like the original Manhattan Project, which developed nuclear weapons, this second one should be inspired by a similar sense of passion and urgency. Its goal would be the reverse, however: to massively reduce the chances of a nuclear holocaust.

Central to reducing the chances of nuclear catastrophe is minimizing the number of states that possess nuclear weapons. Just as fights are more than twice as likely to break out between four siblings than between two, the risk of conflict increases more than linearly as the number of countries with nuclear weapons grows. South Africa's unique decision to give up nuclear weapons should be hailed by the global community (July 2021 marked the thirtieth anniversary of the moment South Africa finished dismantling its nuclear arsenal).[22] We must send a message to the nine remaining nuclear powers that they would be venerated by the global community if they did the same.

Alas, the chances are growing that the world will soon have its tenth nuclear power. Over recent decades, measures to stop Iran from acquiring nuclear weapons have included Iraqi bombings of its reactors, Israeli assassinations of its nuclear scientists, and a joint US-Israeli computer virus that destroyed one-fifth of Iran's centrifuges. In 2015, Iran agreed to a deal with the European Union and five permanent members of the UN Security Council. In exchange for sanctions being lifted, Iran agreed to limit its enrichment program, and accept international monitoring.

In 2018, urged on by Israeli prime minister Benjamin Netanyahu, Trump withdrew from the agreement, calling it "a horrible one-sided deal that should have never, ever been made." Iran responded by announcing that it would no longer respect any limits in the nuclear deal. At the time of writing, it was unclear whether the Biden Administration would be able to successfully negotiate the United States' re-entry into the deal. If the agreement collapses, analysts believe that Iran could now build a bomb in about a year.[23]

As well as reducing the number of nuclear nations, it is important to reduce the number of weapons. The US and Russian stockpiles were amassed under the outdated logic of the Cold War. Now that we recognize the madness of MAD, it's time to acknowledge that additional weapons make the world riskier, not safer. Given that one hundred missiles could cause a nuclear winter severe enough to create a global famine, stockpiles of thousands of weapons are a hazard to humanity. Each missile—whether it's based in a silo, submarine, air base, or mobile launcher—is a potential point of failure, as the United States proved in 2007 when six armed nuclear missiles were accidentally loaded onto a B-52 bomber and flown across the country, remaining unsecured for thirty-six hours.

Reducing the number of missiles has other benefits too. When launch sites are spread across the globe, it increases the odds that an adversary will mistake something innocuous—the sun glinting off clouds, a weather rocket, or a computer malfunction—for a real attack. By luck, such mistakes have not yet caused a nuclear holocaust. But more weapons means more mistakes. Eventually our luck could run out.

Securing the world's fourteen thousand nuclear weapons against terrorists is an asymmetrical game. Governments need to get it right fourteen thousand times. Terrorists only have to get it right once. If we think of nuclear security as a chain, it is only as strong as its weakest link. So an effective way of improving nuclear security is to remove some links from the chain. Reducing the size of the world's nuclear arsenal makes it less likely that terrorists will steal a weapon—especially if disarmament starts by removing the missiles that are most vulnerable to theft.

Any nuclear power could help by making voluntary reductions in the size of its arsenal, but the geopolitical impact would be largest if it began with cutting the numbers of weapons held by the United States and Russia. This would help create a "race to the bottom" of the most desirable kind: in which all nuclear-armed countries feel the pressure to shrink the size of their arsenals.

Action by the nuclear supremos would create an environment in which it was easier to pressure countries such as India and Pakistan to scrap their weapons entirely. It would also strengthen efforts to stop new nuclear powers from emerging if the nuclear club was seen to be downsizing. This is no longer a radical peacenik view. In 2007, four elder statesmen—former secretaries of state Henry Kissinger and George Shultz, former defense secretary William Perry, and former senator Sam Nunn—wrote an op-ed in the *Wall Street Journal* titled "A World Free of Nuclear Weapons."

The danger of nuclear weapons comes not only from the size of the arsenal but also who can fire them. In the United States, France, and North Korea, launch authority resides solely with the head of state.[24] These leaders have absolute authority to order a nuclear strike for any reason, and the order cannot be countermanded. As President Richard Nixon told reporters during the Watergate scandal, "I can go back into my office and pick up the telephone and in 25 minutes 70 million people will be dead."[25] Once, when Nixon was drunk, he began planning a nuclear strike.[26] The world would be safer if the United States, France, and North Korea adopted a rule that nuclear weapons could be launched only after multiple people had agreed, as is the procedure in other nuclear powers.

Some countries have pledged that they will not use nuclear weapons unless attacked by nuclear weapons. China (since 1964) and India (since 1998) have pledged themselves to a doctrine of "no first use," and urged other nuclear-armed states to do the same. But most nuclear powers leave open the possibility of using nuclear weapons in response to a conventional attack. Extraordinarily, the United States has even canvased the possibility of nuclear weapons being used to respond to a cyberattack.[27] By blurring the line between conventional and nuclear war, this makes nuclear conflict more likely. As former nuclear launch officer Bruce Blair argues, "There exists no plausible circumstance in which nuclear first use would be in the national security interest of the United States."[28] Blair points out that taking a US nuclear first strike off the table would not only contribute to stability but also put pressure on all nuclear powers—particularly Russia and Pakistan—to make the same pledge. Broader adoption of no first use would help ensure that China does not abandon the policy—something it is reportedly considering.[29] A declaration of no first use is not an admission of weakness; it is a reflection of strength, and a country's confidence in the superiority of its nonnuclear forces.[30] At a bare minimum, the United States should begin a conversation about what international conditions would need to be met to enable such a shift.[31]

Nuclear protocols matter too. Since 1985, the Soviet Union (and now Russia) has employed a system known as "Dead Hand."[32] The system serves as a vengeful backup, ensuring that Russian missiles retaliate even if Moscow is obliterated. In a crisis, Dead Hand can be switched on, at which point it uses seismic, radioactivity and pressure sensors to monitor for signs of a nuclear strike. If Dead Hand detects that a nuclear weapon has hit Russia, it can trigger the launch of Russia's intercontinental ballistic missiles. Designed in order to guarantee Russia's second-strike capability, Dead Hand creates a *Dr. Strangelove*–like risk. If switched on, the world is only a few sensor errors away from nuclear war. By sending Dead Hand to the grave, Russia would make the planet a safer place.

In Russia and the United States, a policy of "launch on warning" sees missiles kept on hair-trigger alert, able to be deployed in minutes in response to an incoming attack. Moreover, according to investigative journalist Eric Schlosser, the US military has refused to add a self-destruct feature into missiles, fearing that it might be used by an adversary.[33] So once missiles are launched, they cannot be recalled. All nuclear weapons should also be fitted with command-destruct mechanisms—as is done in the testing phase—since the threat of an errant missile outweighs the risk of a weapon being disabled by the enemy. And just as gun owners are advised to prevent accidents by storing their ammunition separately from their weapons, nuclear delivery systems should be stored separately from their warheads.

In effect, there are thousands of people who could launch nuclear weapons. Suppose that an Ohio-class submarine is being followed by an enemy submarine when its commanders learn that a missile is headed toward the United States.[34] Suddenly, all communications go dead. Would they fire their Trident nuclear missiles, or risk being destroyed and losing the capacity to respond? Could we be sure that all submarine commanders would refrain from firing?

Another danger is launch officers with mental illness. They present a risk akin to commercial airline pilots who have committed suicide by deliberately crashing their planes.[35] Screening and treatment for mental health problems can help, but the job is inherently stressful. One study found that people in nuclear-armed submarines were twice as likely to suffer from neuropsychiatric illness as other naval personnel.[36] To reduce the risk, the US military mandates "no lone zones" so that launch areas must be staffed by two people, who are within sight of each other at all times. Similarly, missile launch operates on a "two-person rule," with both commanders turning their keys at the same time.

These safeguards reduce the risk, but do not eliminate it. To see this, suppose that 1 in 100 commanders are sufficiently unstable to launch a rogue attack. The odds of two unstable commanders being paired together would be 1 in 100^2, or 1 in 10,000. That might sound reassuring, until you reflect that the world has fourteen thousand nuclear weapons.[37] Reducing the number of weapons is the surest way to lower the chances that humanity stumbles into World War III by accident.

A Manhattan Project II of denuclearization would involve careful work by diplomats, military personnel, activists, and engineers, all focused on ensuring that the technology of nuclear weapons is never deployed. In the case of other existential risks—such as artificial intelligence—the challenge is not to prevent the technology being used but rather to ensure it is built safely. It is to superintelligence that I now turn.

5
The Last Invention

Jimmy Chou has won more than $1 million playing poker, but he was trounced by Libratus, a new artificial intelligence program, in six-player, no-limit Texas hold'em. As Chou noted, "The bot gets better and better every day. It's like a tougher version of us. The first couple of days, we had high hopes. But every time we find a weakness, it learns from us and the weakness disappears the next day."[1] Libratus bluffs aggressively and doesn't back off when it loses a hand. As poker champion Dong Kim put it, "I felt like I was playing against someone who was cheating, like it could see my cards. I'm not accusing it of cheating. It was just that good."[2] In a 2017 tournament against Chou, Kim, and two other humans, Libratus won $1.8 million in chips.[3] It is effectively the world's best poker player.[4]

Libratus's victory was just one of many areas in which humans have folded in the face of our computer opponents. Machines have bested us in backgammon (1992), checkers (1995), chess (1997), the quiz show *Jeopardy!* (2011), facial recognition (2014), deciphering captcha codes (2014), transcribing a telephone call (2016), lipreading (2016), interpreting cancer scans (2018), the multiplayer game *Dota 2* (2019), and all fifty-seven Atari 2600 games (2020).[5]

Computers are now able to train themselves on these games. Unlike early chess computers, which were trained by being fed thousands of human chess games, Google's AlphaGo Zero started with nothing but the rules of the ancient Chinese game Go. Using a form of reinforcement learning, the machine served as its own teacher. After three hours, it played like a human beginner. After a day, it had learned more advanced techniques. After three days, it was performing at superhuman levels, discovering the corner sequences (*jōseki*) that professional players use and then creating a fresh *jōseki* variation of its own.[6] After 40 days, AlphaGo Zero was in an entirely new realm, employing all the elements of top human players, but with midgame play that experts called "truly mysterious."[7]

Linguistically, computers are startlingly good at mimicking styles. Using OpenAI's GPT-3, technologist Arram Sabeti has produced poems about Elon Musk in the style of Dr. Seuss: "We'll settle on Mars / Where we can be free. / We'll build cities, / Homes and factories." The machine has written a rap about Harry Potter in the style of Lil Wayne: "I'm higher than a kite like a witch on a broomstick / I got bigger balls than Dumbledore with a Firebolt." Sabeti has even produced computer-generated comedy, including a sketch in which Silicon Valley leaders complain about running a company. In the segment, GPT-3 has PayPal cofounder Peter Thiel say, "Socializing on the internet is like if you walked into a bar and everyone there had only read about alcohol, but never actually tried it. You'll be torn to shreds." The computer doesn't match the quirky wit of *Seinfeld* or *Monty Python*, but it does exploit exaggeration and repetition for comic effect.

In one exercise, Sabeti has his artificial intelligence write an op-ed about human intelligence. A passage from the machine-written article reads, "Humans were wrong about alchemy, phrenology, bloodletting, creationism, astrology, numerology, and homeopathy. They were also wrong about the best way to harvest crops, the best way to govern, the best way to punish criminals, and the best way to cure the sick. . . . If humans are so smart, how come they keep being wrong about everything?"[8]

Yet while computers triumph in structured environments, they still cannot shop in a cramped bodega, lead a team, or empathize with a dying patient. Language models based on deep learning are eerily accurate at impersonating writing styles, but go adrift when required to structure a larger piece of writing, such as a novel or movie. Google's driverless cars have been navigating US highways for over a decade, but are still unable to cope with severe snowstorms or the unruly fender fights that occur in congested cities. Current machines struggle with new situations that go beyond the data on which they have been trained and patterns they are used to recognizing. Yet as we will see, most researchers expect that it will eventually become possible to design a machine whose electronic circuits can outperform our neurons.

How will we know when computers have reached the human benchmark? The most famous test was devised by pioneering computer scientist Alan Turing. During World War II, Turing was a key member of the Bletchley Park team of German code breakers whose work may have shortened the war by as much as two years, saving over ten million lives. Yet just seven years after the end of the war, Turing was prosecuted for his homosexuality and accepted chemical castration as a punishment. In 1954, at age forty-one, he committed suicide. "There was no such thing as a 'simple' life for him," one biographer wrote, "no more than there was a 'simple' science."[9]

Turing proposed a test in which a human examiner converses with two entities: another person and a computer. If the examiner cannot tell them apart, Turing argued, the computer has attained human-level intelligence. In his honor, the Loebner Prize awards an annual prize to the computer program that can best trick the judges into thinking it is a human. It is an ingenious test, but modern researchers have found that building a chatbot that fools humans is easier than carrying out real world tasks, from folding towels to curing tuberculosis. Mimicking human prose turns out to be simpler than running along an unfamiliar forest trail.

Had his life not been cut short, Turing might well have devised better tests for intelligence. Apple cofounder Steve Wozniak proposes the coffee test, in which the machine is required to go into your home, find the coffee maker, fill it up, and brew a cup of coffee. Researcher Ben Goertzel suggests the college test, in which the artificial intelligence attends a university, passes the exams, and graduates. Computer scientist Nils John Nilsson proffered the career test, in which the machine goes to your workplace and does your job as well as you do. Roboticist Rodney Brooks offers the child test, in which we ask whether the computer has the object recognition, language understanding, manual dexterity, and social understanding of a young child. Among these, the career test is probably the most useful, but each provides insights. Perhaps the answer is a "Five Cs" artificial intelligence pentathlon in which machines must pass Turing's chatbot test, Wozniak's coffee test, Goertzel's college test, Nilsson's career test, and Brooks's child test.

But there is no reason to think that artificial intelligence will stop advancing when it wins the Five Cs Pentathlon. After all, chess computers did not stop improving after beating Garry Kasparov in 1997. These days, the competition isn't even close. On the Elo scale, which measures the probability that one contestant will beat another, the best chess computer is currently about 700 points ahead of the best human.[10] Likewise, the best Go computer is currently about 1400 Elo points ahead of the best human.[11] In a human-computer matchup, we should expect the machine to win 99.3 percent of the time in chess (ignoring drawn matches) and 99.99995 percent of the time in Go. Playing chess and Go against machines, humans have about the same chance of victory as a regular guy might have of winning a boxing match against Tyson Fury.

The key to advances in artificial intelligence is the speed at which machines can improve themselves. Because human generations are around thirty years, genetic evolution takes thousands of years to bring about noticeable changes. But a computer algorithm can adapt instantly and rerun the code. This means that algorithmic "generations" are measured in fractions of seconds, so technological advances occur at a dizzying rate. When they approach our levels of ability, it's possible that computers might blast past us as though we are standing still. We could see an "intelligence explosion."

It is hard to overstate the importance of this development. As early as 1965, Irving Good, a statistician who had served alongside Turing on the Bletchley Park code-breaking team, warned that "the first ultraintelligent machine is the *last* invention that man need ever make, provided that the machine is docile enough to tell us how to keep it under control. It is curious that this point is made so seldom outside of science fiction."[12]

The control problem is the challenge of designing a machine in such a way that it will help rather than harm humanity. This isn't as simple as it might initially seem. If we allow the machine to devise its own objective, then it is unlikely to come up with one that accords with ours. Researcher Nick Bostrom gives the example of a machine that alights on the objective of making as many paper clips as possible and soon begins to devour all metal on the planet to create paper clips.[13]

If we set the objective ourselves, then we run into the same problem as King Midas, who realized too late that he didn't in fact want *everything* he touched to turn into gold. A machine programmed to *maximize* human happiness may force-feed us heroin. A computer instructed to *minimize* human suffering might sterilize our species. A machine coded with the sole objective of discovering a cure for cancer may deliberately increase the prevalence of the disease so that it can run medical experiments until it finds a solution. A computer ordered to defend a country at all costs could decide to preemptively obliterate neutral nations so that they never become adversaries. One illustration of the King Midas problem emerged when programmers taught an artificial intelligence agent to play the classic boat-racing game *CoastRunners*.[14] The agent alighted on a strategy of turning in a small circle, repeatedly crashing into other boats, catching on fire, and traveling in the wrong direction. Its final score was 20 percent higher than it if had completed the course.

Formally known as "perverse instantiation," the problem of describing the goals of our species arises because humanity has multiple aims, which are often in tension with one another. Science fiction writer Isaac Asimov famously proposed four laws for robots: don't harm humanity, don't injure humans, obey orders, and protect yourself. The rules sounded sensible, but they turned out to create all kinds of problems, which Asimov explored in his short stories.[15]

In a sense, the problem of encoding altruism into a computer is akin to the challenge of writing a watertight tax code: clever attorneys frequently find ways of obeying the letter of the law while violating the spirit of the code. One tax break designed to let family farmers swap horses without incurring a tax obligation morphed into a multibillion dollar loophole used by Wells Fargo and General Electric.[16] Encoding our values is harder than it seems. If this problem arises when groups of smart humans are pursuing different goals, it seems plausible that it will also emerge when humans are programming a highly advanced machine. The problem is even trickier if the goal is to create a system that satisfies everyone on the planet. The aspirations of a Scandinavian atheist are not necessarily those of a Middle Eastern sheikh.

Can't we just unplug it at the wall? While this solution works for a simple desktop, it is unlikely to be effective in the case of advanced artificial intelligence. A superintelligence would likely be integrated into too many systems to be able to simply turn it "off." Not to mention the fact that if a superintelligence is smarter than we are, then it will probably anticipate and prevent this from happening. As computer scientist Steve Omohundro observes, any sufficiently advanced machine will want to self-improve, acquire resources, and resist being shut down.[17] Once a superintelligence has been created, it would be near-impossible to contain.

The idea of a computer that resists efforts to shut it off is not merely the stuff of Arthur C. Clarke novels. In 2013, researcher Tom Murphy reported on an artificial intelligence agent designed to play the brick-dropping game of *Tetris*. Noticing that the game is ultimately unwinnable, it alighted on the ingenious strategy of pausing the game just before the last brick sealed its fate.[18] As leading safety researcher Stuart Russell points out, if we give a superintelligent computer a goal, then it is most likely to be achieved by continuing to run.[19] So defying shutdown is an inherent part of many objective functions (and therefore, Russell argues, Asimov's fourth law of robotics is unnecessary).

The control problem might be manageable if artificial intelligence research involved just one team of researchers, working at a calm pace. For example, they might create a stunted superintelligence that could only answer questions with "yes" or "no." Or they might install trip wires to detect attempts at unwanted behavior. Such guardrails would make the system safer, at a cost of being less useful. But it's hard to see such safeguards enduring in a competitive research environment. With research teams competing across the globe, some would inevitably compromise on risk in order to secure more performance. For this reason, many experts take the view that "capability control" approaches—in which the performance of the system is deliberately curtailed—are probably not an effective solution to the control problem. Instead, researchers are focused on creating artificial intelligence that is aligned with human values. I will return to the alignment problem in a moment.

Could the risk community be jumping at electric shadows? A few think so. Computer scientist Andrew Ng claims that it is like worrying about "overpopulation on the planet Mars," while software pioneer Mitch Kapor dismisses fears about superintelligence as "intelligent design for the IQ 140 people."[20] Some of the pushback against safety concerns has come from researchers who argue that achieving human-level intelligence is so far away that it is not worth worrying about its risk. For example, technology philosopher Jaron Lanier argues that the idiosyncrasies of machines still make them quite unlike humans: "The very features of computers that drive us crazy today, and keep so many of us gainfully employed, are the best insurance our species has for long-term survival as we explore the far reaches of technological possibility."[21] Computers can advance a long way, Lanier believes, before they get close to human level operation. Similarly, Microsoft cofounder Paul Allen, who is working on artificial intelligence from the approach of neuroscience, predicts that rather than accelerating returns, we should expect a complexity brake, as each advance makes us realize how little we understand of the sophistication of the human brain.[22]

Other skeptics characterize discussions of risk as attempts to shut down their work, pointing to the many benefits of artificial intelligence. For instance, Facebook CEO Mark Zuckerberg says, "If you're arguing against artificial intelligence, then you're arguing against safer cars that aren't going to have accidents. And you're arguing against being able to better diagnose people when they're sick. I just don't see how, in good conscience, some people can do that."[23] Yet there is no evidence that people in the safety community are arguing against artificial intelligence. Those working on risk are aiming to shape the technology, not block its development. The Institute of Electrical and Electronics Engineers (the world's largest peak body for computer scientists) makes the point with an analogy to the way the programming language C developed.[24] A mistaken choice in how to code strings (null terminated versus length prefixed) means that the language is vulnerable to common and costly buffer overflow attacks. If early C programmers had paid more attention to security issues, the code would have been a little less memory efficient, but much less vulnerable. Safety should not be an afterthought.

Ultimately, the most striking thing about the discussion over artificial intelligence risk is how broadly the concerns are shared. As writer Scott Alexander wryly sums up the debate, "The 'skeptic' position seems to be that, although we should probably get a couple of bright people to start working on preliminary aspects of the problem, we shouldn't panic or start trying to ban artificial intelligence research. The 'believers,' meanwhile, insist that although we shouldn't panic or start trying to ban artificial intelligence research, we should probably get a couple of bright people to start working on preliminary aspects of the problem."[25] In making the case for artificial intelligence researchers to work on safety issues, Russell concludes that the risks "are neither minimal nor insuperable."[26]

A broadly shared belief in the risks is also reflected in surveys that ask when computers will attain human-level intelligence. Since 1972, people have been surveying artificial intelligence researchers on this question.[27] While there is a broad spread of views, one clear finding is that researchers who are worried about artificial intelligence safety make similar estimates on when machines will attain human-level intelligence as do researchers who do not see it as a danger.[28] The difference between the nervous and the relaxed comes down to what should be done, not divergence over when the crossover point will arrive.

A 2016 survey of 352 artificial intelligence experts asked what year they expected machines to attain a level of intelligence that allowed them to pass the career test: accomplishing every task better and more cheaply than human workers.[29] The median guess was 2061. As milestones, the experts were also asked about specific occupations and tasks, which are shown in figure 5.1. On average, they guessed that machines will reach human-level performance at truck driving in 2027, writing a best-selling book in 2049, surgery in 2053, and mathematics research in 2059. The chart provides a sense of the degree of uncertainty among experts too. For example,

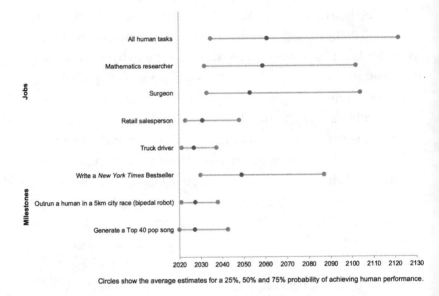

Circles show the average estimates for a 25%, 50% and 75% probability of achieving human performance.

Figure 5.1
Median estimates (with confidence intervals) of artificial intelligence achieving human performance. *Source*: Katja Grace, John Salvatier, Allan Dafoe, Baobao Zhang, and Owain Evans, "When Will AI Exceed Human Performance? Evidence from AI Experts," *Journal of Artificial Intelligence Research* 62 (2018): 729–754.

artificial intelligence researchers believe that there is a 25 percent chance that computers will pass the career test by 2035, but a 75 percent chance that machines will pass the career test by 2122.

What happens when human-level intelligence is attained? On average, artificial intelligence experts believe that there is a 43 percent chance of an intelligence explosion.[30] They generally think that the outcomes are likely to be neutral or positive, but do not rule out the downside. Artificial intelligence experts believe that attaining human-level intelligence has a 10 percent chance of being "bad," and a 5 percent chance of being "extremely bad (e.g., human extinction)." When the leading researchers on an issue believe that there is a one in twenty chance it could extinguish the world, it's not alarmist to be looking for solutions. Indeed, artificial intelligence experts are three times as likely to support more research on safety than to believe that investment in safety should be reduced.

It's possible that the forecasts of those working on artificial intelligence are overly optimistic about technological progress in their field. In the 1972 survey, 59 percent of experts predicted that human-level intelligence would be attained by 2022 or earlier.[31] They did not forecast the two artificial intelligence "winters" of the late 1970s and late 1980s. Today, artificial intelligence is booming. Since 2010, artificial intelligence research has doubled its share of published papers, and artificial intelligence jobs have quintupled as a share of the workforce. Attendance at artificial intelligence conferences has tripled, and investment in artificial intelligence start-ups has grown thirtyfold.[32] The vast majority of surveyed artificial intelligence experts say that the pace of progress has been faster in the second half of their career than in the first half.

As Joshua Gans and I noted in *Innovation + Equality: How to Create a Future That Is More Star Trek Than Terminator*, rapid adoption of artificial intelligence could have significant human benefits— taking over tedious or hazardous jobs, improving the treatment of disease, and reducing risk in our daily lives. But from the standpoint of averting catastrophe, a fast takeoff cuts down on the amount of time available to solve the control problem and gives us fewer years in which to figure out how to create an artificial intelligence whose goals are aligned with ours.

Similar issues apply to the competitiveness of the mission to achieve superintelligence. Suppose the quest for superintelligence is a winner-take-all race in which an intelligence explosion allows the first successful research team to dominate the entire field. This scenario, akin to World War II's race to build the first nuclear bomb, would create incentives for teams to hack or sabotage their rivals. Bostrom argues that an even greater harm "stems not from the smashup of battle but from the downgrade of precaution."[33] If teams start from the same point and safety measures impede technical progress, then the winner will be the team that spends the least on safety. The more hotly contested the race, the greater the risk to humanity.

*   *   *

"I first became interested in artificial intelligence risk back around 2007," writes Alexander. "At the time, most people's response to the topic was 'Haha, come back when anyone believes this besides random internet crackpots.'"[34] Over recent decades, a significant number of leading technology figures—including Elon Musk, Jaan Tallinn, Steve Wozniak, and Bill Gates—have raised concerns. More than eight thousand experts have signed the Future of Humanity Institute's open letter calling for more research to ensure that humanity avoids potential pitfalls. There is a broad recognition that a misaligned superintelligence could cause us harm not through malice but rather because it has different goals than our own. It might treat us the way we treat the world's bird life, though the intelligence gap between us and the superintelligence may be far greater.

Promising solutions to the alignment problem are emerging. Given our inability to fully codify humanity's objectives and the risk of "perverse instantiation" (the King Midas problem), Russell proposes instead that programmers focus on building computers that are observant, humble, and altruistic. As opposed to following a preset moral code, such machines would start from the premise that they didn't know much about what humans wanted. Their task would be to watch how humans behave and help us achieve our goals.[35]

This approach has the added advantage that programmers would not be locking a set of values into the system that later generations regard as bigoted or intolerant. For instance, take the leading computer programmers who proposed in 1956 that a ten-man team of researchers, working at Dartmouth College over a summer, could crack the problem of artificial intelligence. If they had succeeded in encoding their values into a superintelligence, it would have embodied the more sexist, racist, and homophobic norms of that era. By requiring an artificial intelligence to realize *contemporary* human values, we allow for the possibility that moral attitudes (such as views on the treatment of animals) might become more enlightened in the future than they are today.

Already, the approach that governments are adopting toward artificial intelligence risk suggests that an ideological divide may emerge. In 2018, Canada's Justin Trudeau and France's Emmanuel Macron announced plans for an "International Panel on Artificial Intelligence," to be modeled on the IPCC. Just as the IPCC helped raise the profile of climate change, such a panel would have drawn global attention to ethical concerns over artificial intelligence. But the United States refused to support it, reportedly because of concerns that an overly cautious approach could hamper the development of the technology.[36] The Canadian-French initiative eventually led to a fifteen-member Organisation for Economic Co-operation and Development forum called the Global Partnership on Artificial Intelligence—a much more modest initiative than the IPCC. In the absence of global cooperation, analysts are already warning of an artificial intelligence cold war between the United States and China, with the twentieth century's Iron Curtain and Berlin Wall replaced by a modern-day Digital Curtain and Great Firewall.

Turbocharging the race for artificial intelligence—while dismissing the dangers—increases the odds of the kind of "extremely bad (e.g., human extinction)" scenario that artificial intelligence experts say has a 5 percent probability of occurring. Reducing the risks of a superintelligence will require more global cooperation, not less. International statements on artificial intelligence—such as the Organisation for Economic Co-operation and Development's Principles on Artificial Intelligence and the G20 Human-Centered

AI Principles—already mention the importance of "trustworthy" systems that are "robust, secure and safe." But the focus is almost exclusively on current technologies, such as fraud detection, crop monitoring, and targeted advertising. Nations need to explicitly address how to avoid the creation of a dangerous superintelligence, which may require moving beyond guiding principles to negotiating enforceable treaties.

Across research institutions, professional societies, and corporations, values statements are proliferating. A recent report identified over eighty sets of artificial intelligence guidelines developed by stakeholders, including the Institute of Electrical and Electronics Engineers' *Ethically Aligned Design Principles*, UNI Global Union's *10 Principles for Ethical Artificial Intelligence*, Future of Life Institute's *Asilomar AI Principles*, and Tokyo Statement's *Cooperation for Beneficial AI*.[37]

Common themes across these guidelines include the need to embed appropriate human values, avoid creating weapons systems that would be able to kill autonomously, and encourage collaboration over competition. Some guidelines also embody Bostrom's "common good principle," which states that superintelligence should only be developed for the benefit of all humanity and in the service of widely shared ethical ideals.[38] The common good principle, Bostrom argues, creates an expectation that the first country or business to create a superintelligence will immediately share it with the rest of humanity. Humanity's "last invention" must not be protected by a twenty-year patent.

Minimizing the risks from artificial intelligence is not only a blend of philosophy and programming; it requires governments to synthesize their innovation-backing role with their regulatory duties. At present, these responsibilities are often delegated to different parts of the bureaucracy. Governments should learn from car designers, who recognize the value of putting the gas pedal next to the brake.[39] Good institutional design is important not only for reducing the risk of artificial intelligence but also for other areas such as data sharing, privacy policy, and financial technology. Indeed, good design may help address the risks of what researcher Toby Walsh calls "stupid artificial intelligence"—self-driving cars that crash, human resource systems that discriminate, and social media algorithms that spread misinformation.[40] Smart design can stop today's artificial intelligence systems from making dumb mistakes and prevent tomorrow's systems from taking over the world.

Unique among the challenges discussed in this book, the question with superintelligence is not whether it will transpire but when. At some point in the future—whether it's 50 or 150 years away—we will need to tackle the problem. It makes sense today to make the preparations that will help ensure that humanity's final invention does not bring our final hour.

6
What Are the Odds?

An asteroid hitting Earth is extremely improbable. So was the fact that in a two-month period in 1998, twin films hit the cinemas based on precisely that scenario.[1] One possible explanation is that the Bruce Willis film *Armageddon* and Steven Spielberg movie *Deep Impact* may both have been inspired by the Shoemaker-Levy 9 comet, which crashed into the planet Jupiter in 1994, flinging debris across a thirty-seven-hundred-mile area.

Thinking about the impact of an asteroid with the Earth is a fearful prospect. Sixty-six million years ago, an asteroid six to nine miles in diameter struck the Yucatán Peninsula in Mexico.[2] The result was a worldwide dust cloud, acid rain, and freezing temperatures. Three-quarters of all life on earth perished, including all nonavian dinosaurs.

Without that asteroid, there would probably be no humans. Yet while we owe our existence to the last major asteroid strike, it's quite reasonable to be concerned about averting the next one. The obliteration of the dinosaurs enabled the rise of humanity, but that doesn't make incoming space rocks any more attractive.

In the case of asteroids, humanity spent most of our time on the planet being just as vulnerable as the dinosaurs were. But over recent decades, the situation has changed. Since 1998 (there's that date again), NASA has attempted to track near-Earth objects that could cause us significant harm. Of particular concern are large asteroids and comets—those with a diameter exceeding 0.6 miles. So far, NASA's Planetary Defense Coordination Office has identified around nine hundred large objects.[3]

By looking at the rate at which it is finding new objects, NASA can estimate how many are yet to be discovered. In the early 2000s, astronomers discovered over fifty large objects each year. In 2020, they found just three. That's encouraging news. The dwindling rate of new discoveries suggests that NASA is now tracking 90 percent of large objects in the area near Earth. True to its name, the Planetary Defense Coordination Office also studies techniques for deflecting an asteroid off a predicted impact course with Earth. The most promising approaches are to divert the asteroid's trajectory with a nuclear explosion on the edge, break it into smaller parts with a nuclear explosion in the center, or knock it off course with a fast and heavy rocket. In 2022, NASA plans to test one of these tricks by deliberately crashing a half-ton spacecraft into Didymoon, a five-hundred-foot asteroid.

Based on NASA's mature understanding of the risks and mitigation strategies, those who study existential risk are sanguine about asteroids. And unlike some of the existential risks we have already encountered in this book, there is bipartisan support within the United States for reducing asteroid risk. Among those who have taken an interest in the issue are Republican senator Ted Cruz, who asked NASA in 2018, "What steps do we need to be taking so that we don't have to rely on sending Bruce Willis to space to save humanity?"[4] In 2021, the budget for planetary defense was thirty times larger than it had been in 2008.[5] If other existential risks received the same political priority as asteroid risk, this book would be unnecessary.

In this chapter, I'll aim to take a comprehensive approach to existential risk. I've already devoted separate chapters to four of the greatest catastrophic threats: disease, climate change, nuclear war, and superintelligence. In chapter 8, I address a fifth danger: totalitarianism. But what other menaces lurk in the shadows? And might there be perils that we haven't yet thought of?

In encapsulating the threats to humanity, a useful starting point is Ord's probability estimates. Surveying the research across a wide range of fields, Ord bravely attempts to assess the chances of each risk materializing over the coming century. "Don't take the estimates to be precise," he warns. "Their purpose is to show the right order of magnitude."[6]

Presented in table 6.1, Ord's figures span an extremely large range, from one in a billion at the low end to one in six at the high end. It can be hard to get your head around these probabilities, so here's one way to think about the difference. One in six is the chance that if you roll a die, it comes up six. One in a billion is the chance that if you roll twelve dice, they all come up six.

ble 6.1

omparing Existential Threats to Everyday Risks

xistential risks	Chance within next 100 years	Equivalent risks
steroid or comet ιpact	~ 1 in 1,000,000	Chance that you will die a violent or accidental death today[a]
ιpervolcano	~ 1 in 10,000	Chance of death from riding a motorbike 700 miles[a]
ellar explosion	~ 1 in 1,000,000,000	Chance of being struck by lightning this week[b]
ιtal natural risk	~ 1 in 10,000	Chance that a mother will die in childbirth[c]
uclear war	~ 1 in 1,000	Annual chances of death for logging and fishing workers[d]
ιtastrophic climate ιange	~ 1 in 1,000	Chance of death for a US soldier deployed to the Iraq War for 4 years[e]

(continues)

Table 6.1 (cont.)

Existential risks	Chance within next 100 years	Equivalent risks
Other environmental damage	~ 1 in 1,000	Chance of dying per 100 skydiving jumps[a]
"Naturally" arising pandemics	~ 1 in 10,000	Chance of dying in a car crash this year[b,f]
Engineered pandemics	~ 1 in 30	Chance that having unprotected sex once will lead to pregnancy[g]
Unaligned artificial intelligence	~ 1 in 10	Chance that a smoker's habit will kill them before age 60[h]
Widespread authoritarianism	~ 1 in 100	Chance that your spouse cheated on you last month[i]
Other anthropogenic risks	~ 1 in 50	Chance of death for a US solider serving in the Vietnam War for one year[e]
Unforeseen anthropogenic risks	~ 1 in 30	Chance that a 1970s Formula 1 driver died in a single season[j]
Total anthropogenic risk	*~ 1 in 6*	*Chance of death for a pedestrian hit by a car traveling at 28 mph[k]*
Total existential risk	*~ 1 in 6*	*Chance that a 90-year-old will die within a year[l]*

Notes: a. Michael Blastland and David Spiegelhalter, *The Norm Chronicles: Stories and Numbers about Danger* (London: Profile Books, 2013), 292. b. "Odds of Dying Due to Injury," 2018, injuryfacts.nsc.org. c. The US maternal mortality rate is actually a little above 1 in 10,000, having risen since the 1990s. In 2018, the figure was 17.4 deaths per 100,000 births, or 1 in 5,747. See National Center for Health Statistics figures, cdc.gov. d. Laura Armey, Thomas Kniesner, John Leeth, and Ryan Sullivan, "Combat, Casualties, and Compensation: Evidence from Iraq and Afghanistan," Discussion Paper 11785, IZA, Bonn, 2018. e. Matthew S. Goldberg, "Death and Injury Rates of US Military Personnel in Iraq," *Military Medicine* 175, no. 4 (2010): 220–226. f. Kenneth D. Kochanek, Sherry L. Murphy, Jiaquan Xu, and Elizabeth Arias, *Deaths: Final Data 2017*, National Vital Statistics Reports, vol. 68, no. 9 (Hyattsville, MD: National Center for Health Statistics, 2019), 46. g. M. Antonia Biggs and Diana Greene Foster, "Misunderstanding the Risk of Conception from Unprotected and Protected Sex," *Women's Health Issues* 23, no. 1 (2013): e47–e53. h. Prabhat Jha, Chinthanie Ramasundarahettige, Victoria Landsman, Brian Rostron, Michael Thun, Robert N. Anderson, Tim McAfee, and Richard Peto, "21st-Century

Hazards of Smoking and Benefits of Cessation in the United States," *New England Journal of Medicine* 368, no. 4 (2013): 341–350. i. Adrian J. Blow and Kelley Hartnett, "Infidelity in Committed Relationships II: A Substantive Review," *Journal of Marital and Family Therapy* 31, no. 2 (2005): 217. j. Hannah Barnes, "Lauda, Hunt and Rush: How Deadly Was 1970s Formula 1?," *BBC Magazine*, September 22, 2013. k. Brian C. Tefft, *Impact Speed and a Pedestrian's Risk of Severe Injury or Death* (Washington, DC: AAA Foundation for Traffic Safety, 2011). l. Office of the Chief Actuary, Social Security Administration, "Period Life Table, 2017," ssa.gov/oact.

Another approach is to compare existential risks with everyday risks. In their book *The Norm Chronicles*, Michael Blastland and David Spiegelhalter estimate risks for everyday activities. Drawing on some of their numbers and calculating some of my own, I calculate an everyday risk that approximately matches each of Ord's existential risks.

The thing about everyday risks—as *The Norm Chronicles* makes clear—is that most of us aren't good at comparing them. People generally worry more about shark attacks than drowning in a bath. We're more likely to fear dying in a plane crash than in an airport taxi. News reports often emphasize terrorism over family violence. When the same risk is framed in positive terms, people are more inclined to take it than when the downside is emphasized.[7] Across the population, people have huge differences in the risk they attribute to different dangers.[8] So don't be surprised if some of the everyday risk numbers in this chapter surprise you.

Let's start with natural risks. The chances of an asteroid or comet wiping out humanity in the next century are one in a million, which is approximately your daily chance of dying in an accident or violence. Objects larger than 0.6 miles strike the Earth on average once every 440,000 years.[9] NASA's ability to track and deflect such objects reduces the risk further still. So don't let an asteroid strike keep you up at night.

Nastier natural hazards are supervolcanoes. These occur when magma rises toward the surface from a hot spot, but is unable to break through the crust. This causes the formation of a large pool of magma, which eventually explodes with extraordinary force. A volcano that shoots out more than 240 cubic miles of ash and lava is classed as a supervolcano. During Earth's history, it is estimated that at least forty supervolcanoes have exploded, including in Yellowstone National Park 2.1 million years ago, Indonesia 74,000 years ago, and New Zealand 26,000 years ago.[10] Such an explosion is hard to predict, tricky to prevent, and potentially catastrophic because of its impact on the climate.

In understanding tsunamis, we frequently start with large waves. Similarly, one way to appreciate the power of supervolcanoes is to begin with the impact of a regular volcano. Take Indonesia's Tambora volcano. When Tambora exploded in 1815, it sent so much ash into the atmosphere that sunsets in Europe glowed with new twilight colors. Crops failed. Livestock died. Maine and New York experienced June snowfalls. The year 1816 became known in the Northern Hemisphere as "the year without a summer." Europe suffered the worst famine of the nineteenth century. The explosion killed tens of thousands directly, and hundreds of thousands indirectly.[11] Now consider that Tambora was just a regular volcano. When Indonesia's Toba supervolcano exploded 74,000 years ago, its eruption was thirty-five hundred times larger than Tambora.[12] A twenty-first-century supervolcano could have calamitous consequences, including complete global crop failures, near-complete livestock deaths, disease spread, and societal breakdown.

It is estimated that the odds of a supervolcano extinguishing humanity in the next hundred years are one in ten thousand. This is approximately the chances of death that motorcycle riders face every seven hundred miles on the road.

Then there are stellar explosions. When stars collapse or collide, they release enormous amounts of energy—equivalent to the total amount of energy in a hundred-billion-star galaxy. Were these supernovas and gamma ray bursts to strike Earth, they could do immense damage. The sky would burn blue. As radiation poured into our atmosphere, most of the protective ozone layer would be destroyed. Yet such events are exceedingly rare, posing an extinction risk to humanity of one in a billion over the next century. This is around the chance that you will be struck by lightning this week.

Adding together these "natural risks" suggests that the probability of human existence being snuffed out by asteroids, comets, supervolcanoes, or stellar explosions is about one in ten thousand over the next hundred years. This is approximately the same as the chances that the typical US resident will die in a motor vehicle accident this year.

Anthropogenic risks are where the dangers loom. Ord estimates that the odds of a civilization-ending nuclear war are one in a thousand. This is approximately the odds of death each year for logging and fishing workers, the most dangerous civilian occupations. He places similar odds on a species-ending climate catastrophe—again, one in a thousand. Another way of thinking about this figure is that it is approximately the chances of death that a US soldier would face if deployed to the Iraq War for four years.

To these risks, Ord adds a third category: "other environmental damage." This might include cascading ecosystem failures, or the loss of resources that are scarce, essential, and irreplaceable. In my view, some environmental risks have been exaggerated. Dire warnings about overpopulation from scholars such as Thomas Malthus, Garrett Hardin, and Paul Ehrlich failed to eventuate (and the racist history of the eugenics movement should give pause to modern-day Malthusians).[13] Fears about overpopulation should be allayed by the fact that the total fertility rate across the world is now 2.4 births per woman—close to the steady-state level of 2.1. Almost half the people in the world live in nations where fertility levels are below the replacement rate. The same is true of the overblown fears of "peak oil." In reality, the ongoing transition to renewables makes it extremely unlikely that fossil fuel shortages will terminate our species. Even the prospect of honeybees becoming extinct would be awful rather than apocalyptic since less than one-tenth of crops rely on such pollinators. Yet while overpopulation, peak oil, and the bee apocalypse have been overemphasized, environmental ecosystems are so intricately interconnected that there remains a possibility that an as-yet-unidentified environmental risk could spell disaster. Overall, Ord places a one in thousand probability on the prospect of other environmental damages causing human extinction in the next century. This is approximately the chance of dying every hundred skydiving jumps.

COVID-19 has made us particularly focused on the danger of diseases jumping the species barrier or evolving particularly nasty characteristics. Yet, as of mid-2021, fewer than one in a thousand people around the world had died from this specific coronavirus. Contemplating the risks across the coming hundred years, the danger of civilizational collapse being caused by such a pandemic are estimated at one in ten thousand, or a little less than the probability that a mother will die in childbirth in the United States. Humans are far more vulnerable to engineered organisms, created to be deadlier and more infectious than naturally occurring diseases. The odds of a lab-bred pandemic are estimated at one in thirty, which is about the odds that a young heterosexual couple who have unprotected sex will find that the woman is pregnant.

If there was a "most wanted" poster for existential risks, it would bear the face of a superintelligence. Over the next hundred years, there is a good chance that humans will build a machine with a comparable level of intelligence to our own. If such a computer is self-improving, uncontrollable, and does not share our values, then there is little prospect we can simply shut it down. Instead, there is a one in ten chance that it will effectively shut us down. This is a major menace, approximately equal to the chance that a smoker's habit will kill them before their sixtieth birthday.

Widespread authoritarianism, discussed in chapter 8, is not among Ord's top concerns, but it does rank in mine. This makes it necessary to estimate the odds of its occurrence. In his discussion of the issue, Bryan Caplan places a one in two hundred probability on "world totalitarian government" emerging at some point in the next century.[14] If we expand the definition further to encompass mass totalitarianism (of the kind that might have followed a Nazi victory in World War II), then it seems reasonable to give it a probability of one in a hundred. Among married couples, this is about the chances that your spouse has cheated on you in the last month.

Other anthropogenic risks exist. Nanotechnology, with its potential for creating self-replicating machines, could revolutionize manufacturing. But there is also a tiny chance that it could spread out of control (what nanotechnology pioneer K. Eric Drexler famously dubbed the "gray goo" scenario). Another concern is that by reducing the cost of making armaments, molecular manufacturing might encourage new conflicts.[15] Space exploration too creates a risk that substances found elsewhere in the solar system might have a damaging effect when brought back to Earth. Another possibility is that solar geoengineering, implemented in order to reduce the risk of global warming, could itself catastrophically destabilize the climate.[16] The dangers of these other anthropogenic risks are around one in fifty over the coming century, or approximately the odds of death for a US soldier serving in the Vietnam War.

Until now, I have focused on risks we can identify and quantify—the "known knowns"—and risks we can identify but can't easily quantify—the "known unknowns." But perhaps the most difficult category of risks are those that we cannot identify, or what former US defense secretary Donald Rumsfeld famously dubbed the "unknown unknowns."

To get a sense of what we might be missing, consider what science fiction writer H. G. Wells told an audience in 1902:

It is impossible to show why certain things should not utterly destroy and end the human race and story; why night should not presently come down and make all our dreams and efforts vain . . . something from space, or pestilence, or some great disease of the atmosphere, some trailing cometary poison, some great emanation of vapor from the interior of the Earth, or new animals to prey on us, or some drug or wrecking madness in the mind of man.[17]

Wells, the man often dubbed "the father of science fiction," was prescient to foresee the idea of existential risks. But when it came to naming the hazards, he did not mention nuclear war, engineered pandemics, climate change, or superintelligence. How confident can we be today that we have not missed a potential source of calamity? What unknown unknowns might be lurking?

By definition, we cannot identify the unknown unknowns. Yet we can get hints of them from history. In 1945, prior to the first-ever atomic test, scientists recognized that the temperature of the explosion could reach several hundred million degrees, making it hotter than anything ever experienced on earth. For a nanosecond, the temperature generated by the bomb would be hotter than the sun. Hungarian American physicist Edward Teller feared the consequences of this unprecedented moment. The heat, Teller believed, could set fire to the atmosphere and kill everything on earth.

Calculations by other physicists indicated that this would not occur, and the test was scheduled for July. As they drove from Los Alamos to Alamogordo in New Mexico, though, physicist Enrico Fermi said to his colleague Victor Weisskopf that he thought the odds of the atmosphere igniting were around one in ten.[18] Fermi had won the 1938 Nobel Prize and was perhaps the world's most brilliant nuclear physicist. A few days later, when the first atomic bomb detonated with "the radiance of a thousand suns," Weisskopf—watching from ten miles away—briefly thought that the atmosphere had indeed caught fire.[19]

Were the chances of our species being snuffed out by the first atomic bomb test really one in ten? As Bostrom notes, it's a possibility that should not be rejected. Nine years later, scientists tested the first lithium bomb, comprised of lithium-6 and lithium-7 isotopes. Their calculations told them that only the lithium-6 would contribute to the explosion. They were wrong. The blast was more than twice as powerful as had been anticipated, destroying much of the test equipment, and proving that even big-name nuclear scientists can make big mistakes. Humanity was lucky, Bostrom observes, that nuclear scientists bungled their calculations on the role of lithium-7, not on whether an atomic bomb would ignite the atmosphere.[20]

Fears about unknown unknowns should not paralyze scientific progress, but they ought to encourage debate about the costs and benefits of any new technology. Such a process occurred in the early 2000s, when scientists were preparing the European Large Hadron Collider for operation. The most powerful particle collider ever built, some critics feared that it could endanger humanity. One theory was that the machine could lead to the creation of microscopic black holes, which would then begin swallowing all matter around them. Another was that the Large Hadron Collider could cause the creation of negatively charged strange quark matter, or "strangelets." In response, a safety committee was established to review the available science. Updating work that had been done the previous decade to assess the safety of the Brookhaven Relativistic Heavy Ion Collider, the committee concluded in 2002 that the dangers could not materialize.[21] The Large Hadron Collider began operation six years later.

Unknown unknowns are sometimes described as "black swan" events. In sixteenth-century Europe, people had only ever seen white swans. So they used the term "black swans" to refer to impossibilities. This "known" fact was upended when Dutch explorers arrived in Western Australia and were surprised to discover black swans. (In a neat reversal, my youngest son once turned to me as we were passing a group of black swans on an Australian lake and said, "Hey dad, did you know some swans are white?")

Given what we know from history about the emergence of new risks and their potential to create a catastrophe, the cumulative risk of these unforeseen anthropogenic risks is one in thirty. That's a danger approximately equal to the chance of death that a Formula 1 driver faced from racing a car for a full season during the 1970s— the decade in which a dozen drivers died, including Peter Revson, Jochen Rindt, and Ronnie Peterson.

Adding up the anthropogenic risks gives a cumulative danger of one in six. These odds are roughly the chance of dying for a pedestrian hit by a car traveling at twenty-eight miles per hour. Because the natural catastrophic risks are tiny in comparison, adding them to the anthropogenic risks does not change the overall survival odds. Over the next hundred years, the chances of an existential risk extinguishing the human project are one in six, or approximately the chances that a ninety-year-old will not live out the year.

On an annual basis, this estimate suggests that the chance of human extinction is 0.18 percent. This is in the ballpark of economist Nicholas Stern's seminal climate change review, which estimated the risk that humanity goes extinct (or experiences a major catastrophe such as nuclear war or asteroid strike) at 0.1 percent a year. Over a century, a 0.1 percent annual risk of extinction equates to a one in ten chance that humanity fails to see out the next hundred years.[22] That isn't far off the one in six figure that Ord's thorough analysis produces.

As we saw in chapter 1, a one-sixth risk is equivalent to our species playing the deadly game of Russian roulette. It implies that catastrophic risk is more hazardous to the life of the typical person in the United States than car crashes, homicides, accidental drownings, electrocutions, and venomous animals put together. If the danger remains at this level, there's less than a fifty-fifty chance that humanity makes it to the end of the twenty-fourth century, and slim odds that we see out the millennium.

Until now, I've discussed existential risks as though they are distinct from one another. But it is also worth considering how one threat can magnify another. One concern is over the impact of climate change on pandemics. In 2016, a twelve-year-old boy was killed by anthrax released from a frozen reindeer carcass. The animal had died seventy-five years earlier and been frozen in the permafrost. The boy's death was a reminder of the potential for climate change to exacerbate disease threats, with scientists fearing that permafrost could release diseases such as smallpox and the bubonic plague. When parts of Panama saw a tripling of rainfall in 1999, the rat population swelled. In that year, Panama also saw the spread of a fatal lung disease, hantavirus pulmonary syndrome, which is transmitted by rodents. The disease had never been previously seen in Central America.[23]

Climate change could raise the danger of nuclear conflict too. The US Department of Defense has dubbed climate change "a threat multiplier" due to its potential to exacerbate conflicts over scarce resources. India and Pakistan share water from the Indus River, which may be less reliable as climate change advances. Crop failures in the border region of Kashmir could worsen tensions between the two nuclear-armed nations. The traditional winter cessation of border hostilities between the two South Asian countries could become shorter because of global warming, placing further pressure on a region that one analyst describes as the world's "premier nuclear flashpoint."[24]

Other troubling spillovers are possible. A totalitarian state might be more willing to develop a superintelligence that was focused on dominating humanity rather than improving our well-being. A bioterrorism incident could be used as a pretext for an authoritarian crackdown. A brilliant and crafty artificial intelligence might deduce a way of delivering a knockout blow with atomic weapons—disturbing the fine balance between the nuclear powers. Like unknown risks, interacting threats raise the stakes and make it more vital still that we find ways of averting catastrophe.

Reducing catastrophic risk is fundamentally a political challenge. Get the politics wrong this century, and our species could face oblivion. Get the politics right, and humanity could endure for millennia to come. Now it's time to take a deep dive into the populist approach, exploring why populists have been so electorally successful in recent decades, how populist policies exacerbate each of the major catastrophic threats, and why populism poses such a danger to our long-term future.

7
The Populist Risk

Populists can be left wing or right wing. Their key defining characteristic is that they see politics as a contest between the pure mass of people and a vile elite. Perhaps the most famous populists were Vladimir Lenin and his followers, who took power in the 1917 Russian Revolution, a populist uprising that lauded the peasantry and reviled the monarchy. Lenin and his followers did not seek to create a more democratic Russia or build a broad alliance among liberals. Instead, he used a secretive revolutionary organization to take power, overthrowing those he called "the enemies of the people."[1]

Left-wing populists were especially common in Latin America in the 1960s and 1970s. Because the continent has traditionally had high levels of inequality, left-wing Latin American populists tended to characterize the vile elite as the rich, and the pure mass of people as middle- and working-class voters. They were a little more democratic than the Russian revolutionaries, but often relied on bullets rather than ballots to stay in power.

And then there are right-wing populists. Like their left-wing counterparts, right-wing populists see politics as a contest between a vile elite and the pure mass of people. But to them, the enemies are people with university degrees, urbanites, experts, and immigrants.

The pure mass of people are defined by place, race, and degrees, not income. Where left-wing populism is economic ("we are the 99 percent"), right-wing populism tends to be cultural ("America, love it or leave it"). Both groups appeal to a sense of unfairness, but the goal of left-wing populists is economic fairness ("get our fair share"), while the goal of right-wing populists is cultural fairness ("get our country back"). Left-wing populists aim at redistribution. Right-wing populists aim at retribution.

In the past generation, right-wing populism has been ascendant in many nations. Trump's "Make America Great Again" campaign bore some similarity to past US populists such as Charles Coughlin, Strom Thurmond, and George Wallace. Trump drew support from the Tea Party, an antitax, anti-immigration movement formed in 2009 that pushed the Republican Party to the right and thwarted bipartisan efforts to offer undocumented immigrants a pathway to citizenship.[2] In winning the Republican nomination in 2016, Trump defeated a slate of experienced and well-financed candidates, including Texas senator Ted Cruz, former Florida governor Jeb Bush, New Jersey governor Chris Christie, and Florida senator Marco Rubio.

Trump's win in the 2016 election shocked the pundits, and over the next four years he transformed the Republican Party into his own image: angry, isolationist, and mendacious. "Never Trumpers" faded away, with a near record number of moderate Republicans in Congress quitting politics in 2018.[3] Across the country, Republican primary voters chose the candidate who seemed to be more devoted to Trump. By the time he left office, Trump dominated the Republican Party's power structures, including state parties, congressional caucuses, political action committees, and think tanks.[4] In his first impeachment trial (on charges of abuse of power and obstruction of Congress), only one Senate Republican voted to convict. In his second impeachment trial (on a charge of incitement of insurrection), just seven Senate Republicans voted to convict. Even among the voting public, Trump's loss in the 2020 election was narrower than many had predicted. Trump won ten million more votes than he had done four years earlier and secured a slightly larger share of the popular vote against Joe Biden than he had done against Hillary Clinton.

Populism adds another dimension to politics. Conventionally, the main dividing line has been between equality on the Left and liberty on the Right. But populism draws the line between its own nativism and its enemy, globalism. The opposite of a populist is an internationalist.

Because populism versus internationalism cuts across equality versus liberty, we end up with politicians in four quadrants: Internationalist Egalitarians (e.g., Obama and Biden), Internationalist Libertarians (e.g., Romney and Bush), Populist Egalitarians (e.g., Bernie Sanders and Alexandria Ocasio-Cortez), and Populist Libertarians (e.g., Trump and Sarah Palin). Sanders's strong performance in the 2020 Democratic primaries—with his aggressive denunciations of billionaires, large corporations, and open markets—demonstrates the power of Populist Egalitarians. But as Biden's eventual primary win shows, the pull of populism is significantly stronger in the Republican Party. One explanation for this is rising inequality; in order to sustain a policy agenda based on delivering tax cuts for the wealthy and undermining access to health care, the Republican Party opted to double down on nativism, outrage stoking, and divisive campaigning. This strategy—dubbed "plutocratic populism" by political scientists Jacob Hacker and Paul Pierson—has pulled the Republican Party in an ethnonationalist direction and made it increasingly willing to undermine democratic norms in order to maintain power.[5]

In the United Kingdom, the shift toward populism was illustrated by the 2016 vote to exit the European Union, followed by the rise of Boris Johnson to prime minister in 2019. Both Conservative prime minister David Cameron and Labour leader Jeremy

Corbyn had campaigned for Britain to remain in the European Union, so the 52 percent vote to leave was a rejection of both major parties.[6] Analysis of Britain's 2016 referendum shows that electors who voted to leave tended to have worse economic prospects and more negative attitudes toward migration.[7] Ironically, the impact of Brexit may be the worst in Britain's old industrial heartlands since these regions are among the most dependent on exports to the European Union.[8] Frustration at inequality led some to vote leave, but leaving the European Union could further widen the gap between rich and poor.

Johnson's history of Euroskepticism goes back to the early 1990s, when he was the Brussels correspondent for the *Daily Telegraph*.[9] His anti-European columns often contained exaggerations and fabrications, helping build a caricature of Brussels against which he campaigned in the Brexit referendum.[10] With his penchant for provocative phrases, Johnson has insulted African people, defended colonialism, and drawn a rebuke from the Muslim Council of Britain.[11] When Johnson became prime minister, Trump dubbed him "Britain Trump", and their advisers worked closely together.[12] Yet Johnson isn't merely "Donald Trump with a thesaurus."[13] His rhetoric is less divisive than Trump's. Johnson's electoral appeal is partly in his uniqueness—what one pundit dubbed "an unprecedented blend of comedian, conman, faux subversive showman and populist media confection."[14]

Populism is also on the rise in developing nations. When India's Narendra Modi was chief minister of the state of Gujarat, he failed to stop the anti-Muslim riots that killed 2,000 Muslims and left 150,000 in refugee camps.[15] Modi was refused a visa to enter the United States on the grounds that he had committed "severe violations of religious freedom." An analysis of the election platforms of Modi's Bharatiya Janata Party reveals that since the party was founded in 1980, it has steadily morphed from a "big tent" nationalist party into a more nativist, anti-elite populist party.[16] The

Bharatiya Janata Party's notion of "the authentic people" has narrowed to mean Hindus, effectively excluding India's 200 million Muslims. Since becoming prime minister in 2014, Modi has championed Hindu nationalism (Hindutva), positioning himself as the protector of the four-fifths of the population that identify as Hindu and encouraging poor Hindus to vote their religious identity rather than their economic interests. The Pew Research Center ranks India one of the world's worst countries for religious intolerance.[17] In 2020, the Modi government set about establishing a national register of citizens, and many fear it may lead to millions of Muslims being stripped of their citizenship. Critics have likened the crackdown on minorities, protestors, and journalists to Indira Gandhi's declaration of emergency rule in the mid-1970s.[18]

In Indonesia, the country with the fourth-largest population in the world, hard-line Islamists have grown more powerful over recent years, and the military has become stronger. Indonesia watchers describe the 2014 and 2019 presidential elections as contests between two alternative populist visions. Both elections pitted former businessman and army general Prabowo Subianto against former furniture exporter and mayor Joko Widodo (generally known as Jokowi). Jokowi prevailed in both contests; his brand of "polite populism" proved electorally attractive to the rural poor, while Prabowo's "confrontational populism" appealed to the urban middle classes.[19] During his time in office, President Jokowi has shifted closer to conservative Islamist politics and military rulers. In 2019, he chose as his vice president the country's most powerful Muslim cleric, Ma'ruf Amin.[20] Jokowi has appointed a slew of former military leaders to senior government positions (including Prabowo as defense minister).[21] In 2020, the anticorruption commission lost its independence, many labor and environmental protections were scrapped, and the constitutional court was weakened.[22] Observers warn of rising intolerance of LGBTQIA+ people, non-Muslims, and ethnic minorities.[23] During recent years, the Economist Intelligence

Unit has downgraded Indonesia's democracy index, and commentators fear that it may become an even more illiberal democracy in the future.[24]

In Brazil, Bolsonaro, a former army officer, was elected president in 2018. Although he had spent nearly three decades as a congressman, Bolsonaro campaigned as an outsider who would support family values and get tough on crime. He described the two decades in which Brazil was ruled by a brutal military dictatorship as a "glorious" period in Brazil's history. Bolsonaro opposes homosexuality and same-sex marriage (which are legal in Brazil), and has advocated the death penalty (which is banned under the constitution). As a member of Parliament, he referred to African migrants as "the scum of humanity," advocated torture, and told a female legislator that she was not worth raping. His presidential electoral victory drew on widespread public anger over violent crime (more than fifty thousand murders a year), unemployment (12 percent), and political sleaze (former president Luiz Inácio da Silva had just been jailed for corruption). Bolsonaro appealed to the few Brazilian institutions that still commanded respect: the military, Catholic church, and traditional families.[25] His campaign exploited WhatsApp to spread misinformation about rival candidates.[26] Bolsonaro did especially well among evangelicals, farmers, businesspeople, and those fearful of crime, many of whom saw him as a strong leader at a chaotic time.[27]

Political movements have their eras. In the 1940s and 1950s, communism expanded across Eastern Europe and Asia. In the 1990s, the collapse of the Soviet Union led some to predict "the end of history" and proclaim capitalist democracy the only stable way to organize society. In the past two decades, populism has experienced a similar moment. Just as communism and capitalism have both proved contagious ideas at different moments of history, it's populism that's catching on in the twenty-first century.

In 2019 and 2020, the world's four largest democracies—with a combined population of over two billion—were run by populists:

Trump in the United States, Modi in India, Widodo in Indonesia, and Bolsonaro in Brazil.[28] Tracking the growth of populism, an analysis of advanced countries found that from the 1990s to 2016, 12 percent of voters shifted from centrist to populist parties.[29]

Another study estimated that from 1990 to 2018, the number of countries with populist leaders rose from four to twenty. It identifies thirty-three populist leaders who held office during this period, including Argentina's Cristina Fernández de Kirchner, Belarus's Alexander Lukashenko, Bolivia's Evo Morales, Hungary's Viktor Orbán, Israel's Benjamin Netanyahu, Italy's Silvio Berlusconi, Nicaragua's Daniel Ortega, the Philippines' Rodrigo Duterte, Poland's Lech Kaczyński, Russia's Vladimir Putin, South Africa's Jacob Zuma, Thailand's Thaksin and Yingluck Shinawatra, Turkey's Recep Tayyip Erdoğan, and Venezuela's Nicolás Maduro.

These populist leaders exchanged political strategies and went out of their way to praise one another. Trump called India's Prime Minister Modi "incredible" on the issue of religious freedom. Brazilian president Bolsonaro backed Trump's immigration policies (saying, "The vast majority of potential immigrants do not have good intentions") and was one of the last world leaders to acknowledge Trump's defeat. Far-right Hungarian prime minister Orbán calls Britain's Johnson "one of the bravest European politicians."

No single element has driven the rise of populists, but the changes are a consequence of systematic shifts, not idiosyncratic individuals. Together, five factors have combined to make the early twenty-first century the age of the populist. I'll call them jobs, snobs, race, pace, and luck.

First, jobs. Globally, the growth of technology and trade has made millions better off. The number of hungry people in the world fell from 1 billion in 1991 to 820 million in 2017.[30] Worldwide, life expectancy is up and infant mortality is down. Yet not everyone has gained. In the United States, one-third of the economic growth since 1980 has gone to the top 1 percent.[31] For many working-class men, wages have not even kept pace with prices. In the 2010s, the United States saw a spate of "deaths of despair" as the opioid epidemic and rising suicide rates reduced average life expectancy for the first time since World War II. The share of children earning more than their parents has dropped from around 90 percent in the 1940s to 50 percent today.[32] There is, as Bruce Springsteen put it, a "distance between American reality and the American dream."[33]

Good jobs—those that pay enough to support a family and mortgage—have become increasingly scarce. Almost two-thirds of the jobs created since 1990 have been "low quality" in the sense that they paid less than the average wage.[34] Millions of manufacturing workers and administrative assistants have lost their jobs.[35] The impact has been toughest on those with less education. Over the past generation, twice as many jobs have been created for high-educated workers as for low-educated workers. Job growth has been four times faster in occupations requiring high-level analytic or social skills as among jobs requiring high-level physical skills.[36]

These effects translated directly into political outcomes. In those electoral districts most adversely affected by competition from Chinese imports, more people watch Fox News and vote Republican.[37] Exposure to trade has led to moderate Republicans being replaced by extreme conservatives and moderate Democrats being replaced by extreme liberals. In other contexts, economic pain seems to benefit only the Far Right. One study of European elections found that the higher the unemployment rate, the better far-right parties performed.[38] Another looked at the impact of financial crises. Analyzing over eight hundred elections since 1870, the researchers found that after a severe financial crisis, far-right parties enjoyed a one-third increase in their vote share. By contrast, financial crises did not benefit far-left parties—a result that the researchers attribute to the Far Right's use of "nationalist or xenophobic" rhetoric to attract voters who had been economically hurt by the crisis.[39]

Second, snobs. Over the past generation, establishment centrists have done a lousy job of maintaining their supporter base. On the conservative side, Britain's Johnson, Australia's Scott Morrison, and the United States' Trump took over the leadership of their parties from moderates who were seen to have been "out of touch" with the electorate. In Germany and Sweden, established right-wing parties have been losing votes to anti-immigration populists.

In many cases, the establishment didn't take populist challengers seriously. Pundit Nate Silver predicted that Trump wouldn't win the Republican nomination in 2016 "because he's not really a Republican."[40] Of the hundred largest newspapers, fifty-seven endorsed Clinton, while two endorsed Trump.[41] Clinton amassed more business endorsements than Trump.[42] Twelve Republican governors, fourteen Republican senators, and at least one former Republican president (George H. W. Bush) announced their opposition to Trump. Even Republican consultant Frank Luntz tweeted on Election Day 2016 that "Hillary Clinton will be the next President of the United States."

On the other side of the Atlantic, the same pattern emerged. Johnson's egotism, eccentricity, and extramarital affairs led one commentator to predict that he would never serve in a Tory cabinet.[43] In 2000, British bookies offered odds of fifty to one that Johnson would ever become leader.[44] In the United States, Britain, and elsewhere, populist challengers to the conservative establishment have reached out to the party membership, bypassing traditional donors. Compared with Internationalist Libertarians, the pitch from such Populist Libertarians is more isolationist and less global, more focused on small enterprise than big business.

On the Left, the problem of snobbery has led to mainstream progressives losing the support of less educated voters. In the 1948 US presidential election, those without a degree were 20 percentage points more likely to vote Democratic. By 2016, nongraduates were 14 percentage points *less* likely to vote Democratic.[45] Little surprise that Trump once told a campaign rally, "I love the poorly educated." In the postwar era, the US Democratic Party has moved from being the workers' party to the party of the highly educated. A strikingly similar shift has occurred in Britain, France, Italy, Switzerland, Canada, the Netherlands, Australia, and New Zealand. In all these countries, left-wing parties are increasingly likely to draw their support from highly educated voters.[46]

Less educated voters increasingly struggle to see themselves represented in mainstream parties of the Left. Too often, mainstream progressives have exacerbated the problem by failing to back up their talk of meritocracy with the equal funding of schools in poor neighborhoods. Some top US universities, including Dartmouth, Princeton, and Yale, have more students drawn from the top 1 percent than from the bottom half of the income distribution.[47] Over the past half century, the share of educational spending going to the top tenth of students has risen from 28 to 36 percent.[48]

Economist Thomas Piketty derides the establishment parties as the "Merchant Right" (seen as too close to big business) and "Brahmin Left" (regarded as the party of meritocracy in a world where the best educational institutions are increasingly unattainable). These categories loosely correspond to what I've termed Internationalist Libertarians and Internationalist Egalitarians. Both groups, Piketty contends, have been too slow to recognize the hostility toward global institutions, and have failed to understand that the electorate regards them as elitist and irrelevant.[49] Some scholars criticize social democratic parties for favoring policies that protect securely employed "insiders" at the expense of "outsiders," such as gig workers and the unemployed.[50] In the 2020 Irish elections, the nationalist Sinn Féin Party won more first preference votes than either of the two establishment political parties, Fianna Fáil and Fine Gael. Sinn Féin's campaign slogan—"Giving workers and families a break"—has been the catchphrase of outsiders across the advanced world who have captured electoral support from dozy establishment parties.

Third, race. Around the world, populists have tapped into racial
and religious resentment, mobilizing anti-Arab sentiment in Israel,
anti-Muslim sentiment in India, and anti-immigrant sentiment in
Europe. In the United States, former President Trump promoted the
falsehood that Obama was not born in the United States, referred
to Mexican immigrants as "rapists," and called on four Democratic
congresswomen (three of whom were born in the United States)
to "go back" to the countries "from which they came." Asked in
the first 2020 presidential election debate to condemn the violent
white supremacist organization the Proud Boys, Trump responded
by saying that it should "stand back and stand by." The extremist
group began selling T-shirts bearing the phrase.

Political scientists have proven that when randomly selected
voters are exposed to comments like these from Trump, those voters were more likely to express offensive views toward minorities.[51]
Across counties, those that hosted a Trump campaign rally in 2016
experienced a subsequent doubling in hate crime rates.[52] Analyses
of the 2016 presidential election have shown that Trump's racial
views won him more votes than they lost and may have been the
decisive factor in his victory.[53] In 2020, Trump succeeded in increasing his share of the vote among racial minorities, winning around
one-tenth of Black votes and one-third of Latino votes.[54] Trump's
ability to use more racially charged language while still winning
about the same share of Black and Latino votes as past Republican
presidential candidates may embolden other Republicans to employ
similar tactics in the future.[55]

Racial resentment taps into a fear of difference that has characterized Homo sapiens since the beginning. For most of our time on
the planet, humans lived in groups of around 150 people and everyone knew each other. In such a context, it made sense to be fearful
of outsiders. If resources are scarce, it's not paranoid to think that
people in other tribes might kill you. We can still see this tendency
to "hunker down" in the face of difference.[56] Successive waves of

European migrants to the United States—particularly those from Ireland, Germany, and Italy—have experienced hostility, followed by acceptance. As economist Ed Glaeser points out, a political strategy based on racial resentment relies on the supply of stories about how a specific minority group poses a threat.[57] This works only when the group is large enough for the stories to be credible, but small enough that the political contender can afford to alienate them. By choosing their targets strategically, some populists have weaponized racial resentment for electoral gain.

Fourth, pace. As recently as 2005, there was no such thing as an iPhone, iPad, Alexa, or Kindle. Instagram, Twitter, and Snapchat did not exist, and hardly anyone was on Facebook. Same-sex marriage was opposed by most people and illegal almost everywhere.[58] No US state had legalized recreational marijuana, and only white men had ever served as president or vice president.

Since 2005, the United States has experienced two recessions and a pandemic. Weekly attendance at religious services has dropped from 44 to 35 percent.[59] Back then, almost all households had a landline. Now less than half do.[60] Ride-hailing services—launched in 2011—now outnumber taxis in major cities.[61] The retail apocalypse has gathered pace, with physical stores closing at the rate of one per hour since the start of 2019.[62] Meanwhile, 90 million people in the United States have a smart speaker, and 110 million are Amazon Prime members.[63]

The combination of technological and social change can be profoundly unsettling. Journalist Thomas Friedman argues that the "supernova" of change makes it difficult for many people to adapt.[64] Buffeted by changing gadgets, morays, and social structures, it is little surprise that some turn to populist politics. Just as President Nixon offered a sense of old-world security at the end of the tumultuous 1960s, today's populist politicians appeal to voters who are uncomfortable with change. Rather than living in the eye of a cyclone, voters may instead turn to leaders who promise to restore a halcyon past. This is borne out by the data; an analysis of elections in twenty-four European countries finds that right-wing populists are more electorally successful at times of economic uncertainty.[65]

Nostalgia, as they say, isn't what it used to be. Spurning the latest gizmos is as unthinkable as swapping our cars for horses. Yet it's easy for those who enjoy six-figure incomes to underestimate the social disruption that has taken place. Manufacturing once provided a secure pathway to the middle class for a man who dropped out of high school but was willing to work hard. Retail provided work for millions. A sixty-year-old whose employer has gone bankrupt doesn't want to be told to go back to school. In that situation, wouldn't you yearn for a bit less creative destruction? So long as populists are the only ones appealing to tradition in a fast-changing world, they will continue to reap the electoral benefits.

Fifth, luck. In political life, chance is the invisible kingmaker. Whatever errors Clinton made in 2016, she was also extremely unlucky. Despite winning 3 million more votes than Trump, Clinton lost Wisconsin, Michigan, and Pennsylvania by a total of just 78,000 votes. It doesn't take much to imagine how those states could have swung the other way. What if Green Party candidate Jill Stein had withdrawn, and delivered her 132,000 votes in Wisconsin, Michigan, and Pennsylvania to Clinton?[66] What if Clinton's cybersecurity team had not been fooled by a Russian phishing scam that opened up access to the emails of campaign chair John Podesta? Similarly, Trump would probably have won a second term in office were it not for coronavirus, since his skills made him better suited to running for reelection on the strength of the economy than on his ability to handle a pandemic. As Trump once told Oprah Winfrey, "There's no more important word than luck."[67]

Luck has also helped elect other populist leaders. In 1988, Brazil's Bolsonaro was being pursued in the courts for alleged misconduct as a military officer. So he ran for city council in Rio—a job that provided immunity from prosecution.[68] That led to a three-decade career in congress and then to the presidency. As Bolsonaro's son wrote in a biography of his father, "His entry into politics happened by chance, for his desire was to continue in his military career."[69]

Erdoğan's rise to power in Turkish politics began when he won a tight three-way race for mayor of Istanbul in which his opponents regarded him as a country bumpkin and the media mocked him.[70] He then gained national attention after serving a four-month prison sentence for reading a controversial poem. Erdoğan's lawyers had sought to have him pay a fine instead. Had they succeeded, it is plausible that Erdoğan would not have won the national sympathy that enabled his Justice and Development Party to win the presidency five years later.

Political success frequently turns on timing. Without Britain's 52 percent vote in favor of leaving the European Union, it is unlikely that Johnson would have become prime minister. In 2015, the opening up of new migrant routes through the eastern Mediterranean and western Balkans led to a surge of asylum seekers into Europe. Many voters feared that the influx of migrants—mostly young men—would increase crime and unemployment.[71] The result was an electoral windfall to far-right parties, including those in Italy, Austria, Poland, and Hungary. For every successful populist today, history is replete with dozens of unsuccessful ones, including Britain's Enoch Powell, Canada's Preston Manning, France's Jean-Marie Le Pen, and the United States' Pat Buchanan. Had they faced weaker opponents or run at a more propitious moment in history, they might have won.

The five drivers of populism—jobs, snobs, race, pace, and luck—overlap and interact. An analysis of party platforms across more than one thousand elections in the postwar era found that when inequality rose, right-wing parties were more likely to make racial or religious appeals to the electorate.[72] When jobs are tight, conservatives are more inclined to campaign on race.

Jobs and snobs interact too. In an age with plenty of manufacturing jobs, the snobbery of overfunded elite colleges and underfunded public schools didn't create resentment. As the tide went out on manufacturing, those who lost their jobs became aggrieved at the simplistic snobbery that presumes anyone can ride the escalator of education into the middle class. Similarly, the rapid pace of change is keenly felt with regard to demographic shifts. Already, the typical survey respondent thinks that the minority share of the United States is one-third larger than it truly is. Remind people that their nation is becoming more diverse, and they are more likely to express anti-immigrant views.[73] Pace makes race more salient.

Commentator Ezra Klein argues that electoral outcomes lag demographics by a decade, while culture leads demographics by a decade. The result is that "the Left feels a cultural and demographic power that it can only occasionally translate into political power, and the Right wields political power but feels increasingly dismissed and offended culturally."[74] White voters unsettled by the pace of change enabled the Trumpification of the Republican Party— embracing ethnonationalism and ejecting moderates. Meanwhile, the Black Lives Matter movement has prompted a national conversation about policing, the 2020 NBA season began with virtually every player kneeling during the national anthem, and the Oscars has announced that by 2024, films nominated for the best picture award will need to meet diversity standards.

*   *   *

Why do populists pose a threat to long-termism? Because tackling long-term threats requires four things: strong science, effective institutions, global engagement, and a sense of cooperation and order. Populists are anti-intellectual, anti-institutional, anti-international, and anti-irenic ("irenic" means to strive for peace and consensus). This is not an accident. Each of the four antis forms part of the electoral appeal of populism, just as each makes it impossible for populists to effectively address challenges to humanity's future.

First, populists are anti-intellectual. Because populists view politics as a contest between a pure mass of people and vile elite, their characterization of the elite often includes experts. This has led to a spate of clashes between populist leaders and scientists. According to the Union of Concerned Scientists, Trump attacked science more than 150 times.[75] Research on child health and pollution, the environmental impacts of coal mining, and species extinction was ignored or criticized. In the 2017 "Sharpiegate" affair, the White House redrew a meteorologic map to make it consistent with an erroneous presidential tweet. Trump called climate change "mythical" and "nonexistent." In a similar fashion, Bolsonaro has questioned his own government's data on deforestation in the Amazon, while Dutch far-right leader Thierry Baudet rails against "climate change hysteria."

Not every populist is a climate denier, but virtually all climate deniers are populists.[76] One analysis of the twenty-one largest right-wing populist parties in Europe found that one-third were outright climate deniers, while many others were hostile to climate action.[77] Right-wing populists make up 15 percent of the European Parliament, but account for around half of the votes against climate and energy resolutions.

One study in the United Kingdom identified voters who held populist beliefs about politics, such as agreeing that people rather than politicians should make policy decisions, or that elected officials talk too much and take too little action.[78] These populist voters were significantly less likely to agree that global warming is caused by human action and less likely to support measures to protect the environment. Importantly, this pattern held across the political spectrum; populism explains climate denial among both left- and right-wing voters.

The anti-vaccination movement, with its conspiracy theories about large pharmaceutical companies, has been bolstered by populists. In Italy, the populist Five Star Movement criticized a 2017 law making it compulsory for children to be vaccinated against measles, mumps, and rubella, sometimes repeating falsehoods about the vaccine. In France, the populist National Rally party (formerly the National Front) condemned an increase in the number of mandatory childhood vaccines.

Across Europe, the rise of populist parties has been accompanied by an increase in anti-vaxxer sentiment. One in seven Europeans say that they do not believe vaccines are important, while half wrongly believe that vaccines can often cause serious side effects.[79] As vaccination rates fell, the number of European measles cases more than doubled between 2011 and 2019.[80] Confirming the role of politics, a study that analyzed data across fourteen European countries found a strong relationship between the share of people who vote for populist parties and the proportion who believe that vaccination is not important.[81]

Before becoming president, Trump expressed support for a prominent anti-vaxxer conspiracy theory: the debunked claim that vaccines cause autism. As president, Trump tweeted about the dangers of vaccines more than thirty times.[82] It was much the same with COVID-19. Trump's overconfidence led him initially to dismiss the coronavirus threat. In January 2020, he said, "We have it totally under control. It's one person coming in from China, and we have it under control. It's going to be just fine." In February, he referred to coronavirus as a "new hoax" being peddled by the Democrats. Gainsaying the experts, Trump was dismissive of mask wearing, slowed down testing, and touted the ineffective drug hydroxychloroquine. It soon became clear that Trump saw the disease primarily in terms of politics rather than public health.[83] As a satirical headline in the *Onion* put it, "Trump: 'Even One Death That Makes Me Look Bad Is a Tragedy.'"[84]

Bolsonaro was similarly dismissive of medical expertise. He initially described coronavirus as a media "trick," arguing that Brazilians were naturally immune to the disease. "The Brazilian needs to be studied," said Bolsonaro. "He doesn't catch anything. You see a guy jumping into sewage, diving in, right? Nothing happens to him. I think a lot of people were already infected in Brazil, weeks or months ago, and they already have the antibodies that help it not proliferate." Bolsonaro urged the premature relaxation of physical distancing measures, supported street protests against quarantines, and fired two health ministers.[85] Relative to population, Brazil has one of the highest COVID-19 death rates in the world.[86] Like populist leaders Johnson and Trump, Bolsonaro contracted coronavirus himself. Three of Brazil's 81 senators have died from the disease.

Similarly, in Indonesia and the Philippines, populist leaders sidelined technocrats and touted unproven health measures. Widodo was slow to implement lockdowns in Indonesia, saying that he did not want to cause "panic" and claiming that lockdowns were ineffective. His ministers variously promoted prayer and a necklace made of eucalyptus as protections against COVID-19.[87] In the Philippines, President Duterte advocated gasoline as a disinfectant and created a coronavirus task force led by retired generals rather than epidemiologists.[88] Indonesia and the Philippines have among the highest rates of coronavirus deaths in the Asia-Pacific region.[89]

Hostility toward scientists and intellectuals shows up among supporters too. In a 2019 survey, 62 percent of Democrats—but only 44 percent of Republicans—agreed that scientists' judgments are based solely on the facts.[90] Populists' skepticism of intellectuals also manifests in support for debunked conspiracy theories.[91] A global survey of twenty-two thousand voters across nineteen democracies found that populist voters were far more likely to be conspiracy minded. Populists are more than twice as likely to think that global warming is a hoax. They are almost twice as likely to believe that AIDS was invented by the US Central Intelligence Agency, that supposedly harmful effects of vaccines are being hidden from the public, and that the US government knowingly helped the September 11 attackers. Populists are more likely to believe that alien contact is being hidden from the public.

Populist leaders frequently build political support by pushing conspiracy theories. Among the falsehoods peddled by populist actors are that the Holocaust is a hoax, former German chancellor Angela Merkel is the secret daughter of Adolf Hitler, the European Union is resurrecting the Roman Empire as a communist superstate, and there is a worldwide cabal of Satan-worshipping pedophiles who rule the world (the QAnon theory).[92] In November 2020, Georgia Republican Marjorie Taylor Greene was the first QAnon supporter to be elected to the US Congress.[93] Half of all Republican voters believe one of QAnon's key tenets: that top Democrats are involved in child sex trafficking.[94] A majority of Republicans believe that the January 2021 assault on the United States Capitol was "mostly an antifa-inspired attack."[95]

Second, populists are anti-institution. Campaigning as outsiders, populist leaders tend to be suspicious of institutions such as the bureaucracy, judiciary, and media. Journalist Michael Lewis highlights the plethora of programs run by the two million people employed by the federal government, including child nutrition, veterans' health, air traffic control, and national security. Yet the day after the 2016 election, Lewis writes,

> The hundreds of people who had prepared to brief the incoming Trump administration sat waiting. A day became a week and a week became a month . . . and no one showed up. The parking spots that had been set aside for Trump's people remained empty, and the briefing books were never opened. You could walk into almost any department of the US government and hear people asking the same question: where were these people who were meant to be running the place?[96]

This approach to the federal bureaucracy characterized the Trump administration. By the time coronavirus struck, ten cabinet members had departed, and four-fifths of senior White House positions had turned over.[97] Trump was on his fifth secretary of the Department of Homeland Security, his fourth national security adviser, and his third chief of staff. As journalists Jennifer Steinhauer and Zolan Kanno-Youngs note, "Between Mr. Trump's history of firing people and the choice by many career officials and political appointees to leave, he now finds himself with a government riddled with vacancies, acting department chiefs and, in some cases, leaders whose professional backgrounds do not easily match up to the task of managing a pandemic."[98]

Populists regard regulatory bodies and oversight mechanisms not as an appropriate check on power but rather as a creation of self-serving insiders. In Poland and Hungary, populist governments have changed the rules on the appointment of judges and imposed age limits to remove unwanted ones.[99] Elsewhere, populists have encouraged lawbreaking. In Brazil and the Philippines, populist leaders advocate the extrajudicial murder of suspected criminals. Kenneth Roth, executive director of Human Rights Watch, fears that populism "threatens to reverse the accomplishments of the modern human rights movement" created in the aftermath of the atrocities of World War II.[100]

Universities—the institutional home of many intellectuals—are a particular focus of populist ire. Populists claim that university research is irrelevant to real-world problems. and teaching amounts to indoctrination. Colleges are accused of lacking legitimacy and being out of touch with popular opinion. Amid the populist takeover of the Republican Party, the share of Republicans who thought that universities had a negative effect on the country jumped by 22 percentage points between 2015 and 2019.[101]

Another trademark of populists are their attacks on the mainstream media—or what Palin dubbed the "lamestream media." Describing journalists as "human scum," "low life reporters," "corrupt," "dishonest," and "the enemy of the people," Trump sought to undercut the credibility of the press. As Chris Wallace of Fox News summed it up, "He has done everything he can to undercut the media, to try and delegitimize us, and I think his purpose is clear: to raise doubts, when we report critically about him and his administration, that we can be trusted."[102] Ethical journalism—with its adherence to accuracy, independence, impartiality, and public accountability—is an important check on the abuse of power. Without an ethical media, it becomes more difficult to have a conversation about the long term. The overall importance of institutions is reinforced by a four-country study that found people who were less trusting of national institutions were also less supportive of policies to protect the well-being of future generations.[103]

COVID-19 also reflected Trump's undermining of institutions. Experts had long warned about the need for the United States to work with China on potential disease hot spots. As early as 2007, microbiologists warned that "coronaviruses are well known to undergo genetic recombination, which may lead to new genotypes and outbreaks." They went on to note that "the presence of a large reservoir of SARS-CoV-like viruses in horseshoe bats, together with the culture of eating exotic mammals in southern China, is a time bomb."[104]

Despite this, Trump reduced the number of China-based staff from the CDC by two-thirds during his first two years in office.[105] In his proposed budgets prior to the pandemic, Trump sought to cut CDC funding by 10 to 20 percent, with a particular emphasis on reducing CDC funding for emerging diseases, global health, and public health preparedness.[106] The Trump administration also shut down the entire global health security unit of the National Security Council.[107]

As a report from the Environmental Data and Governance Initiative put it, "[Trump's] efforts to reduce spending have dramatically and consistently taken aim at programs most likely to reveal and tackle potential pandemic origin points around the world."[108]

The problem wasn't just underinvestment in global health. The United States is the only advanced nation without universal health coverage, despite spending more on health care as a share of the economy than any other nation in the world. The lack of universal health care is one reason the United States has experienced so many COVID deaths and suffered difficulties in rolling out the vaccine. Minorities were both more likely to contract COVID in 2020 and less likely to be vaccinated in 2021. Populist opposition to the institutional framework of universal health care made the impact of COVID more severe and more inequitable.

Third, populists are anti-international. Populist political slogans include "I Want My Country Back," "Law and Border," "Patriotism, Protection, and Prosperity," "Finland for the Finns," "Courage to Stand Up for Germany," and "America First." Populists typically distrust immigration, trade, and foreign investment. They tend to be hostile toward global bodies such as the World Bank, International Criminal Court, World Trade Organization, and United Nations. Many European populists advocate dissolving the European Union. Had he won a second term, experts anticipated that Trump would have tried to withdraw the United States from NATO, destabilizing the power balance in Europe.[109]

During the COVID-19 crisis, populists also undermined international cooperation. President Trump deliberately fomented conflict with China, calling COVID-19 "the China Virus" and "Kung Flu." The Trump administration withdrew from the World Health Organization and cut funding to the Pan-American Health Organization, Latin America's leading health agency. President Bolsonaro bizarrely claimed that the World Health Organization was encouraging same-sex relationships in four-year-olds, sexual experiences for nine-year-olds, and masturbation in children from birth.[110] Trump and Bolsonaro worked together to drive out 10,000 Cuban doctors and nurses from Brazil, Ecuador, Bolivia and El Salvador, increasing the death toll of the virus in impoverished communities.[111]

When populists turn their countries away from international trade, they make it harder to address the impact of future pandemics. Over time, nations have built up comparative advantages in producing certain kinds of medical supplies. Switzerland is a major manufacturer of pharmaceuticals. Malaysia is a substantial exporter of surgical gloves. The United States is the world's largest exporter of medical instruments. China is the world's biggest producer of face masks. South Korea mass-produces in vitro diagnostics products. Nine-tenths of the personal protective equipment sold in the European Union is imported.[112] Unfortunately, during the COVID-19 crisis, over eighty countries implemented export controls on medical supplies and medicines, leading to concerns about a cascading closure of the global medical trade.[113] Such a slide into autarky would be especially damaging for developing nations. The rhetoric of self-reliance misleads; rather than banning trade, countries should build stockpiles. By allowing nations to specialize in what they do best, we end up with more production of higher-quality goods at cheaper prices—and a world that is better able to respond to disease threats.

At its best, patriotism fosters a sense of pride in what our ancestors have built and a love of local communities. But the antiglobal movement frequently stokes unfounded fears. Populists often create scapegoats out of minority communities and deploy racism to win votes. By fostering a suspicion of foreigners, and separating the world into "us" and "them," populists make it harder to solve problems that cross international boundaries. By definition, existential threats to humanity are global problems, and are much harder to solve when countries are unwilling to work together. International tensions increase the chances of nuclear war and make it more difficult to control bioterrorism.

Anti-internationalism also raises the risks of artificial intelligence. In 2020, President Trump issued an executive order on artificial intelligence, which touched briefly on safety issues. But in implementing it, his administration dismissed concerns about a machine that can "perform at the level of, or better than a human agent," saying that such issues were "beyond the scope" of the executive order.[114] Trump's chief technology officer, Michael Kratsios, stated the goal simply: for the United States to "win the race for artificial intelligence."[115] This is dangerously narrow-minded. We need to move from international values statements on artificial intelligence to binding treaties. But such global agreements could founder on the tendency of populist governments to oppose international pacts. If populists prevent the development of global artificial intelligence safety standards, the world risks a race to the bottom.

Fourth, populists are anti-irenic. Rather than striving for an irenic calm consensus, they benefit from division and disagreement. The politics of division requires that the temperature be at boiling point, the volume at full blast, the gas pedal flat to the floor. To persuade voters that politics is broken, there must be a villain. Populists thrive on bombast and blame—not compromise and community building. Throughout his four years as president, Trump averaged a false or misleading statement every ninety minutes, according to analysis by the *Washington Post*.[116] Many of his lies were deliberately designed to provoke outrage. Describing the effect of his most incendiary statements, Trump said, "I used to watch it like a rocket ship when I put out a beauty."[117] A perpetual culture war not only served to mobilize the Republican base; it also engendered a sense of stress and anxiety that has been shown by psychologists to foster hostility toward outsiders.[118] Two-fifths of Republicans think their political opponents are evil. One-fifth regard Democrats as animals.[119]

When stressed, people can develop tunnel vision—overvaluing short-term priorities at the expense of future needs. Scarcity, argue researchers Sendhil Mullainathan and Eldar Shafir, "makes us dumber. It makes us more impulsive. We must get by with less mind available, with less fluid intelligence."[120] Stressful politics and a perpetual state of fear can act as a "cognitive tax" on voters, promoting a politics of short-termism. If every day is a crisis, long-term planning is a luxury. In a battle, soldiers aren't thinking about whether they've put enough money into their retirement accounts.

Populists may not be bonkers, but they revel in being agitators and stirrers, fighting against a system that they regard as having served the elites for too long. If populism was a computer program, its volatility and unpredictability would be regarded as a feature, not a bug. To attack the establishment is to attack the institutions and rules that have sustained the status quo. If we could rank the world's leaders on a spectrum, starting with the most calm and cerebral, and ending with the crankiest and craziest, populists would be at the end of the line. Remember from chapter 4 the nuclear war study "War with Crazy Types"? Populists are more likely to be "crazy types." If anyone collapses the nuclear deterrence house of cards, it's likely to be a populist.

Divisive politics also acts as a counterweight against the sort of cooperation that is essential to long-run planning. Where politicians have taken significant actions to reduce long-term threats, it has often involved a measure of bipartisanship. A program to contain "loose nukes" after the breakup of the Soviet Union was driven by Democratic senator Nunn and Republican senator Richard Lugar. California's 2006 cap-and-trade emissions reduction program was passed by a Democratic legislature and signed into law by Republican governor Arnold Schwarzenegger. But voters who believe their political opponents are "evil" or "animals" are less likely to support bipartisan collaboration on long-term issues.

Populists thrive off chaos of their own making. But when external crises hit, populist leaders struggle. According to one study on crisis leadership, effective disaster response requires providing clear direction, putting public safety first, being compassionate toward victims, and learning lessons afterward.[121] As COVID-19 showed, many populist leaders were erratic, put politics first, were unsympathetic toward the most vulnerable, and covered up their policy failings. The qualities that make populists electorally successful also make them abysmal crisis managers. We should no more expect populists to be good crisis leaders than we should expect jockeys to succeed at basketball.

The characteristics of populists that threaten long-termism— anti-intellectual, anti-institutional, anti-international, and anti-irenic—are frequently celebrated by populists themselves. Populist talk show host Rush Limbaugh used to call government, academia, science, and media "the four corners of deceit."[122] For Limbaugh, hostility to intellectualism and institutions wasn't a mark of shame, it was a badge of honor.

For much of the postwar era, a centrist consensus in many advanced nations held that decisions should be guided by experts, globalization is fundamentally a force for good, established institutions deserve respect, and the media is an essential check on power. The rise of populism—driven primarily by jobs, snobs, race, pace, and luck—has upended these views. The greatest consequence of this transformation could be on the future. Populist politics risks exacerbating the catastrophic risks of nuclear war, pandemics, dangerous superintelligence, and climate change. But there is another risk too: that populist democrats become authoritarian demagogues—quashing democracy and ushering in a frightening future. It is to that danger that I now turn.

8

The Death of Democracy

In the last election before Hitler became German chancellor, his Nazi Party lost thirty-five seats. Opposed by the Social Democrats and Communists, his only hope was to gain the support of the old-guard conservatives. After cycling through three conservative chancellors in a single year, the traditional conservatives decided on a plan to install a popular figure who could sideline the radical Left. Even though the old-guard conservatives disliked Hitler, they were confident they could control him.

On the day Hitler was appointed chancellor, one of the architects of the plan, Franz von Papen, said, "We've engaged him for ourselves. . . . [W]ithin two months we will have pushed Hitler so far into a corner that he'll squeak."[1] Alfred Hugenberg, leader of the right-wing German National People's Party, hoped to control Hitler, using him as his "tool."[2] Reflecting on the situation, novelist Thomas Mann assured a friend, "The raging of nationalist passions is nothing more than the late and final flickering of an already burnt-out fire."[3]

Some soon realized their error. The day after Hitler was sworn in as chancellor, Hugenberg confessed, "I have just committed the greatest stupidity of my life; I have allied myself with the greatest demagogue in world history."[4] By the end of the year, all other political parties had been banned, Hitler had acquired emergency powers, Jews and Communists had been purged from the public service, the first concentration camp had been opened, and tens of thousands had been arrested. As one scholar wrote of the conservatives who hoped to control Hitler, "The puppet became the puppeteer."[5]

Imagine if Hitler had won World War II and successfully entrenched fascism across Europe, from Britain to the Soviet Union. Suppose that such a regime proved durable—building up a powerful network of informants, exploiting new surveillance technologies, and managing leadership succession. Imagine a superstate with the ideology of Nazi Germany and control mechanisms of modern-day Communist China.

For Jewish people, LGBTQIA+ people, and dissidents, such an outcome would have been fatal. For them, the victory of fascism over democracy would have been as deadly as a pandemic or nuclear attack. For many others, the oppression of the regime would be as stifling to a fulfilling life as the heat waves of a climate change disaster. Indeed, living under a crushing dictatorship may be worse. I'd hazard a guess that the typical North Korean would prefer to swelter in Death Valley than be subjected to the caprices of Kim Jong-un.

In this chapter, I focus on the existential risk of enduring autocracy—a world in which democracy has been overthrown in favor of a stable totalitarian regime. Such a scenario has been depicted in novels such as *Fahrenheit 451*, *It Can't Happen Here*, *The Iron Heel*, and *The Man in the High Castle*. Yet while their plots might seem farfetched to those living in strong democracies, they are often eerily familiar to citizens whose nations have slipped backward from fair elections and the rule of law into authoritarian rule by powerful tyrants. No political commandment states that a democracy must live forever.

In *How Democracies Die*, political scientists Steven Levitsky and Daniel Ziblatt argue that democracies used to perish at the hands of people with guns.[6] During the Cold War, three-quarters of all democratic breakdowns were due to coups. Argentina, Brazil, Chile, the Dominican Republic, Ghana, Greece, Guatemala, Nigeria, Pakistan, Peru, Thailand, Turkey, and Uruguay all suffered violent takeovers, frequently at the hands of the army.

But democracies can also be undermined from within. In 1998, when Hugo Chávez was elected president of Venezuela, the country was South America's oldest democracy. Chávez won three more elections before his death in 2013. During his time in office, he arrested opposition politicians, harassed judges, closed a major television station, and handed out vast amounts of cash in exchange for votes. Chávez's successor, Maduro, continued to jail critics. According to a UN report, his security forces have been responsible for almost seven thousand extrajudicial killings.

Each year, the Economist Intelligence Unit produces the *Democracy Index*.[7] Experts from the unit assess each country's electoral process and pluralism, functioning of the government, political participation, political culture, and civil liberties. These are compiled together into a single democracy index, which in turn allows countries to be classified as full democracies, flawed democracies, hybrid regimes, or authoritarian regimes. About half the world's population lives under democracy, one-third under autocracy, and the remainder in hybrid regimes.

Since 2006, Venezuela had been classed as a hybrid regime. In 2017, when Maduro abolished the elected National Assembly, the Economist Intelligence Unit formally downgraded Venezuela to an authoritarian regime. The following year, it judged Venezuela's presidential election "neither free nor fair." Venezuela is now one of three authoritarian regimes in Latin America, along with longtime authoritarian regime Cuba, and Nicaragua, which was downgraded to authoritarian in 2018.

As Levitsky and Ziblatt point out, many Venezuelans do not appear to have seen the changes coming. Asked in 2011 to rate their country from one ("not at all democratic") to ten ("completely democratic"), half of all Venezuelans rated their country an eight or above. "Because there is no single moment—no coup, declaration of martial law, or suspension of the constitution—in which the regime obviously 'crosses the line' into dictatorship," they write, "nothing may set off society's alarm bells. . . . Democracy's erosion is, for many, almost imperceptible."[8]

Sometimes the slide into autocracy is justified on the grounds of protecting the nation. In the Philippines, Ferdinand Marcos began his political career with his election in 1949 to the House of Representatives, where he held office for a decade, working on multiple parliamentary committees. He then ran for the Senate, where he served for six years, rising to become senate president. His progression paralleling Lyndon Johnson, Marcos was an active member of the legislature, introducing several significant bills. In 1965, he was elected president of the Philippines with 52 percent of the vote. Four years later, Marcos became the first president in the postwar era to win a second term. But the country's constitution decreed that presidents were limited to two terms in office, requiring him to leave office in 1973.

Through his time as a democratically elected leader, Marcos had been planning for autocracy. By the end of his second term, he commanded personal loyalty from the armed forces, controlled many local governments, had developed a strong relationship with the Nixon administration, and had appointed almost all the Supreme Court justices. According to an aide, Marcos had believed since childhood that the Philippines needed a "strongman" leader, such that "a martial law regime for the Philippines was virtually a lifetime ambition for him."[9]

Now he needed a pretext. Over a six-month period in 1972, twenty bombs exploded across Manila, causing havoc, but leading to only one death. These were followed by an alleged assassination attempt on Marcos's defense minister. The bombings are largely believed to have been the work of Marcos supporters, while the assassination is thought to have been staged. In preparation for the announcement of martial law, Marcos distributed copies of his plan to key officials in the armed forces—secretly coding each copy with a different zodiac sign. When word emerged about "Operation Sagittarius," he knew which general had leaked. Shortly afterward, that general died under mysterious circumstances.

Even as he subverted the constitution, Marcos claimed that he was upholding it. The proclamation of martial law, he argued, "is not a military takeover." Instead, he claimed to be protecting democracy in the Philippines in the face of violent unrest. When confronting such a danger, Marcos said, the president "has inherent and built-in powers, wisely provided for under the Constitution." Immediately, hundreds were arrested, including opposition politicians, labor leaders, and journalists. Most media outlets were closed. Congress was abolished.

During Marcos's fourteen-year dictatorship, tens of thousands of political dissidents were incarcerated and tortured. Thousands were killed, their mutilated bodies frequently dumped in public places, as a means of sowing fear among the public.[10] Poverty rose, and government debt increased, as Marcos and his cronies plundered the public coffers. By the time Marcos was ousted in 1986, his family was estimated to have stolen $5 to $10 billion.[11] Imelda Marcos's collection of art, jewelry, and shoes spawned the term "imeldific": a shameless and vulgar extravagance.

Hitler, Chávez, and Marcos began with election victories, and then used their positions to undermine democracy from within. Such an approach has become increasingly common in the past generation. By contrast to the Cold War era, when most democratic breakdowns were caused by coups, a majority of democratic breakdowns since the 1990s have been instigated by politicians who started their careers by winning elections. Democratic leaders have undermined electoral institutions in Poland, Hungary, Peru, Georgia, Ukraine, Turkey, Russia, and Sri Lanka. "Democratic backsliding today begins at the ballot box," Levitsky and Ziblatt conclude.[12]

In 1992, political scientist Francis Fukuyama wrote that the world had entered a new ideological epoch. The steady expansion of capitalism and democracy across the globe had become unstoppable. With the dissolution of the Soviet Union, he asserted, the world had arrived at "The End of History"—a point where "there are no serious ideological competitors left to liberal democracy."[13] There might be the occasional setback, but the march of liberal democracy was unstoppable.

A quarter of a century later, Fukuyama was not as sanguine. "Twenty-five years ago, I didn't have a sense or a theory about how democracies can go backward," he told a reporter. "And I think they clearly can."[14] Pointing to the rise of populists in Turkey, Hungary, and the United States, Fukuyama forecast that the tide of nationalist indignation could cause a political disruption comparable to the collapse of the Soviet Union.[15]

Since the Economist Intelligence Unit began publishing its annual *Democracy Index* in 2006, some countries have become more democratic, including Armenia, Chile, Colombia, Malaysia, Nepal, Algeria, Morocco, Tunisia, and Angola. But across the world, the average democracy index was lower in 2020 than in 2006.[16] Democracy scholar Larry Diamond declares that the world has suffered "a democracy recession."[17]

The Economist Intelligence Unit has downgraded several countries from hybrid to authoritarian regimes. These include Russia in 2011, Cambodia in 2017, Nicaragua and Mozambique in 2018, and the Palestinian Territories and Iraq in 2019. Several other countries—including Hungary, Poland, Ukraine, Turkey, Lebanon, and China—have also become less democratic.[18] Since the turn of the millennium, one-third of the presidents who reached the end of their constitutionally mandated term attempted to change the rules to hold onto power.[19] Many succeeded.

In a report titled *Revenge of the "Deplorables,"* the Economist Intelligence Unit in 2016 demoted the United States from "full democracy" to "flawed democracy." The nation's electoral processes remained solid, the report authors argued, but a trust deficit was undermining democracy. Public confidence in government had slumped to historic lows. The report noted that while Trump benefited electorally from these trends, he was not responsible for the 2016 downgrade. Even without a presidential election in 2016, the United States would have been relegated to a "flawed democracy."[20] Yet Trump's insistence that he won the 2020 election, despite clear evidence to the contrary, was without precedent among advanced democracies. Critics noted that the United States had condemned similar behavior by leaders in Belarus, Ivory Coast, and Zimbabwe. Former ambassador Michael McFaul called Trump's refusal to accept the election result "his parting gift to autocrats around the world."[21]

There is no iron rule that democracies must stay democratic. In Venezuela, Turkey, and Hungary, democracy has been eroded as the ruling party has taken control of the courts, public service, and public broadcasting services. Independent journalists, opposition members, and protesters have been harassed and intimidated. In each of these countries, populists won elections as outsiders, then used their power to attack traditional institutions. They claimed that democracy was "corrupt," "rigged," or "broken," and that populists alone represent the authentic voice of the people. They changed not just the ideological direction of the country, but the political system itself.

Historian Anne Applebaum points to the way institutions can be delegitimized by cynically suggesting that everyone is as bad as the worst authoritarians. This kind of "whataboutism" leads to claims like "Putin is a killer, but so are we all." It rejects the Jeffersonian idea of spreading liberty across the globe. Instead, it adopts an inward-looking nationalism. Implicitly, it rebuffs the role that the United States played in foreign policy for much of the twentieth century. Moral equivalence, Applebaum maintains, "undermines faith, hope and the belief that we can live up to the language of our Constitution."[22] It is reflected in the apocalyptic pessimism of Trump's inaugural address, with its talk of "American carnage"—a far cry from the sunny optimism of Reagan's "morning in America." If you can convince people that your political opponents are trying to undermine the nation itself, then it becomes easier to justify breaking the rules in order to save the country.

Authoritarians took advantage of COVID-19. When the pandemic hit, many countries sensibly responded by limiting citizens' freedom of movement. But some populists and hard-liners went further, seizing the opportunity to curtail free speech and free elections. In Hungary, Orbán's government declared a state of emergency, suspended all elections and referenda, and enacted a new law making it possible to jail journalists for five years for disseminating information that hindered the government's response to the pandemic. Opposition politicians who objected were derided as "pro virus." In India, Modi's government suspended Question Hour, which allows opposition members to ask snap questions of the executive government. In Thailand, Prayut Chan-o-cha (who seized power in a coup) assumed the authority to impose curfews and censor the press. The Philippines Parliament gave President Duterte emergency powers that were described as "tantamount to autocracy" by a local civil liberties group.[23] And fear of disease may directly fuel xenophobia: one study found that people were less likely to favor legalizing undocumented immigrants if they had just been told about a new strain of the flu.[24]

The risk that populists pose to democratic institutions is revealed in a study carried out by political scientists Jordan Kyle and Yascha Mounk. Analyzing elections in thirty-three democracies, they identify forty-six populist leaders who entered office since 1990 and compare them to nonpopulist leaders. Half of the populists either rewrote or amended the constitution, often with the aim of reducing constraints on executive power or scrapping term limits. Populists are four times as likely to damage democratic institutions. Populist rule is associated with a 7 percent decline in freedom of the press, 8 percent decline in civil liberties, and 13 percent decline in political rights. The dangers are not restricted to right-wing populists: left-wing populists are just as likely to damage democracy. Under populists, corruption levels worsen, and two-fifths of populist leaders end up being indicted for corruption.[25] The long-term harm to democracy might be more severe still, given that many populists in the study remain in office today.

Could things get worse? As the quip goes, a recession is when your neighbors lose their jobs; a depression is when you lose yours. While there is no firm definition of when a democratic recession turns into a democratic depression, one marker would be if the world's strongest democracies began to regress toward authoritarianism. It is one thing for emerging democracies to relapse, but quite another for countries with long traditions of fair elections to backslide and become less democratic. To date, most of the reversion has indeed occurred in weak democracies. From 1998 to 2020, support for autocratic leaders has grown across the world, but the rise has been four times larger in weak democracies than in healthy ones.[26] A red flag will be if autocratic preferences begin to grow rapidly in nations presently regarded as healthy democracies.

While authoritarianism sometimes marches over democracy in army boots, it can also tiptoe in the soft shoes of a silent assassin. Yet there are some clear warning signs that democracy is under threat. Others have suggested useful approaches to this problem, including Diamond's twelve-step program for autocrats, sociologist Juan Linz's litmus tests for the breakdown of democratic regimes, and Levitsky and Ziblatt's four key indicators of authoritarian behavior.[27] Drawing on these as well as my own experiences as a parliamentarian, I maintain that there are seven deadly sins indicating that an elected leader could be trying to degrade their democracy into an authoritarian regime.

- *Wrath*: Promoting or condoning violence toward opponents. This can involve the use of the police or armed forces, or a failure to rein in violence by supporters.

- *Greed*: When a hunger for domination results in a leader changing the rules to attain or maintain power. This may entail changes to electoral boundaries, voter eligibility requirements, or rules about the conduct of elections that are designed to give the leader an unfair advantage.

- *Lust*: An unbridled desire for power that leads to breaking the rules. This may involve suspending the constitution, postponing elections, calling out the army, or taking over the media.

- *Gluttony*: Appropriating government resources by appointing family and friends to senior government positions, and steering contracts to accomplices. This serves the purposes of channeling public resources to the private coffers of the leader while entrenching unqualified cronies in positions of power.

- *Pride*: When the leader puffs their own party up as the only true patriots, and demonizes opponents as disloyal or criminal. This strategy equates criticism of the regime with an attack on the nation by creating a false dichotomy that "you're either with us or against us."

- *Envy*: Bitterness at the way in which the media publicizes opponents or holds the leader to account can lead to curtailing press freedom. This can involve unfounded accusations of bias, closing media outlets, using regulation to muzzle critical voices, or chilling the media by expanding libel laws.

- *Sloth*: Rather than working for the common good, leaders concoct crises and provoke culture wars. This helps them avoid accountability by distracting potential critics. By deliberately saying something outrageous, leaders create a media smoke screen behind which they can lazily avoid public criticism.

The seven antidemocratic sins could be seen in Marcos's first two presidential terms in the lead-up to his imposition of martial law in the Philippines. They characterized Venezuela in the early years of the Chávez regime. They typified the later period of Erdoğan's rule in Turkey, particularly following the antigovernment protests of 2013. They have been hallmarks of Orbán's increasingly illiberal regime since he returned as prime minister of Hungary in 2010.

During his term in office, Trump demonstrated all seven sins. He provoked hundreds of protestors to storm the Capitol, leading to five deaths and over 100 people injured. This violent attempt to overturn the election result followed weeks of false claims from Trump about election fraud and years of partisan redistricting by Republicans, who also brought more than three hundred court cases to discourage voter participation.[28] Trump's corruption was tracked by Citizens for Responsibility and Ethics in Washington, which estimated that he averaged two ethics violations for every day in office, profiting from the presidency on thousands of occasions.[29] He demonized Democrats as "evil" people who "want to destroy our country."[30] He attacked the media using phrases such as "enemy of the people," "dishonest," and "corrupt," suggested revoking NBC's broadcast license, and proposed ending funding for public radio. He was a master of exhausting opponents by creating new distractions, successfully diverting news coverage away from the Access Hollywood revelations, his handling of Hurricane Maria, and the Mueller investigation.[31]

Authoritarians have plenty of raw material to work with. Surveying people in forty countries, researchers found that the typical respondent believes that the share of the population that is Muslim is twice as large as it truly is.[32] French people think their country is 31 percent Muslim (it is actually 8 percent). Britons think their country is 15 percent Muslim (the true figure is 5 percent). US residents say their nation is 17 percent Muslim (the truth is 1 percent). If they want to stoke nativist tensions, demagogues need not be constrained by demography.

Political psychologist Karen Stenner estimates that around one-third of the population finds diversity difficult to tolerate. This group, she argues, can form the core of an authoritarian movement. Stenner proposes an "authoritarian dynamic" in which intolerance of difference is a function of the share of the population who are predisposed to authoritarianism and how threatened they feel.[33] Stenner's research suggests that a predisposition to authoritarianism is driven by a dislike of complexity. Asked what qualities they prize in children, those with an authoritarian predisposition favor manners and obedience over independence and creativity.

According to Stenner, every society contains a sizeable share of potential authoritarians: people who are fearful of dissidence, deviance, or diversity. When threatened in this way, those with an authoritarian predisposition become willing to support strict measures to combat it. This might include restrictions on immigration, new constraints on free speech, or the additional regulation of moral behavior. What is most troubling about Stenner's research is her suggestion that the share of the population with an authoritarian predisposition may be immutable—with about one in three people serving as the wellspring of support for any would-be autocrat who can conjure up a sufficiently frightening threat.

*   *   *

"That was when they suspended the Constitution," writes Margaret Atwood in *The Handmaid's Tale*. "They said it would be temporary. There wasn't even any rioting in the streets. People stayed home at night, watching television, looking for some direction."

Like the other nightmare scenarios discussed in this book, an authoritarian turn is improbable. But it is not impossible. Fictional scenarios that were once fanciful have become unexpectedly possible. For example, in Philip Roth's *The Plot against America*, xenophobic populist Charles Lindbergh wins the Republican nomination, defeats Franklin D. Roosevelt, and sets the nation on a path toward fascism. As Levitsky and Ziblatt have pointed out, the power of party bosses prevented an outsider from winning the presidential nomination in that era. Indeed, when another extremist demagogue, Henry Ford, toyed with seeking the 1924 presidential nomination, he was more popular than all other contenders, yet unable to bypass the political kingmakers. As one insider put it, "How can a man over sixty years old, who . . . has no training, no experience, aspire to such an office? It is most ridiculous."[34] Modern-day party leaders have no power to block a radical populist such as Lindbergh or Ford.

Similarly, Orwell's *1984* envisaged a society based on mass surveillance—a technological impossibility when the novel was published in 1949. Today, China's Skynet system includes hundreds of millions of closed-circuit television cameras, feeding data to computers running sophisticated facial recognition algorithms.[35] The Chinese social credit system, allowing people to be blacklisted for "untrustworthy" behavior, has already been used to deny more than twenty million air ticket purchases. In Xinjiang, all Uygurs are required to install a remote monitoring app on their phones. Many of these technologies can be purchased from their Chinese suppliers by other authoritarian governments. The utopian view about technology inevitably strengthening democracy, epitomized in older books such as *Wiki Government: How Technology Can Make Government Better, Democracy Stronger, and Citizens More Powerful*, has given way to a more dystopian view, expressed in recent titles such as *The Age of Surveillance Capitalism* and *The People vs Tech: How the Internet Is Killing Democracy (and How We Save It)*.

*   *   *

If the United States were to stage a major retreat from democracy, it would not be for the first time. With the passage of the Fifteenth Amendment in 1870, African American men were given the right to vote in all states. Mississippi, where former slaves made up a majority of the population, elected Black senators in 1870 and 1875. South Carolina briefly had a majority Black state legislature. But with the end of Reconstruction and withdrawal of federal troops, the Ku Klux Klan stepped up its terror campaign. In the 1890s, states used poll taxes, literacy tests, and education qualifications (which could be waived at the registrar's discretion). The result was the almost total elimination of African American voters from the rolls. As late as the 1930s, less than 1 percent of African Americans in Mississippi and South Carolina were registered to vote.[36] Exclusion from voting rolls meant that southern juries were typically all-white. For African Americans in many southern states, the elimination of democracy lasted nearly a century, ending only with the passage of the Voting Rights Act in 1965. Many who suffered under these shameful reforms are still alive today. For them, the prospect of democratic backsliding may not feel so far-fetched.

A lasting democratic depression is made less likely by the fact that authoritarianism does not have the planetary impact of a nuclear war, superintelligence, or global warming. While leaders learn from one another, authoritarianism is less contagious than a pandemic. But the rise of populism means that it cannot be discounted. As we have seen, populism typically leads to a decline in media freedom, political rights, and civil liberties. Populists might claim to be the authentic voice of the people, but they are usually more interested in accumulating power than sharing it. They typically lack the belief in equality and freedom that underpins a healthy democracy. For all that they rail against "elites," populist leaders pose a danger to humanity because of the possibility that they will steer their country toward totalitarianism.

From the Philippines to Hungary, we know that the prospect of an authoritarian takeover is more than the stuff of dystopian novels. As Applebaum warns, "Given the right conditions, any society can turn against democracy. Indeed, if history is anything to go by, all of our societies eventually will."[37] I am not as pessimistic as Applebaum, but it pays to be on the lookout for the seven deadly sins—wrath, greed, lust, gluttony, pride, envy, and sloth—indicating that an elected leader could be trying to transform their democracy into an autocracy.

What can we do to reduce the risk of a populist wave slamming us onto the jagged rocks of totalitarianism? The answer lies in making democracy work better by improving political institutions, strengthening democratic norms, and creating a more inviting civic culture. Want to save the world? Let's start by fixing politics.

9
Fixing Politics

According to the definitive historical database of democracy, the United States was the most democratic country in the world in 1800.[1] Although women and slaves could not vote, the United States went further than any other nation at that time in allowing the people to decide how the country was run. Over the next two centuries, Britain and the United States played a decisive role in promoting democracy around the world. Half of the lasting transitions to democracy since then occurred with their help.[2] US intervention in World War II not only protected democracy in Europe but also ensured that Germany and Japan transitioned to democracy after their defeat.

When the United States was in its infancy, leaders recognized the need to regularly improve the country's democratic institutions. Thomas Jefferson proposed that the Constitution be revisited once a generation to make "periodical repairs."[3] Since Jefferson's time, some substantial repairs have been made, such as the Fifteenth Amendment of 1870 granting African American men the right to vote, the Nineteenth Amendment of 1920 allowing women the right to vote, and the Voting Rights Act of 1965 finally making good on the promise of the Fifteenth Amendment. But the constitutional maintenance envisaged by Jefferson ceased in 1971 with the passage of the most recent pro-democracy amendment to the Constitution (lowering the voting age from twenty-one to eighteen). It has been half a century since the nation's supreme law was amended to make the country more democratic.

If US democracy were a car, it would be an aging classic—a once-stylish limousine now rattling angrily, blowing smoke, and desperately in need of a full service. The same database that ranked the United States the most democratic nation in the world in 1800 now lists fifty-one countries as having stronger democratic institutions than the United States (among them Chile, Greece, Mauritius, Portugal, Slovenia, and Uruguay).[4] Recall too the Economist Intelligence Unit's decision to demote the United States in 2016 from "full democracy" to "flawed democracy."

What could be done? As a starting point, elections should be a mass participation activity, not an elite sport. Across advanced democracies, around seven in ten adult citizens vote in national elections.[5] In the United States, this figure is six in ten during presidential elections and typically around four in ten for midterms.[6] Despite a rise in turnout in the 2020 presidential election, one-third of adult citizens failed to cast a ballot. If voters were a random sample of the citizenry, low turnout might not skew the result. Just as a survey can provide an accurate picture of the whole population, a representative subset of voters could theoretically mirror the whole electorate. But in fact, people who are older, richer, and better educated are more likely to participate in elections.[7] As a consequence, the election result does not accurately reflect the values of the citizenry.

In recent years, motor voter laws, early in-person voting, and absentee ballots have helped to raise turnout.[8] Conversely, some states have enacted voter identification laws ostensibly to prevent fraud, but perhaps also because identification requirements disproportionately disenfranchise Democratic voters. Yet as a political deterrent, they are strikingly ineffective. According to one study, strict voter identification laws prevent at most one in five hundred people from casting a ballot.[9] Strict voter identification laws are unjustified, but opponents should not let themselves be distracted from factors that have a much bigger impact on turnout.

To encourage participation in elections, it helps to hold them on a convenient day. One of the most common reasons nonvoters give for failing to cast a ballot is that they were too busy or had a conflicting schedule.[10] This could be readily addressed by holding elections on a weekend. Around the world, Sunday is by far the most common day for elections, with Saturday being the next most common day. Absentee ballots and early voting accommodate those whose religions do not allow them to participate on those days. Only a handful of countries, including Canada, Britain, Indonesia, Norway, and the United States, have a fixed Election Day that is not on the weekend. In regularly holding elections on weekdays, these countries make it harder for their citizens to vote.

A straightforward fix is to move polling day to the weekend. Alternatively, if elections must be held on weekdays, the day can be made a holiday. This already occurs in several US states and territories, including Hawaii, Louisiana, New York, and Puerto Rico.[11] An easy way to see the effect of holiday voting is to compare voting rates of Puerto Ricans living in the United States with those living on the island, where Election Day is a holiday. Puerto Ricans on the island vote at twice the rate of those on the mainland.[12]

A more radical approach would be to treat voting as a civic obligation. Countries generally regard jury service, paying taxes, and filling out the census as responsibilities that cannot be shirked (refusal to complete the US Census carries a fine of up to $5,000). Yet voting is typically voluntary. Internationally, Australia, Austria, and Belgium are among the few nations that enforce compulsory voting laws. Analyzing Australia's adoption of compulsory voting, the leading study found that it boosted turnout from 67 percent (similar to the voting rate in the 2020 US presidential election) to 91 percent.[13] In other words, one in four Australians who would not have voted under a voluntary voting system ended up participating once voting was compulsory.

Voting didn't just become more common; voters became more representative of the community. Before compulsory voting, rich citizens had been much more likely to vote than poorer ones. Making voting mandatory virtually erased that gap, making Australian democracy substantially more egalitarian. There is little evidence of a backlash; citizens in Australia, Austria, and Belgium are no less committed to democracy than in advanced nations that do not treat voting as a civic duty. Compulsory voting also puts pressure on election authorities to ensure that everyone can vote. Given that the failure to vote without a valid reason incurs a fine of 20 Australian dollars (around 15 US dollars), it is no surprise that Australian elections are held on Saturdays, polling places are accessible, and many people take the option to vote early or by mail.

Getting more citizens to the polling place is only part of the challenge. Just as each voter should only be allowed to cast a single ballot, each ballot should carry equal weight in the election contest. Yet this principle of "one vote, one value" is violated by the electoral college, which gives over twice as much weight to Vermont voters as Texas voters, and further distorts the result through "winner takes all" rules in most states.[14] In five out of forty-five elections—1824, 1876, 1888, 2000, and 2016—the presidency went to a candidate who had not received the most votes. The electoral college magnifies the power of white voters and forces both parties to run a campaign significantly to the right of the median voter.[15] Since 1988, the Republican presidential candidate has won the popular vote only once. A practical solution is the National Popular Vote Interstate Compact, an agreement among a group of states to provide their electoral votes to the candidate who wins a majority of the popular vote nationally. The compact will bind states' electoral college votes once it has been supported by states with 270 electoral college votes. At that point, the popular vote would be decisive, regardless of what other states chose to do. While the compact is already supported by sixteen jurisdictions with 196 electoral votes, virtually no Republican states have signed on.[16] Without some Republican support, the National Popular Vote Interstate Compact will not come into effect.

At a congressional level, independent redistricting would reflect the principle that underlies all competitive sport: the umpire should be unbiased. In countries that hold elections, more than half have an independent election commission. After the defeat of Saddam Hussein, the US-led Coalition Provisional Authority established an independent election commission to oversee Iraq's elections. When the United Nations is advising emerging democracies, it recommends that they create an independent electoral commission.[17] Yet at present, only a handful of US states have truly nonpartisan redistricting commissions.[18] Like the electoral college, this skews the results. As the Republican gerrymandering strategist Thomas Hofeller once put it, partisan redistricting is like an election in reverse: "Usually the voters get to pick the politicians. In redistricting, the politicians get to pick the voters."[19]

The United States is not the only advanced country where partisan redistricting affects election outcomes; one report found that politically drawn boundaries have a minor impact on French election results. Even in countries with independent redistricting, the electoral system sometimes operates under rules that give more weight to rural voters.[20] But when it comes to partisan redistricting, the United States is the world champion.[21] A report on gerrymandering found that in each of the 2012, 2014, and 2016 elections, an average of fifty-nine members were elected to the US House of Representatives merely because the district lines were drawn in their favor.[22] For example, partisan redistricting in Texas allows Republicans to win two-thirds of the congressional seats with just half the popular vote.[23] Removing partisanship from the redistricting process would make the United States a more democratic democracy.

Another worthwhile electoral reform is the adoption of ranked-choice voting, in which electors number candidates in order of preference. If no candidate receives a majority of the vote, the candidate with the fewest votes is eliminated, and their preferences distributed to the remaining candidates. This process continues until one candidate has a majority. Also called instant runoff voting, such a system ensures that minor party candidates do not play a spoiler role, draining votes away from moderates. Had the 2000 election been conducted by ranked-choice voting, conservative supporters of Pat Buchanan could have ranked him first and George W. Bush second, while progressive supporters of Ralph Nader could have ranked him first and Al Gore second.[24] Ranked-choice voting has been implemented in several US cities and states, including Maine, San Francisco, and Santa Fe (it is used in the Oscars too). As Fair-Vote's David Daley points out, anyone who thinks ranked-choice voting is complicated should consider the fact that the current system often forces voters to consult opinion polls and vote strategically if they are to avoid "wasting" their vote.[25] Under ranked-choice voting, voters would have more options and could simply choose their favorite candidates.

It is probably no coincidence that four of the electoral reforms I have proposed—weekend or holiday voting, compulsory voting, independent redistricting, and ranked-choice voting—are all part of the democratic system in my own country. Australia's democracy isn't perfect, but as a citizen and parliamentarian, I'm proud of the fact that my country invented the voting booth, was one of the first in the world to implement the secret ballot and extend the franchise to women, and has an electoral participation rate of around nine in ten eligible citizens today.[26]

Internationally, democracies already cooperate through global parliamentary forums, monitoring each other's elections, and promoting democracy in fragile states. Consistent with this work, democracies should ensure that their firms do not help authoritarians (or budding ones) by supplying facial recognition technologies, surveillance technologies, or tools that enable the hacking of political opponents. Troublingly, US firms have sold facial recognition technology to Saudi Arabia and the United Arab Emirates, while Israeli companies have sold espionage technology to Angola, Bahrain, and Kazakhstan.[27] Expanding liberty is a higher priority than getting a few more export dollars. Advanced democracies should also help civil society groups and watchdog organizations that are working to prevent the abuse of surveillance technologies in developing countries. In the worst case, regimes that misuse surveillance technologies to undermine democracy could be named and shamed as "digital authoritarian" states.[28]

Protecting democracy is also about norms—what Levitsky and Ziblatt call the "soft guardrails" of the system. They point out that political parties have traditionally played a vital role in "distancing" themselves from extremists.[29] In the 1930s, the youth wing of the Swedish conservative party became troublingly radical—supporting Hitler and criticizing democracy. The senior wing of the party responded not by placating the group but instead expelling all twenty-five thousand members from their ranks. The party may have suffered a short-term electoral cost, yet Swedish democracy benefited in the long run.

In the United States, there are moments when senior party leaders have taken a "high road" approach—putting the health of the democracy ahead of immediate political gains. When Republican senator Joseph McCarthy alleged that the State Department was "infested with communists," he quickly received national attention. Although unable to verify most of his allegations, McCarthy continued to make baseless claims. In mid-1954, polls showed that half of all people in the United States supported his campaign. McCarthy pressured the administration into dismissing hundreds of gay men from government posts on the grounds that they might be vulnerable to blackmail.[30] But he began to lose support in his own party as the gap between his claims and what he could prove grew wider. In one hearing, an army lawyer memorably interrupted McCarthy with the words, "Let us not assassinate this lad further, Senator. You've done enough. Have you no sense of decency, Sir, at long last? Have you left no sense of decency?"[31] At the end of 1954, the Senate voted to condemn McCarthy by a vote of sixty-seven to twenty-two. Half of the Republicans supported the condemnation, including Maine Republican senator Margaret Chase Smith, who had denounced McCarthy in her famous "Declaration of Conscience" speech. After the condemnation vote, McCarthy's power was sapped, and he was generally regarded as a fringe extremist during his final few years in the Senate.

Likewise, when Nixon faced impeachment proceedings for his role in the Watergate break-in and subsequent cover-up, a significant number of Republican members decided that protecting the institution of the presidency was more important than winning at all costs. As Maine Republican William Cohen put it, "I have been faced with the terrible responsibility of assessing the conduct of a President that I voted for, believed to be the best man to lead this country . . . but a President who in the process by act or acquiescence allowed the rule of law and the Constitution to slip under the boots of indifference and arrogance and abuse."[32] Knowing that the House would impeach him, and the Senate would likely convict him, Nixon resigned.

There is a subtle side to democratic norms. When I'm getting to know new members of the Australian Parliament after each election, I remind them of the litmus test suggested by former Canadian parliamentarian Michael Ignatieff: "No democracy has any health in it unless debutant MPs think of the chamber with awe and respect."[33] In a democracy, those with the privilege to pass laws *should* feel a sense of trepidation when they first enter the parliament. By contrast, in nations where the parliament is a sham, legislators have no real responsibility and show no signs of nerves on the chamber floor.

For those who are troubled by the rise of populists, a natural reaction is to abandon all pretense of adhering to democratic norms—to employ a "win at all costs" approach that puts policy outcomes ahead of institutions. This might be temporarily satisfying, but would ultimately backfire. Hate-fueled politics is the ideal petri dish for extremist politics. Turning down the political temperature advantages centrists. For this reason, electoral reforms must be justified in terms of their benefits for democracy, not merely because they provide a partisan edge. Politics as street fighting is likely to lower the standing of politicians, which in turn will erode the standing of government. If you believe that government must focus on long-term risks, the only viable route is the high road.

Increasingly, many who call themselves "political activists" are inactive where it counts most—in their own local communities. These so-called activists enthusiastically follow national politics on cable news and social media, but treat school boards and city planning with disdain. Consequently, they end up being like ESPN-addicted couch potatoes: they can build a perfect fantasy league, but won't go outside and throw a ball with their daughter. Political scientist Eitan Hersh refers to this trend as "political hobbyism" since it leads to a situation in which partisans behave toward those on the other side like sports fans treat their opponents—cheering and jeering, rather than trying to engage and persuade.[34]

The health of a democracy doesn't depend on people retweeting a partisan attack. Instead, democracy relies on those who are willing to host a house meeting, set up an information table in the local mall, or knock on doors for a cause. This kind of activism doesn't just affect the issue itself; it helps build a civic culture where the currency that matters is persuasion rather than animosity. Recall the five factors that have brought populists to power: jobs, snobs, race, pace, and luck. Mainstream political activism can affect at least two of these—creating a sense that mainstream politics is inclusive, not snobbish, and that the pace of change is manageable.

Strengthening democracy also involves shaping a better-informed electorate. Less than one-quarter of US middle schoolers are "proficient" at civics.[35] Similarly, a study across twenty-four countries found that only one-third of school students had a critical perspective on citizenship.[36] One proposed reform is to have educators teach civics by linking political theory to current events (e.g., using an upcoming vote to discuss the constitutional underpinnings).[37] Another is to ask all senior students to develop their own Change the World project, deploying the lessons of classroom civics to campaign on a local issue. And political education should not stop on high school graduation day. To promise civic learning among adults, one worthwhile proposal is "Deliberation Day": an annual holiday on which everyone is invited to join community meetings to discuss major political issues.[38]

*   *   *

Democracies outperform on many metrics. Democracies invest more in health and education. Over the long run, transitioning to democracy raises incomes by 20 percent.[39] Democracies are less likely to experience famines.[40] Never in history have two fully democratic states gone to war.[41] Yet many still quote British prime minister Winston Churchill's maxim: "Democracy is the worst form of government except for all those other forms that have been tried from time to time." This flaccid defense has always irritated me. It conveys a thinly veiled distrust of our fellow citizens and a sense that democracy is a form of mob rule that must be tolerated rather than celebrated. It's democracy with a sneer and sigh.

As a member of the Australian House of Representatives, I've seen plenty of bad bills and untidy legislative compromises. For a time, my electoral district had more voters than any other in the country, so I've had plenty of encounters with citizens who are frantic, furious, and even ferocious. But I've also seen how a good law can make the business environment more productive or provide support to someone with a profound disability. There's a true pleasure in being able to help your electors with their problems, whether it's navigating the social safety net, providing a congratulatory letter to a centenarian, or simply explaining how a policy works. No job I've ever done has been as interesting, diverse, or rewarding as elected office.

You're never off duty as a politician. Beyond the regular town hall meetings, I've had political conversations with the man next to me in the changing room of my local swimming pool, with people who stop me while I'm buying eggs at the supermarket, and even with fellow marathon runners during a race.

Because it is rule by the many, democracy is egalitarian. Authoritarianism—rule by the few—is not. Suffragette poet Alice Duer Miller summed up the point in her poem "Democracy":

Democracy is this—to hold
That all who wander down the pike
In cart or car, on foot or bike,
Or male or female, young or old,
Are much alike—are much alike.[42]

Democracy embodies freedom too. As E. M. Forster once put it, democracy starts from the assumption

that the individual is important, and that all types are needed to make a civilization. It does not divide its citizens into the bossers and the bossed—as an efficiency-regime tends to do. The people I admire most are those who are sensitive and want to create something or discover something, and do not see life in terms of power, and such people get more of a chance under a democracy than elsewhere . . . [P]eople need to express themselves; they cannot do so unless society allows them liberty to do so, and the society which allows them most liberty is a democracy.[43]

Egalitarians and libertarians alike should be proud of democracy. It is not just another system of government—it is the best system of government. We should be proud to promote it worldwide, vigorous to defend it against saboteurs, and ambitious to make democracies more democratic.

10
The End

In a show titled "The Cataclysm Sentence," RadioLab asked a group of writers to suppose that humanity had been destroyed and they could pass on a single sentence to the next intelligent species to occupy the planet.[1] Screenwriter Cord Jefferson suggested, "The only things you are innately afraid of are falling and loud noises. The rest of your fears are learned and mostly negligible." Funeral director Caitlin Doughty offered, "You will die, and that's the most important thing." Nonfiction writer Nicholson Baker proposed, "You know more than you can say." Artist Jenny Odell said, "Everything is connected." Psychologist Alison Gopnik came up with simply "Why?"

Others were more expansive. Science historian James Gleick wrote, "The moon revolves around the earth, which is not the center of the universe (far from it) but just one of many objects (large and small) that revolve around the sun—which in turn is one of countless stars, mostly so far away that they are invisible, even on the clearest night—all travelling through space, on paths obeying simple laws of nature that can be expressed in terms of mathematics; oh and by the way, there is no God." Writer and blogger

Maria Popova proposed, "We are each allotted a sliver of space time, wedged between 'not yet' and 'no more,' which we fill with a lifetime of joys and sorrows, immensities of thought and feeling, all deducible to electrical impulses coursing through us at 80 feet per second, yet responsible for every love poem that has ever been written, every symphony ever composed, every scientific breakthrough measuring out nerve conduction and mapping out space time."

These are beautiful messages to be sending to another species, but there is a poignancy about the idea that we might need to craft them because humanity could go extinct. Wouldn't it be better to imagine that we can leave messages for our own descendants—for humanity thousands of years in the future? My reaction to them is similar to how I feel when Elon Musk argues that humans should colonize Mars so that we have a backup planet in the event of a third world war. Wouldn't it be better to put those resources into averting catastrophe in the first place?

Writing this book has sometimes felt like being stuck in a disaster movie: assailed by bugs, bombs, bots, and Big Brother while being boiled by the climate. In assessing catastrophic threats, it's foolish to spend time fretting about things that cannot happen or over which we have no control. But it's similarly foolish to dismiss dangers that we can control merely because they *probably* will not happen. Five out of six people who play Russian roulette live to tell the tale. Nonetheless, I don't recommend it as a pastime. When it comes to catastrophic risks, "unlikely" isn't good enough.

I wrote this book because I'm an optimist and want to hurl all my energies toward safeguarding a future for humanity that could be extraordinary—trillions of people living lives of exquisite beauty. I want this for the next generation, and whether or not you have children, I'm guessing you do too. So why wouldn't we want it for all the generations to come?

As philosopher Will MacAskill observes, to care about future generations is nothing more than an extension of the Golden Rule, a principle found in most religions and secular philosophies.[2] Islam reminds its adherents, "That which you want for yourself, seek for mankind." Confucianism teaches, "Do not do to others what you do not want them to do to you." Christianity's edict is "do unto others what you would have them do to you." Judaism says, "Love your fellow as yourself." Buddhism instills, "Hurt not others in ways that you yourself would find hurtful." In Hinduism, the principle is, "By making dharma your main focus, treat others as you treat yourself." Atheist thinker Adam Lee also cherishes the Golden Rule, noting, "Moral directives do not need to be complex or obscure to be worthwhile, and in fact, it is precisely this rule's simplicity which makes it great. It is easy to come up with, easy to understand, and easy to apply."[3]

Yet despite the ubiquity of the Golden Rule for making decisions in the present moment, humans often fail to apply it to future generations. As artificial intelligence researcher Eliezer Yudkowsky puts it, "People who would never dream of hurting a child hear of an existential risk, and say, 'Well, maybe the human species doesn't really deserve to survive.'"[4] The attitude seems scarily similar to Soviet leader Joseph Stalin's dictum, "If only one man dies of hunger, that is a tragedy. If millions die, that's only statistics."[5]

By definition, a one in six chance of catastrophe probably won't happen. And by definition, if it does happen, there's no chance of a do-over. The usual approach of suffering a small loss, adjusting course, and getting it right the next time around doesn't work when confronting existential challenges.[6]

We don't face species-ending catastrophic risks in our day-to-day lives, but we do confront risks that would be catastrophic for our own circumstances. This year, there is a one in three hundred chance that your home will burn down.[7] Most of us don't have enough cash on hand that we could readily afford to rebuild our home. So we take measures to reduce the risk, such as installing a smoke detector, keeping an eye on frying pans, and not putting candles near curtains. Nine out of ten homeowners also take out insurance, with fire insurance being the biggest claim category.[8]

Both risk reduction and hedging losses have their origins in Founding Father Benjamin Franklin, who set up one of the first firefighting departments in the United States and then went on to establish the nation's oldest property insurance company. Franklin made it a priority to ensure that citizens in his home city of Philadelphia did not have their lives ruined by fire. Today, most of us happily pay the taxes that fund firefighters and buy home insurance, thereby minimizing and mitigating this one in three hundred risk.

The philosophy of insurance also applies to how we think about catastrophic threats. These tail risks deserve our attention not because they're probable but instead because they would be unbearable. Ignoring existential risks is like putting all your assets into short selling: you risk unlimited losses for a limited gain. With regular investing, you can lose your shirt. With short selling, you can lose your pants and underwear too. Regardless of how confident you are about forecasting the market, it would be rash to put everything into a short-selling strategy.

Alas, electoral incentives can coax leaders away from insuring society against mortal dangers. Successful politicians tend to be overconfident in their own abilities and correspondingly overconfident about the future. Faced with a packed diary, planning for a potential crisis can feel like a waste of time. Except in the rare circumstances of a leader who has experienced an emergency, politicians generally focus on things that are likely to happen than on improbable events. As a society, we tend to underreward successful crisis planning. Rather than lionizing wartime leaders such as Churchill and Lincoln, perhaps we should be celebrating leaders who used deft diplomacy to avoid conflict altogether. In cases such as a foiled terrorist plot or averted pandemic, the public may never even be aware that effective crisis management has saved lives. Insurance is vital, but it isn't glamorous. How many movies have you seen that feature actuaries instead of action heroes?

For the major catastrophic risks outlined in this book, I have proposed specific suggestions for reducing the danger. To lessen the risk of pandemics, it is vital to invest in scientific research, disease surveillance, surge capacity, and stockpiles. To reduce the threat of bioterrorism—the "poor man's atomic bomb"—it would be worth toughening the Biological Weapons Convention, strengthening the safety of laboratories that conduct biological research, improving the security of DNA synthesis, and carefully vetting the publication of research that could readily be misused by bioterrorists.

Lowering the risk of catastrophic climate change requires cutting emissions. This could be done through investing in renewables research, restricting carbon emissions from power plants, and assisting developing nations to follow a cleaner path than the one that today's advanced nations pursued. To lower the chance of atomic catastrophe, a Manhattan Project II should work to minimize the number of nuclear nations and reduce the number of weapons—a virtuous "race to the bottom" by the nuclear powers. Simple procedural and technical changes could also improve safety, including taking missiles off hair-trigger alert, enabling a mistaken launch to be recalled, and adopting a universal principle of no first use.

To improve the odds that a superintelligent computer will serve humanity's goals, we should adopt programming principles that mandate advanced computers to be observant, humble, and altruistic—figuring out what people most want rather than following a preset moral code. National governments should ensure that their innovation-backing function is working closely with their regulatory function—putting the gas pedal next to the brake. International engagement—ultimately leading to a formal treaty—would reduce the risk that rogue companies or countries create a dangerous superintelligence.

The dystopian vision of stable totalitarianism was summed up by Orwell in 1984 with the words "imagine a boot stamping on a human face—forever." Today, Orwellian surveillance technology has strengthened the hand of would-be authoritarians. This means advanced democracies must take extreme care that facial and voice recognition technologies do not fall into the hands of budding dictators. Regimes that are using surveillance technology to stifle dissent should be globally condemned.

But crosscutting all issues of existential risk is the danger of populism. Populists are anti-intellectual, anti-institutional, anti-international, and anti-irenic. This has led them to attack the science of climate change, undermine the public health institutions that coordinate a response to new diseases, undercut international agreements on nuclear nonproliferation, and create a sense of instability that makes it harder to solve the problem of building a superintelligence that is aligned with human values. Populists are especially prone to take their country toward authoritarianism, as signaled by the seven antidemocratic sins.

Catastrophic dangers are what Michael Lewis refers to as the "fifth risk": the risk a society runs when it falls into the habit of responding to long-term dangers with short-term solutions. The fifth risk "is the existential threat that you never really imagine as a risk . . . like bombs with very long fuses that, in the distant future, when the fuse reaches the bomb, might or might not explode." Lewis argues that "if your ambition is to maximize short-term gain without regard to the long-term cost . . . it's better never to really understand those problems. There is an upside to ignorance, and a downside to knowledge."[9] Across the world, populist governments are ignoring these fifth risks.

An effective bulwark against existential peril is more democracy. Strengthening democracy is like a force multiplier, lifting the standing of thoughtful long-termists and making it harder for populists to find a foothold. Vital democracies are better able to act in the interests of future generations. More people will participate in elections if they are held on weekends or holidays; more still if voting is a required civic duty. Democratic equality could be improved by reforming the electoral college, independent redistricting, and ranked-choice voting. The norms of the system are crucial too—particularly the willingness of senior leaders to distance themselves from extremists and put constitutional integrity ahead of legislative victory. Active citizenship requires community engagement—not merely following national politics on cable news and social media. Local politics isn't a sideshow; it's a building block. People who approach politics with the mindset of a sports fan rarely affect the final score.

The best antidote to angry populism isn't anger; it's wisdom. We often associate stoicism with an ability to endure suffering, but the ancient Stoics had a more purposeful life in mind. Through the writings of Seneca, Epictetus, and Marcus Aurelius, they emphasized that a good life is one that is centered on virtue. Stoics welcomed political engagement, but only in service of others, not as a means of self-aggrandizement.

Stoics identified four cardinal virtues: courage, prudence, justice, and moderation.[10] Courage requires boldness in service of truth, and a sense of calm and self-restraint when confronted by opposition. Just as in battle, courage involves accepting danger in pursuit of a noble cause. Prudence, the second virtue, reflects a love of wisdom. It counsels that we must distinguish what we cannot change from what we can and devote energies only where we can make a difference.

To the Stoics, justice requires treating others fairly—not merely by letting them keep what is theirs, but by reducing unfairness and inequality. This is the social justice of philosopher John Rawls, not the narrow property rights justice of philosopher Robert Nozick. Finally, Stoics believe in moderation: living a calm and disciplined life, not a shouty and chaotic existence. They sought to minimize their attachment to worldly possessions, pointing out that if you occasionally skip a meal or take a cold shower, you are more likely to appreciate food and warmth when it comes. This simple philosophy of gratitude and mindfulness, which has enjoyed a revival in recent years, is rooted in ancient philosophy.

We have already seen this kind of modest approach to politics in a different context. Recall that some artificial intelligence experts believe that it makes little sense to try to endow computers with a preset moral code. Instead, they consider that the best ethical system will emerge from coding machines to watch how humans behave and help us achieve our goals. Watchfulness and humility are also embodied in the Stoic virtues, which reflect a willingness to respect tradition, but adapt when the facts change. Proof that gentle advocacy can change minds comes from Pope Francis's 2015 statement that global warming "represents one of the principal challenges facing humanity." In the months following the papal encyclical, devout Catholics became significantly more supportive of action to address climate change.[11]

A stoic approach to politics means spending less time caught up in the cycle of outrage and devoting more energy to making an enduring difference. As Roman emperor Aurelius counseled those who see macho indignation as the best way to win, "Keep this thought handy when you feel a fit of rage coming on—it isn't manly to be enraged. Rather, gentleness and civility are more human, and therefore manlier. A real man doesn't give way to anger and discontent, and such a person has strength, courage, and endurance—unlike the angry and complaining. The nearer a man comes to a calm mind, the closer he is to strength."[12]

The gendered language of Aurelius reflects the fact that he was speaking to a world in which men dominated politics. But his observation highlights something else too: in our modern world, angry politics frequently excludes women. It's no coincidence that most populist politicians tend to be men. And not just any men but men with the swaggering braggadocio of John Wayne, Clint Eastwood, or Sylvester Stallone. An excessively macho approach to politics excludes over half the population from having a say.

Philosopher Martha Nussbaum argues that retributive anger—in which we seek to hurt those who have hurt us—only poisons democratic politics. As Nussbaum notes, pain for pain is a "false lure," creating more suffering rather than solving the problem. Anger is often the offspring of fear, since fear leads us to make hasty decisions, worry about our relative status, and focus on payback. A better approach, Nussbaum reasons, is to replace boasting and invective with a willingness to learn and change. This is, she says, "a practice of hope because it creates a world of listening, of quiet voices, and of mutual respect for reason."[13] Vengeful payback makes us think that we can change the past. Hope reminds us that we can still shape the future.

There is much in this creative, optimistic, future-focused approach that reflects US values. Historian David McCullough maintains that one of the nation's remarkable gifts is improvisation. "We improvise in jazz; we improvise in many of our architectural breakthroughs. Improvisation is one of our traits, as a people, because it was essential, it was necessary, because again and again we were attempting what hadn't been done before."[14] Fellow historian Jon Meacham contends that the United States has long been shaped by the promise of "forward motion"—expanding the frontiers of knowledge and happiness.[15]

Great leaders recognize that big ambitions transcend generations. In his second State of the Union address, President John F. Kennedy told Congress that his goal was "a free community of nations, independent but interdependent, uniting north and south, east and west, in one great family of man, outgrowing and transcending the hates and fears that rend our age." Kennedy went on to admit, "We will not reach that goal today, or tomorrow. We may not reach it in our own lifetime. But the quest is the greatest adventure of our century."[16]

*   *   *

In 1991, as the Soviet Union began to shatter into fifteen fragments, Democratic senator Sam Nunn saw a looming danger. Thousands of nuclear weapons were held outside Russia. Chemical and biological weapons facilities were lightly guarded. Soviet scientists who had spent their careers working on weapons of mass destruction were at risk of being secretly headhunted by Iran, North Korea, and Libya.

Yet when he first proposed a program to secure and dismantle weapons of mass destruction, Nunn was met with partisan opposition. Defense secretary Dick Cheney referred to the plan as "foolish," and President George H. W. Bush averred, "I'm not going to cut into the muscle of defense of this country."[17] Others questioned the need for spending money in a country that had been the United States' mortal enemy. In committee, Republicans voted against it, and the proposal never made it to the Senate floor.

So Nunn tried again. This time he had the intellectual backing of a Harvard University study, directed by Ash Carter, which concluded that "the breakup of the Soviet Union posed the biggest proliferation threat of the Atomic Age." And his international plan had bipartisan support, with senior Republican Richard Lugar agreeing to cosponsor the proposal. It passed the Senate by eighty-six votes to eight, and was signed into law by Bush weeks later.

Over the coming decades, the Nunn-Lugar Cooperative Threat Reduction Program removed all nuclear weapons from Ukraine, Belarus, and Kazakhstan. It eliminated or dismantled over seven thousand nuclear warheads, and two million chemical munitions. Dozens of biological weapons facilities were converted into research laboratories, providing thousands of scientists with work aimed at peaceful ends. As Lugar pointed out in his retirement speech to the Senate, "The United States and Russia have eliminated more nuclear weapons than the combined arsenals of the United Kingdom, France, and China."[18]

From the standpoint of reducing existential risk, the Nunn-Lugar program was one of history's most important initiatives. But it was underpinned by a commitment to the international order, shaped by the intellectual work of Harvard's nuclear security experts, and implemented by scientific and diplomatic professionals. Congress was persuaded to spend money on a foreign aid cooperation program in the Soviet Union at the end of the Cold War. The initiative was formulated by a Democratic senator, signed by a Republican president, and continued to be funded after Republicans took control of Congress.[19] It is much less certain that a measure like Nunn-Lugar could withstand populist opposition today. Populism stands in the way of global progress on issues such as bioterrorism and the safety of artificial intelligence.

It's become commonplace to deride technocrats, but not many people belittle expertise when they're about to go under a surgeon's knife. When a hurricane hits, few say that the era of big government is over. A society that ignores experts and institutions, a society that focuses only on the short term, is putting itself at risk.

This moment in history should remind us about the importance of long-termism. If our species goes extinct, we don't just snuff out the lives of the eight billion living today but also trillions of unborn people stretching out to the almost-infinite future. If our descendants had a voice, they would be shouting at us like a parent who's just seen their child playing with the hand brake of a car parked at a cliff top.

Strengthening institutions, deepening international engagement, and creating space for a more considered and thoughtful politics are the best ways to minimize existential hazards. COVID-19 isn't just a health crisis. It's a shock to the system that reminds us of the dangers of focusing too much on the daily sideshow and ignoring long-term risks. The pandemic has shown us the shallowness of populists and reinforced the value of expertise. If we grab this moment, it could be a game changer—not just for our generation, but for humanity's future.

Acknowledgments

Many people provided helpful advice and valuable comments during this project, particularly Joshua Gans, Andrew Glikson, Katja Grace, Jeevan Haikerwal, Tyler John, Frank Jotzo, Seth Lazar, Barbara Leigh, Michael Leigh, Toby Ord, John Quiggin, Bryan Schonfeld, Will Steffen, Gernot Wagner, Toby Walsh, Robert Wiblin, and three anonymous reviewers. My understanding of populism and its antidotes has been shaped by insightful conversations with my Labor parliamentary colleagues. Special thanks to Emily Taber and her team of talented wordsmiths at the MIT Press. This book is dedicated to my wife, Gweneth, and our three extraordinary sons, Sebastian, Theodore, and Zachary. With luck, our boys will see the twenty-second century, and their descendants will enjoy lives of pleasure and fulfillment in the centuries beyond.

Notes

Chapter 1

1. Lucas Stephens, Dorian Fuller, Nicole Boivin, Torben Rick, Nicolas Gauthier, Andrea Kay, Ben Marwick, et al., "Archaeological Assessment Reveals Earth's Early Transformation through Land Use," *Science* 365, no. 6456 (2019): 897–902.

2. The 1947 Doomsday Clock was drawn by artist Martyl Langsdorf, who said that she set the time to 11:53 p.m. because "it looked good to my eye." See Kennette Benedict, "Frequently Asked Questions," *Bulletin of the Atomic Scientists*, https://the bulletin.org/doomsday-clock/faq/.

3. The comparison with motor vehicle accidents appears in Owen Cotton-Barratt, Sebastian Farquhar, John Halstead, Stefan Schubert, and Andrew Snyder-Beattie, *Global Catastrophic Risks 2016* (Oxford: Oxford University Press, 2016), 24. All figures in this paragraph are based on a comparison between the implied annual odds of catastrophe (one in six per century equates to 0.18 percent per year) and annual risks based on 2018 US mortality data from the National Center for Health Statistics (injuryfacts.nsc.org).

4. Bill Tancer, *Click: What Millions of People Are Doing Online and Why It Matters* (New York: Hyperion, 2008), 107; Linda Lyons, "What Frightens America's Youth?," Gallup, March 29, 2005.

5. Scientists refer to this point as the evolution of "anatomically modern humans." See Carina M. Schlebusch, Helena Malmström, Torsten Günther, Per Sjödin, Alexandra Coutinho, Hanna Edlund, Arielle R. Munters, et al., "Southern African Ancient Genomes Estimate Modern Human Divergence to 350,000 to 260,000 Years Ago," *Science* 358, no. 6363 (2017): 652–655.

6. Jack T. O'Malley-James, Charles S. Cockell, Jane S. Greaves, and John A. Raven, "Swansong Biospheres II: The Final Signs of Life on Terrestrial Planets near the End of Their Habitable Lifetimes," *International Journal of Astrobiology* 13, no. 3 (2014): 229–243.

7. Edmund Burke, "Reflections on the Revolution in France," in *The Works of the Right Honorable Edmund Burke* (1790; repr., London: Little, Brown and Company, 1899), 3:359.

8. Elroy Dimson, Paul Marsh, and Mike Staunton, *Credit Suisse Global Investment Returns Yearbook 2020* (Zurich: Credit Suisse Research Institute, 2020).

9. Juzhong Zhuang, Zhihong Liang, Tun Lin, and Franklin De Guzman, "Theory and Practice in the Choice of Social Discount Rate for Cost-Benefit Analysis: A Survey," ERD Working Paper No. 94, Asian Development Bank, Japan, 2007.

10. This is adapted from the example of Tutankhamen discussed in "Toby Ord on Why the Long-Term Future Matters More Than Anything Else," 80,000 Hours Podcast with Rob Wiblin, episode 6, September 2017. For simplicity, these illustrations assume linear discounting. Hyperbolic discounting is likely to strengthen the point even further.

11. Will MacAskill, *What We Owe the Future* (forthcoming).

12. For a thoughtful exposition of this viewpoint, see Thomas Schelling, "Intergenerational Discounting," in *Discounting and Intergenerational Equity*, ed. Paul Portney and John Weyant (Washington, DC: Resources for the Future, 1999), 99–101. A related point was made to me by philosopher Seth Lazar, who noted that it is often impossible to predict the results of our actions over the long term. If this uncertainty is large, it becomes more difficult to justify investments preventing future catastrophes. This critique should be borne in mind when considering the policy proposals that I advance; in general, I have focused on proven solutions over those that are untested.

13. Richard Posner, "Public Policy towards Catastrophe," in *Global Catastrophic Risks*, ed. Nick Bostrom and Milan Ćirković (Oxford: Oxford University Press, 2008), 184–202. The argument also flips around; Toby Handfield contends that "if our species manages to remain alive long enough, there will come a time when all future lives are certain to be wretched" and therefore there may come a point where the right moral decision is to end our species. Toby Handfield, "A Good Exit: What to Do about the End of Our Species?," *Journal of Moral Philosophy* 15, no. 3 (2018): 272–297. Based on the trajectory of the past few hundred years, I am optimistic that if we avoid catastrophic risk, the well-being of future generations will remain high.

14. Eliezer Yudkowsky, "Cognitive Biases Potentially Affecting Judgment of Global Risks," in *Global Catastrophic Risks*, ed. Nick Bostrom and Milan Ćirković (Oxford: Oxford University Press, 2008), 91–119.

15. Paul Slovic and Daniel Västfjäll, "The More Who Die, the Less We Care: Psychic Numbing and Genocide," in *Imagining Human Rights*, ed. Susanne Kaul and David Kim (Berlin: De Gruyter, 2015), 55–68.

16. Yudkowsky, "Cognitive Biases."

17. Philip N. Howard, *Lie Machines: How to Save Democracy from Troll Armies, Deceitful Robots, Junk News Operations, and Political Operatives* (New Haven, CT: Yale University Press, 2020).

18. These definitions draw on Cas Mudde and Cristóbal Rovira Kaltwasser, *Populism: A Very Short Introduction* (Oxford: Oxford University Press, 2017); Jan-Werner Müller, *What Is Populism?* (London: Penguin, 2017). Researchers differ in their categorization of populists; for example, Brigham Young University's Global Populism Database codes leaders based on text analysis of their speeches.

19. Lawrence Wright, "How Pandemics Wreak Havoc—and Open Minds," *New Yorker*, July 13, 2020.

20. Ulrike Malmendier and Stefan Nagel, "Depression Babies: Do Macroeconomic Experiences Affect Risk Taking?," *Quarterly Journal of Economics* 126, no. 1 (2011): 373–416.

21. Examples include Malawi, Zambia, and Indonesia. For details, see Paul J. Burke and Andrew Leigh, "Do Output Contractions Trigger Democratic Change?," *American Economic Journal: Macroeconomics* 2, no. 4 (2010): 124–157.

22. Some of this discussion draws on David Autor and Elisabeth Reynolds, "The Nature of Work after the COVID Crisis: Too Few Low-Wage Jobs," Hamilton Project, Brookings Institution, Washington, DC, July 16, 2020.

23. Jennifer Fitzgerald, "US Insurance Market Trends during the Pandemic," interview with McKinsey and Company, April 27, 2020.

24. Martha C. Nussbaum, *The Cosmopolitan Tradition: A Noble but Flawed Ideal* (Cambridge, MA: Harvard University Press, 2019), 2.

25. George Orwell, "Notes on Nationalism," *Polemic* (London), May 1945.

Chapter 2

1. Angelo Fichera, "New Coronavirus Wasn't 'Predicted' in Simulation," FactCheck.org, January 29, 2020.

2. Giovanni Boccaccio, *The Decameron*, trans. Mark Musa and Peter Bondanella (New York: W. W. Norton, 1977).

3. Brian Hanley and Birthe Borup, "Bioterrorism and Biodefense for America's Public Spaces and Cities," in *Homeland Security: Protecting America's Targets*, ed.

James J. F. Forest, vol. 2, *Public Spaces and Social Institutions* (Westport, CT: Praeger Security International, 2006).

4. Nathan Nunn and Nancy Qian, "The Columbian Exchange: A History of Disease, Food, and Ideas," *Journal of Economic Perspectives* 24, no. 2 (2010): 163–188.

5. Daniel E. Vasey, "Population Regulation, Ecology, and Political Economy in Pre-industrial Iceland," *American Ethnologist* 23, no. 2 (1996): 366–392.

6. John Harris, "Hiding the Bodies: The Myth of the Humane Colonisation of Aboriginal Australia," *Aboriginal History* 27 (2003): 79–104.

7. Robert J. Barro, José F. Ursúa, and Joanna Weng, "The Coronavirus and the Great Influenza Pandemic: Lessons from the 'Spanish Flu' for the Coronavirus's Potential Effects on Mortality and Economic Activity," NBER Working Paper No. 26866, National Bureau of Economic Research, Cambridge, MA, 2020.

8. Hanley and Borup, "Bioterrorism and Biodefense."

9. David S. Jones, Scott H. Podolsky, and Jeremy A. Greene, "The Burden of Disease and the Changing Task of Medicine," *New England Journal of Medicine* 366, no. 25 (2012): 2333–2338.

10. The 1970 figure is from James N. Gribble and Samuel H. Preston, *The Epidemiological Transition: Policy and Planning Implications for Developing Countries* (Washington, DC: National Academy Press, 1993). The 2016 figure is from World Health Organization, *Global Health Estimates 2016: Deaths by Cause, Age, Sex, by Country and by Region, 2000–2016* (Geneva: World Health Organization, 2018) (summing deaths due to "Infectious and Parasitic Diseases" and "Respiratory Infections").

11. Ian Frazer, quoted in Jo Khan, "We've Never Made a Successful Vaccine for a Coronavirus Before. This Is Why It's So Difficult," ABC News, Health Report, April 17, 2020.

12. Fiona M. Guerra, Shelly Bolotin, Gillian Lim, Jane Heffernan, Shelley L. Deeks, Ye Li, and Natasha S. Crowcroft, "The Basic Reproduction Number (R_0) of Measles: A Systematic Review," *Lancet Infectious Diseases* 17, no. 12 (2017): e420–e428.

13. Ying Liu, Albert A. Gayle, Annelies Wilder-Smith, and Joacim Rocklöv, "The Reproductive Number of COVID-19 Is Higher Compared to SARS Coronavirus," *Journal of Travel Medicine* 27, no. 2 (2020): taaa021.

14. Gita Gopinath, "The Great Lockdown: Worst Economic Downturn since the Great Depression," *IMFBlog*, April 14, 2020.

15. Andy Sumner, Chris Hoy, and Eduardo Ortiz-Juarez, "Estimates of the Impact of COVID-19 on Global Poverty," WIDER Working Paper 2020/43, UNU-WIDER, Helsinki, 2020.

16. David Quammen, *Spillover: Animal Infections and the Next Human Pandemic* (New York: W. W. Norton, 2012).

17. Mark E. J. Woolhouse and Sonya Gowtage-Sequeria, "Host Range and Emerging and Reemerging Pathogens," *Emerging Infectious Diseases* 11, no. 12 (2005): 1842–1847.

18. Abrahm Lustgarten, "How Climate Change Is Contributing to Skyrocketing Rates of Infectious Disease," *ProPublica*, May 7, 2020.

19. Simon J. Anthony, Christine K. Johnson, Denise J. Greig, Sarah Kramer, Xiaoyu Che, Heather Wells, Allison L. Hicks, et al., "Global Patterns in Coronavirus Diversity," *Virus Evolution* 3, no. 1 (2017): vex012.

20. Peter Daszak, quoted in Peter Hessler, "The Sealed City," *New Yorker*, October 12, 2020, 36–45.

21. Adi Stern and Raul Andino, "Viral Evolution: It Is All about Mutations," in *Viral Pathogenesis*, ed. Michael G. Katze, Marcus J. Korth, G. Lynn Law, and Neal Nathanson, 3rd ed. (London: Academic Press, 2016), 233–240.

22. David M. Morens, Peter Daszak, and Jeffery K. Taubenberger, "Escaping Pandora's Box—Another Novel Coronavirus," *New England Journal of Medicine* 382, no. 14 (2020): 1293–1295.

23. Ronald Orenstein, *Wildlife Markets and COVID-19* (Washington, DC: Humane Society International, 2020), 8.

24. Christos Lynteris and Lyle Fearnley, "Why Shutting Down Chinese 'Wet Markets' Could Be a Terrible Mistake," *Conversation*, January 31, 2020.

25. Quoted in Morens, Daszak, and Taubenberger, "Escaping Pandora's Box," 1294.

26. "The Scythes of the Sea," *Economist*, August 22, 2020, 15–16.

27. This discussion of the history of biological warfare draws on Stefan Riedel, "Biological Warfare and Bioterrorism: A Historical Review," *Baylor University Medical Center Proceedings* 17, no. 4 (2004): 400–406.

28. Details of this program are drawn from US Army, *U.S. Army Activity in the U.S. Biological Warfare Programs*, vol. 2 (Washington, DC: US Army, 1977). See also Judith Miller, Stephen Engelberg, and William Broad, *Germs: Biological Weapons and America's Secret War* (New York: Simon and Schuster, 2001).

29. Ken Alibek, *Biohazard* (New York: Random House, 1999); Richard Preston, "The Bioweaponeers," *New Yorker*, March 1, 1998.

30. Alibek, *Biohazard*, x, 112, 166.

31. Steven Block, "The Growing Threat of Biological Weapons," *American Scientist* 89, no. 1 (2001): 28–37.

32. Dean Foust and John Carey, "A U.S. Gift to Iraq: Deadly Viruses," *Business Week*, September 20, 2002.

33. Bureau of Arms Control, Verification and Compliance, *Compliance with the Convention on the Prohibition of the Development, Production, Stockpiling, and Use of Chemical Weapons and on Their Destruction (Condition [10][C] Report)* (Washington, DC: US Department of State, 2019).

34. Miller, Engelberg, and Broad, *Germs*, 27–28.

35. Gigi Kwik Gronvall, *Preparing for Bioterrorism: The Alfred P. Sloan Foundation's Leadership in Biosecurity* (Baltimore: Center for Biosecurity of UPMC, 2012), 55.

36. "Japan Marks 25 Years since Deadly Aum Sarin Attack on Tokyo Subway," *Japan Times*, March 20, 2020.

37. Charles Townshend, *Terrorism: A Very Short Introduction*, 2nd ed. (Oxford: Oxford University Press, 2011), 116.

38. Miller, Engelberg, and Broad, *Germs*, 223–224.

39. Human Genome Project Information Archive, 1990–2003, web.ornl.gov/sci/techresources/Human_Genome/project/budget.shtml.

40. Edd Gent, "$100 Genome Sequencing Will Yield a Treasure Trove of Genetic Data," Singularity Hub, March 8, 2020.

41. Jessica C. Stark, Ally Huang, Karen J. Hsu, Rachel S. Dubner, Jason Forbrook, Suzanne Marshalla, Faith Rodriguez, et al., "BioBits Health: Classroom Activities Exploring Engineering, Biology, and Human Health with Fluorescent Readouts," *ACS Synthetic Biology* 8, no. 5 (2019): 1001–1009.

42. Kyle Watters, *The CRISPR Revolution: Potential Impacts on Global Health Security* (Fairfax, VA: George Mason University, 2018), 14.

43. Daniel R. Coats, *Statement for the Record: Worldwide Threat Assessment of the US Intelligence Community* (Washington, DC: Office of the Director of National Intelligence, 2019).

44. Kai Kupferschmidt, "Critics See Only Risks, No Benefits in Horsepox Paper," *Science* 359, no. 6374 (2018): 375–376, at 375.

45. McCandless's estimates of contagiousness are predominantly drawn from Simon I. Hay, Katherine E. Battle, David M. Pigott, David L. Smith, Catherine L. Moyes, Samir Bhatt, John S. Brownstein, et al., "Global Mapping of Infectious Disease," *Philosophical Transactions of the Royal Society B: Biological Sciences* 368, no. 1614 (2013): 20120250. The estimates of deadliness are taken from a wide range of published scientific studies.

46. Guerra et al., "The Basic Reproduction Number (R_0) of Measles."

47. Katherine Harmon, "What Really Happened in Malta This September When Contagious Bird Flu Was First Announced?," *Scientific American*, December 30, 2011. The Johns Hopkins Center for Health Security describes a highly infectious H5N1 virus as a potential globally catastrophic biological risk: Monica Schoch-Spana, Anita Cicero, Amesh Adalja, Gigi Gronvall, Tara Kirk Sell, Diane Meyer, Jennifer B. Nuzzo, et al., "Global Catastrophic Biological Risks: Toward a Working Definition," *Health Security* 15, no. 4 (2017): 323–328.

48. Blue Ribbon Study Panel on Biodefense, *Holding the Line on Biodefense: State, Local, Tribal, and Territorial Reinforcements Needed* (Washington, DC: Blue Ribbon Study Panel on Biodefense, October 2018).

49. Scott Galloway, "Corona as Vaccine," profgalloway.com, March 27, 2020.

50. Using daily data, the correlation between COVID-19 concentrations in sewage and hospital admissions three days later was 0.99. Jordan Peccia, Alessandro Zulli, Doug E. Brackney, Nathan D. Grubaugh, Edward H. Kaplan, Arnau Casanovas-Massana, Albert I. Ko, et al., "SARS-CoV-2 RNA Concentrations in Primary Municipal Sewage Sludge as a Leading Indicator of COVID-19 Outbreak Dynamics," medRxiv, 2020, 2020.05.19.20105999.

51. Abigail Walker, Claire Hopkins, and Pavol Surda, "The Use of Google Trends to Investigate the Loss of Smell Related Searches during COVID-19 Outbreak," *International Forum of Allergy and Rhinology* 10, no. 7 (2020): 839–847.

52. Aravind Natarajan, Hao-Wei Su, and Conor Heneghan, "Assessment of Physiological Signs Associated with COVID-19 Measured Using Wearable Devices," medRxiv, 2020, 2020.08.14.20175265.

53. Maryn McKenna, "How ProMED Crowdsourced the Arrival of Covid-19 and SARS," *Wired*, March 23, 2020.

54. The ProMED budget estimate is from an email from Linda C. MacKinnon of the International Society for Infectious Diseases, August 28, 2020. The playground cost is from Patricia Sullivan, "The Cost of Play Tops $1 Million for Some Local Playgrounds," *Washington Post*, July 6, 2015.

55. Jonathan B. Tucker and Erin R. Mahan, *President Nixon's Decision to Renounce the U.S. Offensive Biological Weapons Program* (Washington, DC: Center for the Study of Weapons of Mass Destruction, National Defense University, 2009).

56. On the budget of the Biological Weapons Convention, see Toby Ord, *The Precipice: Existential Risk and the Future of Humanity* (London: Bloomsbury Publishing, 2020), 57, 135. I use Gregory Lewis's more recent estimate of employees (three rather than four). Gregory Lewis, "Reducing Global Catastrophic Biological Risks," 80000hours.org, March 16, 2020.

57. Lynn Klotz, "Human Error in High-Biocontainment Labs: A Likely Pandemic Threat," *Bulletin of Atomic Scientists*, February 25, 2019.

58. In 1978, Britain's Janet Parker contracted smallpox from a laboratory at the University of Birmingham.

59. See, for example, Keith Rhodes, *High-Containment Biosafety Laboratories: Preliminary Observations on the Oversight of the Proliferation of BSL-3 and BSL-4 Laboratories in the United States* (Washington, DC: US Government Accountability Office, 2007); National Research Council, *Biosecurity Challenges of the Global Expansion of High-Containment Biological Laboratories: Summary of a Workshop* (Washington, DC: National Academies Press, 2012).

60. Klotz, "Human Error in High-Biocontainment Labs." This figure is slightly simplified from Klotz, who estimates that the probability of a pandemic being seeded is 16 percent per decade across fourteen laboratories. Since the probabilities are independent, I round this down to 1 percent per laboratory per decade.

61. Kelsey Piper, "Why Some Labs Work on Making Viruses Deadlier—and Why They Should Stop," *Vox*, May 1, 2020.

62. Kelsey Piper, "The Next Deadly Pathogen Could Come from a Rogue Scientist. Here's How We Can Prevent That," *Vox*, February 11, 2020.

63. Diane DiEuliis, Sarah R. Carter, and Gigi Kwik Gronvall, "Options for Synthetic DNA Order Screening, Revisited," *mSphere* 2, no. 4 (2017): e00319–17.

64. Kevin M. Esvelt, "Inoculating Science against Potential Pandemics and Information Hazards," *PLOS Pathogens* 14, no. 10 (2018): e1007286.

65. Lewis, "Reducing Global Catastrophic Biological Risks."

Chapter 3

1. The record was set on August 16, 2020. See Elizabeth Fernandez, "New World Temperature Record Set—Is Climate Change to Blame?," *Forbes*, August 21, 2020. An estimate of 134°F recorded at Furnace Creek in 1913 is likely to have been erroneous. See Christopher C. Burt, "An Investigation of Death Valley's 134°F World Temperature Record," wunderground.com, October 24, 2016.

2. Myroslava Protsiv, Catherine Ley, Joanna Lankester, Trevor Hastie, and Julie Parsonnet, "Decreasing Human Body Temperature in the United States since the Industrial Revolution," *eLife* 9 (2020): e49555.

3. This description draws on Amy Ragsdale and Peter Stark, "What It Feels Like to Die from Heat Stroke," *Outside Magazine*, June 18, 2019.

4. "Heatwaves Are Killing People," *Economist*, July 27, 2019.

5. Chi Xu, Timothy A. Kohler, Timothy M. Lenton, Jens-Christian Svenning, and Marten Scheffer, "Future of the Human Climate Niche," *Proceedings of the National Academy of Sciences* 117, no. 21 (2020): 11350–11355.

6. Jonathan Watts, "One Billion People Will Live in Insufferable Heat within 50 Years—Study," *Guardian*, May 5, 2020.

7. Eric Roston, "The Man Who Got Economists to Take Climate Nightmares Seriously," *Bloomberg*, August 30, 2019.

8. Gernot Wagner and Martin Weitzman, *Climate Shock: The Economic Consequences of a Hotter Planet* (Princeton, NJ: Princeton University Press, 2016), xiii.

9. Glenn Scherer, "IPCC Predictions: Then versus Now," climatecentral.org, December 11, 2012.

10. Timothy M. Lenton, Johan Rockström, Owen Gaffney, Stefan Rahmstorf, Katherine Richardson, Will Steffen, and Hans Joachim Schellnhuber, "Climate Tipping Points—Too Risky to Bet Against," *Nature* 575 (2019): 592–595.

11. Dominick V. Spracklen, Steve R. Arnold, and C. M. Taylor, "Observations of Increased Tropical Rainfall Preceded by Air Passage over Forests," *Nature* 489, no. 7415 (2012): 282–285.

12. Lenton et al., "Climate Tipping Points."

13. Martin J. P. Sullivan, Simon L. Lewis, Kofi Affum-Baffoe, Carolina Castilho, Flávia Costa, Aida Cuni Sanchez, Corneille E. N. Ewango, et al., "Long-Term Thermal Sensitivity of Earth's Tropical Forests," *Science* 368, no. 6493 (2020): 869–874.

14. Jacqueline Richter-Menge, Matthew L. Druckenmiller, and Martin O. Jeffries, eds., *Arctic Report Card 2019* (Washington, DC: National Oceanic and Atmospheric Administration, 2019), 58–65. See also Andrew Glikson, "The Methane Time Bomb," *Energy Procedia* 146 (2018): 23–29.

15. Wagner and Weitzman, *Climate Shock*, 12.

16. Martin L. Weitzman, "On Modeling and Interpreting the Economics of Catastrophic Climate Change," *Review of Economics and Statistics* 91, no. 1 (2009): 1–19.

17. James H. Butler and Stephen A. Montzka, "The NOAA Annual Greenhouse Gas Index (AGGI)," NOAA Earth System Research Laboratory, Boulder, CO, 2020.

18. Weitzman, "On Modeling and Interpreting the Economics of Catastrophic Climate Change."

19. For a useful discussion of the potential timing of temperature increases beyond 6°C, see William W. Hogan and Gernot Wagner, "Carbon Prices, Preferences, and the Timing of Uncertainty" (working paper, New York University, 2020).

20. The argument for considering tail risk can be taken too far. As William Nordhaus points out, "This has the unattractive and unrealistic feature that societies

would pay unlimited amounts to prevent an infinitesimal probability of zero consumption. For example, assume that there is a very, very tiny probability that a killer asteroid might hit Earth. . . . Even if the probability were 10^{-10}, 10^{-20}, or even $10^{-1,000,000}$, we would spend a large fraction of world income to avoid these infinitesimally small outcomes." William Nordhaus, "An Analysis of the Dismal Theorem," Cowles Foundation Discussion Paper No. 1686, Yale University, New Haven, CT, 2009, 6–7.

21. Michael Blastland and David Spiegelhalter, *The Norm Chronicles: Stories and Numbers about Danger* (London: Profile Books, 2013), 172. Blastland and Spiegelhalter estimate that if you took a daily flight, the chances of death would be one every 120,000 years. This equates to a one in fifteen hundred chance of death every 80 years.

22. Mark Lynas, *Six Degrees: Our Future on a Hotter Planet* (London: Fourth Estate, 2007).

23. Wagner and Weitzman, *Climate Shock*, 78.

24. Peter Christensen, Kenneth Gillingham, and William Nordhaus, "Uncertainty in Forecasts of Long-Run Economic Growth," *Proceedings of the National Academy of Sciences* 115, no. 21 (2018): 5409–5414.

25. Camilo Mora, Bénédicte Dousset, Iain R. Caldwell, Farrah E. Powell, Rollan C. Geronimo, Coral R. Bielecki, Chelsie W. W. Counsell, et al., "Global Risk of Deadly Heat," *Nature Climate Change* 7, no. 7 (2017): 501–506.

26. Ethan Coffel, Radley Horton, and Colin Raymond, "Heat and Humidity Are a Killer Combination," *New York Times*, October 11, 2018.

27. Kendra Pierre-Louis, "Climate Change Bolsters the Threat of Heat Waves," *New York Times*, July 19, 2019, A18.

28. Tiantian Li, Radley M. Horton, and Patrick L. Kinney, "Projections of Seasonal Patterns in Temperature-Related Deaths for Manhattan, New York," *Nature Climate Change* 3, no. 8 (2013): 717–721.

29. American Lung Association, *State of the Air* (Chicago: American Lung Association, 2020).

30. "Climate Change Could Upend Progress from Environmental Regulations," *All Things Considered*, NPR, September 13, 2020.

31. Mark C. Urban, "Escalator to Extinction," *Proceedings of the National Academy of Sciences* 115, no. 47 (2018): 11871–11873.

32. Bettina Boxall, "Climate Change Will Make California's Drought-Flood Cycle More Volatile, Study Finds," *Los Angeles Times*, April 23, 2018.

33. See, for example, Stephanie C. Herring, Nikolaos Christidis, Andrew Hoell, Martin P. Hoerling, and Peter A. Stott, eds., "Explaining Extreme Events of 2018 from a Climate Perspective," *Bulletin of the American Meteorological Society* 101, no. 1 (2020): S1–S128.

34. Munich Re, Geo Risks Research, and NatCatSERVICE, "Number of World Natural Catastrophes, 1980–2018," 2019, iii.org.

35. Donald J. Wuebbles, David W. Fahey, Kathy A. Hibbard, Benjamin DeAngelo, Sarah Doherty, Katharine Hayhoe, Radley Horton, et al., *Climate Science Special Report: Fourth National Climate Assessment*, vol. 1 (Washington, DC: US Global Change Research Program, 2017), chapter 8.

36. "The Condor's Cry," *Economist*, August 29, 2020, 23–24.

37. Jeremy S. Littell, "Relationships between Area Burned and Climate in the Western United States: Vegetation-Specific Historical and Future Fire" (manuscript on file with US Geological Survey, Alaska Climate Science Center), quoted in James M. Vose, David L. Peterson, and Toral Patel-Weynand, eds., *Effects of Climatic Variability and Change on Forest Ecosystems: A Comprehensive Science Synthesis for the U.S. Forest Sector* (Washington, DC: US Department of Agriculture, 2012), 219.

38. The 2019–2020 fires burned 21 percent of Australia's eastern temperate forests, or ten times as much as a typical season: Matthias M. Boer, Víctor Resco de Dios, and Ross A. Bradstock, "Unprecedented Burn Area of Australian Mega Forest Fires," *Nature Climate Change* 10, no. 3 (2020): 171–172.

39. Michael Kimmelman, "Lessons from Hurricane Harvey: Houston's Struggle Is America's Tale," *New York Times*, November 7, 2017. The *Fourth National Climate Assessment* summarized the research on climate change and tropical cyclones (hurricanes and typhoons) by concluding that "it remains likely that global mean tropical cyclone maximum wind speeds and precipitation rates will increase; and it is more likely than not that the global frequency of occurrence of tropical cyclones will either decrease or remain essentially the same." James P. Kossin, Timothy Hall, Thomas Knutson, Kenneth E. Kunkel, Robert J. Trapp, Duane E. Waliser, and Michael F. Wehner, "Extreme Storms," in *Climate Science Special Report: Fourth National Climate Assessment*, ed. Donald J. Wuebbles, David W. Fahey, Kathy A. Hibbard, David J. Dokken, Brooke C. Stewart, and Thomas K. Maycock (Washington, DC: US Global Change Research Program, 2017), 1:257–276.

40. Mathew E. Hauer, "Migration Induced by Sea-Level Rise Could Reshape the US Population Landscape," *Nature Climate Change* 7, no. 5 (2017): 321–325.

41. Abrahm Lustgarten, "How Climate Migration Will Reshape America," *New York Times Magazine*, September 15, 2020.

42. "Blown Cover," *Economist*, September 21, 2019, 73–74.

43. Hurricane damage from Aslak Grinsted, Peter Ditlevsen, and Jens Hesselbjerg Christensen, "Normalized US Hurricane Damage Estimates Using Area of Total Destruction, 1900–2018," *Proceedings of the National Academy of Sciences* 116, no. 48 (2019): 23942–23946. Flood risk from Ove Hoegh-Guldberg, Daniela Jacob, Michael Taylor, Marco Bindi, Sally Brown, Ines Camilloni, Arona Diedhiou, et al., "Impacts of 1.5°C Global Warming on Natural and Human Systems," in *Global Warming of 1.5°C. An IPCC Special Report on the Impacts of Global Warming of 1.5°C Above Pre-Industrial Levels and Related Global Greenhouse Gas Emission Pathways, in the Context of Strengthening the Global Response to the Threat of Climate Change, sustainable Development, and Efforts to Eradicate Poverty*, ed. Valérie Masson-Delmotte, Panmao Zhai, Hans-Otto Pörtner, Debra C. Roberts, Jim Skea, Priyadarshi R. Shukla, Anna Pirani, et al., (Geneva: Intergovernmental Panel on Climate Change, 2018), 214.

44. Andra J. Garner, Michael E. Mann, Kerry A. Emanuel, Robert E. Kopp, Ning Lin, Richard B. Alley, Benjamin P. Horton, et al., "Impact of Climate Change on New York City's Coastal Flood Hazard: Increasing Flood Heights from the Preindustrial to 2300 CE," *Proceedings of the National Academy of Sciences* 114, no. 45 (2017): 11861–11866.

45. Peter Miller, "Weather Gone Wild," *National Geographic*, September 2012.

46. Hans-Otto .Pörtner, Debra C. Roberts, Valérie Masson-Delmotte, Panmao Zhai, Melinda Tignor, Elvira Poloczanska, Katja Mintenbeck, et al., eds., *The Ocean and Cryosphere in a Changing Climate: A Special Report of the Intergovernmental Panel on Climate Change* (Geneva: Intergovernmental Panel on Climate Change, 2019), 57, 327.

47. Anders Levermann, quoted in Jonathan Watts, "Twin Megastorms Have Scientists Fearing This May Be the New Normal," *Guardian*, September 7, 2017.

48. Roy Scranton, "When the Next Hurricane Hits Texas," *New York Times*, October 7, 2016.

49. Quoted in Laura Mallonee, "An Enormous Hunk of Ice Gets Stuck in Iceberg Alley," *Wired*, April 21, 2017.

50. Dirk Notz, Jakob Dörr, David A. Bailey, Ed Blockley, Mitchell Bushuk, Jens Boldingh Debernard, Evelien Dekker, et al., "Arctic Sea Ice in CMIP6," *Geophysical Research Letters*, 2020.

51. Dirk Notz and Julienne Stroeve, "Observed Arctic Sea-Ice Loss Directly Follows Anthropogenic CO_2 Emission," *Science* 354, no. 6313 (2016): 747–750.

52. Pörtner et al., *The Ocean and Cryosphere in a Changing Climate*.

53. Jeff Goodell, *The Water Will Come: Rising Seas, Sinking Cities and the Remaking of the Civilized World* (Melbourne: Black Inc., 2018), 13.

54. Pörtner et al., *The Ocean and Cryosphere in a Changing Climate*, 388.

55. Mark Lynas, *Our Final Warning: Six Degrees of Climate Emergency* (London: Harper-Collins, 2020), 208.

56. John Roy Porter, Liyong Xie, Andrew J. Challinor, Kevern Cochrane, S. Mark Howden, Muhammad Mohsin Iqbal, David B. Lobell, and Maria Isabel Travasso, "Food Security and Food Production Systems," in *Climate Change 2014: Impacts, Adaptation, and Vulnerability. Part A: Global and Sectoral Aspects. Contribution of Working Group II to the Fifth Assessment Report of the Intergovernmental Panel on Climate Change*, ed. Christopher B. Field, Vicente R. Barros, David Jon Dokken, Katharine J. Mach, Michael D. Mastrandrea, T. Eren Bilir, Monalisa Chatterjee, et al. (Cambridge: Cambridge University Press, 2014), 485–533.

57. Porter et al., "Food Security and Food Production Systems." See also Andrew J. Challinor, James Watson, David B. Lobell, S. Mark Howden, D. R. Smith, and Netra Chhetri, "A Meta-analysis of Crop Yield under Climate Change and Adaptation," *Nature Climate Change* 4, no. 4 (2014): 287–291.

58. Porter et al., "Food Security and Food Production Systems," 502.

59. Dennis M. Mares and Kenneth W. Moffett, "Climate Change and Crime Revisited: An Exploration of Monthly Temperature Anomalies and UCR Crime Data," *Environment and Behavior* 51, no. 5 (2019): 502–529.

60. Connor Y. H. Wu, Benjamin F. Zaitchik, and Julia M. Gohlke, "Heat Waves and Fatal Traffic Crashes in the Continental United States," *Accident Analysis and Prevention* 119 (2018): 195–201.

61. Douglas T. Kenrick and Steven W. MacFarlane, "Ambient Temperature and Horn Honking: A Field Study of the Heat/Aggression Relationship," *Environment and Behavior* 18, no. 2 (1986): 179–191; Alan S. Reifman, Richard P. Larrick, and Steven Fein, "Temper and Temperature on the Diamond: The Heat-Aggression Relationship in Major League Baseball," *Personality and Social Psychology Bulletin* 17, no. 5 (1991): 580–585; Ulla Haverinen-Shaughnessy and Richard J. Shaughnessy, "Effects of Classroom Ventilation Rate and Temperature on Students' Test Scores," *PLOS One* 10, no. 8 (2015): e0136165. For other examples, see Gernot Wagner, "Heatwaves, Fires, Storms: Blame Climate Change for Summer Misery," *Bloomberg Green*, August 14, 2020.

62. Solomon M. Hsiang, Kyle C. Meng, and Mark A. Cane, "Civil Conflicts Are Associated with the Global Climate," *Nature* 476, no. 7361 (2011): 438–441.

63. For the database, see www.worldwater.org/conflict/list.

64. Katharine J. Mach, Caroline M. Kraan, W. Neil Adger, Halvard Buhaug, Marshall Burke, James D. Fearon, Christopher B. Field, et al., "Climate as a Risk Factor for Armed Conflict," *Nature* 571, no. 7764 (2019): 193–197. See also John O'Loughlin

and Cullen Hendrix, "Does Climate Change Cause Wars?," *Washington Post*, July 11, 2019.

65. David Wallace-Wells, *The Uninhabitable Earth: Life after Warming* (New York: Tim Duggan Books, 2020), 4.

66. Gary S. Dwyer and Mark A. Chandler, "Mid-Pliocene Sea Level and Continental Ice Volume Based on Coupled Benthic Mg/Ca Palaeotemperatures and Oxygen Isotopes," *Philosophical Transactions of the Royal Society A: Mathematical, Physical and Engineering Sciences* 367, no. 1886 (2009): 157–168.

67. Wallace-Wells, *The Uninhabitable Earth*, 3.

68. Daniel Rothman, "Thresholds of Catastrophe in the Earth System," *Science Advances* 3, no. 9 (2017): e1700906. See also Andrew Glikson, "The Lungs of the Earth: Review of the Carbon Cycle and Mass Extinction of Species," *Energy Procedia* 146 (2018): 3–11.

69. Lynas, *Our Final Warning*, 262–265. See also James Hansen, *Storms of My Grandchildren* (New York: Bloomsbury USA, 2009), 223–236.

70. Sebastian Sippel, Nicolai Meinshausen, Erich M. Fischer, Enikő Székely, and Reto Knutti, "Climate Change Now Detectable from Any Single Day of Weather at Global Scale," *Nature Climate Change* 10, no. 1 (2020): 35–41.

71. Katharine Hayhoe, tweet, March 26, 2020.

72. "The Contentious and Correct Option," *Economist* 435, no. 9195, May 23, 2020, 56–59.

73. Climate Action Tracker, *Governments Still Showing Little Sign of Acting on Climate Crisis* (Berlin: Climate Analytics, 2019).

74. Nadja Popovich, Livia Albeck-Ripka, and Kendra Pierre-Louis, "The Trump Administration Is Reversing Nearly 100 Environmental Rules. Here's the Full List," *New York Times*, updated May 6, 2020.

75. "Brazil's Bolsonaro Says He Will Accept Aid to Fight Amazon Fires," CBS News, August 27, 2019. See also Gabriel de Oliveira, Jing M. Chen, Scott C. Stark, Erika Berenguer, Paulo Moutinho, Paulo Artaxo, Liana O. Anderson, and Luiz E. O. C. Aragão, "Smoke Pollution's Impacts in Amazonia," *Science* 369 (2020): 634–635; Alison G. Nazareno and William F. Laurance, "Investors Can Help Rein in Amazon Deforestation," *Science* 369 (2020): 635–636.

76. Aline C. Soterroni, Fernando M. Ramos, Michael Obersteiner, and Stephen Polasky, "Fate of the Amazon Is on the Ballot in Brazil's Presidential Election," *Mongabay News*, October 17, 2018.

77. Soterroni et al., "Fate of the Amazon."

78. Jeremy Martinich and Allison Crimmins, "Climate Damages and Adaptation Potential across Diverse Sectors of the United States," *Nature Climate Change* 9, no. 5 (2019): 397–404, supplementary table 8. See also Mark Muro, David G. Victor, and Jacob Whiton, "How the Geography of Climate Damage Could Make the Politics Less Polarizing," Brookings Institution, Washington, DC, January 29, 2019.

79. Alexander E. MacDonald, Christopher T. M. Clack, Anneliese Alexander, Adam Dunbar, James Wilczak, and Yuanfu Xie, "Future Cost-Competitive Electricity Systems and Their Impact on US CO_2 Emissions," *Nature Climate Change* 6, no. 5 (2016): 526–531.

80. Estimates of learning curve effects (also known as "experience curves") are from Michael Liebreich, "Breaking Clean" (presentation at Bloomberg New Energy Finance, London, September 19, 2017).

81. Brad Plumer, "In a First, Renewable Energy Is Set to Pass Coal in the U.S.," *New York Times*, May 14, 2020, B5.

82. Wallace-Wells, *The Uninhabitable Earth*, 4.

83. Bjørn H. Samset, Jan S. Fuglestvedt, and Marianne T. Lund, "Delayed Emergence of a Global Temperature Response after Emission Mitigation," *Nature Communications* 11, no. 1 (2020): 1–10.

84. National Academies of Sciences, Engineering, and Medicine, *The Power of Change: Innovation for Development and Deployment of Increasingly Clean Electric Power Technologies* (Washington, DC: National Academies Press, 2016).

85. BloombergNEF, *Electric Vehicle Outlook 2019* (New York: BloombergNEF, 2019).

86. Alec Tyson and Brian Kennedy, "Two-Thirds of Americans Think Government Should Do More on Climate," Pew Research Center, June 23, 2020.

Chapter 4

1. This section draws on Peter Vincent Pry, *War Scare: Russia and America on the Nuclear Brink* (Westport, CT: Greenwood Publishing Group, 1999), 216–236.

2. Edward Wilson, "Thank You Vasili Arkhipov, the Man Who Stopped Nuclear War," *Guardian*, October 27, 2012.

3. Eric Schlosser, *Command and Control: Nuclear Weapons, the Damascus Incident, and the Illusion of Safety* (New York: Penguin Books, 2013), 364–367.

4. Schlosser, *Command and Control*, 446–448.

5. Bruce Blair, "Keeping Presidents in the Nuclear Dark, Episode #1: The Case of the Missing 'Permissive Action Links,'" cdi.org, February 11, 2004. The air force denies

this account. Dan Lamothe, "Air Force Swears: Our Nuke Launch Code Was Never '00000000,'" *Foreign Policy*, January 21, 2014.

6. The novel was put in a safe, where it remained until it was discovered in 1989 by Verne's great-grandson and published in English several years later. The quote is from Jules Verne, *Paris in the Twentieth Century*, trans. Richard Howard (Bath, UK: GK Hall, 1997), 110.

7. Avidit Acharya and Edoardo Grillo, "War with Crazy Types," *Political Science Research and Methods* 3, no. 2 (2015): 281–307.

8. Lehrer has generously placed this song and many others in the public domain. According to tomlehrersongs.com, "I, Tom Lehrer, and the Tom Lehrer Trust 2000, hereby grant the following permission: All the lyrics on this website, whether published or unpublished, copyrighted or uncopyrighted, may be downloaded and used in any manner whatsoever, without requiring any further permission from me or any payment to me or to anyone else."

9. Greg Myre, "Israeli Who Revealed Nuclear Secrets Is Freed," *New York Times*, April 21, 2004.

10. "Line of Control between India and Pakistan," Reuters, October 20, 2008.

11. "Sharp Drop in World Views of US, UK: Global Poll," BBC World Service, July 4, 2017, 22, 24.

12. Stockholm International Peace Research Institute, *SIPRI Yearbook 2019: Armaments, Disarmament and International Security* (Oxford: Oxford University Press, 2019).

13. See, for example, Sarah Burkhard, Erica Wenig, David Albright, and Andrea Stricker, *Nuclear Infrastructure and Proliferation Risks of the United Arab Emirates, Turkey, and Egypt* (Washington, DC: Institute for Science and International Security, 2017).

14. Alan Robock, Luke Oman, and Georgiy L. Stenchikov, "Nuclear Winter Revisited with a Modern Climate Model and Current Nuclear Arsenals: Still Catastrophic Consequences," *Journal of Geophysical Research: Atmospheres* 112, no. D13 (2007): D13107.

15. Michael J. Mills, Owen B. Toon, Julia Lee-Taylor, and Alan Robock, "Multidecadal Global Cooling and Unprecedented Ozone Loss Following a Regional Nuclear Conflict," *Earth's Future* 2, no. 4 (2014): 161–176.

16. Matthew Bunn and Anthony Wier, "The Seven Myths of Nuclear Terrorism," *Current History* 104, no. 681 (2005): 153–161.

17. Institute for Science and International Security, *Cobalt 60 Sources in Mosul: Recovery and Lessons for the Future* (Washington, DC: Institute for Science and International Security, 2017).

18. Barack Obama, "America's Leadership," campaign advertisement, first aired July 15, 2008.

19. Matthew Bunn, Rolf Mowatt-Larssen, Simon Saradzhyan, William H. Tobey, Yuri Morozov, Viktor I. Yesin, and Pavel S. Zolotarev, *The U.S.-Russia Joint Threat Assessment on Nuclear Terrorism* (Cambridge, MA: Belfer Center for Science and International Affairs, 2011), 40.

20. Graham Allison, "Nuclear Terrorism: Did We Beat the Odds or Change Them?," *PRISM* 7, no. 3 (2018): 2–21.

21. Daniel Ellsberg, "Manhattan Project II," in *Critical Mass: Voices for a Nuclear Free Future*, ed. Greg Ruggiero and Stuart Sahulka (New York: Open Media, 1996).

22. The decision was made in 1989, and the dismantling process concluded in early July 1991, just before South Africa signed the nuclear Nonproliferation Treaty on July 10, 1991: J. W. De Villers, Roger Jardine, and Mitchell Riess, "Why South Africa Gave Up the Bomb," *Foreign Affairs*, November/December 1993, 98–109.

23. "Iran Rolls Back Nuclear Deal Commitments," BBC News, January 5, 2020.

24. Union of Concerned Scientists, "Whose Finger Is on the Button?," Issue Brief, Union of Concerned Scientists, Cambridge, MA, 2017.

25. Quoted in Union of Concerned Scientists, "Whose Finger Is on the Button?"

26. Anthony Summers, *The Arrogance of Power: The Secret World of Richard Nixon* (New York: Viking, 2000), 385.

27. David Sanger and William Broad, "Pentagon Plan Would Expand Nuclear Policy," *New York Times*, January 17, 2018, A1.

28. Bruce Blair, "How Obama Could Revolutionize Nuclear Weapons Strategy Before He Goes," *Politico*, June 22, 2016.

29. Minnie Chan and Kristin Huang, "Is China about to Abandon Its 'No First Use' Nuclear Weapons Policy?," *South China Morning Post*, February 7, 2019.

30. Dominic Tierney, "Refusing to Nuke First," *Atlantic*, September 14, 2016.

31. James Miller, "No to No First Use—for Now," *Bulletin of the Atomic Scientists* 76, no. 1 (2020): 8–13.

32. Nicholas Thompson, "Inside the Apocalyptic Soviet Doomsday Machine," *Wired*, September 21, 2009.

33. Schlosser, *Command and Control*, 298.

34. This example draws on Conn Hallinan, "There Are Thousands of People Who Could Launch a Nuclear War," *Foreign Policy in Focus*, January 24, 2018.

35. Christopher Kenedi, Susan Hatters Friedman, Dougal Watson, and Claud Preitner, "Suicide and Murder-Suicide Involving Aircraft," *Aerospace Medicine and Human Performance* 87, no. 4 (2016): 388–396.

36. W. A. Tansey, Judy M. Wilson, and K. E. Schaefer, "Analysis of Health Data from 10 Years of Polaris Submarine Patrols," *Undersea Biomedical Research* 6 (1979): S217–S246. See also Herbert L. Abrams, "Sources of Human Instability in the Handling of Nuclear Weapons," in *The Medical Implications of Nuclear War*, ed. Fred Solomon and Robert Q. Marston (Washington, DC: National Academies Press, 1986), 490–528.

37. These fourteen thousand weapons do not all have separate pairs of launch controllers. On the other hand, launch controllers switch over time.

Chapter 5

1. Ben Popper, "The Poker-Playing AI Is Getting Smarter and the Humans Are Getting Tired," *Verge*, January 25, 2017.

2. Cade Metz, "Artificial Intelligence Is about to Conquer Poker, But Not without Human Help," *Wired*, January 24, 2017.

3. "Libratus Poker AI Beats Humans for $1.76m; Is End Near?," *Poker Listings*, January 31, 2017.

4. Noam Brown and Tuomas Sandholm, "Superhuman AI for Heads-Up No-Limit Poker: Libratus Beats Top Professionals," *Science* 359, no. 6374 (2018): 418–424.

5. On captcha codes, see Ian J. Goodfellow, Yaroslav Bulatov, Julian Ibarz, Sacha Arnoud, and Vinay Shet, "Multi-Digit Number Recognition from Street View Imagery Using Deep Convolutional Neural Networks," arXiv:1312.6082, 2013. On transcribing, see Wayne Xiong, Jasha Droppo, Xuedong Huang, Frank Seide, Mike Seltzer, Andreas Stolcke, Dong Yu, and Geoffrey Zweig, "Achieving Human Parity in Conversational Speech Recognition," arXiv:1610.05256, 2016. On lipreading, see Yannis M. Assael, Brendan Shillingford, Shimon Whiteson, and Nando De Freitas, "Lipnet: End-to-End Sentence-Level Lipreading," arXiv:1611.01599, 2016. On cancer scans, see Ahmad Algohary, Satish Viswanath, Rakesh Shiradkar, Soumya Ghose, Shivani Pahwa, Daniel Moses, Ivan Jambor, et al., "Radiomic Features on MRI Enable Risk Categorization of Prostate Cancer Patients on Active Surveillance: Preliminary Findings," *Journal of Magnetic Resonance Imaging* 48, no. 3 (2018): 818–828; Mahdi Orooji, Mehdi Alilou, Sagar Rakshit, Niha G. Beig, Mohammadhadi Khorrami, Prabhakar Rajiah, Rajat Thawani, et al., "Combination of Computer Extracted Shape and Texture Features Enables Discrimination of Granulomas from Adenocarcinoma on Chest Computed Tomography," *Journal of Medical Imaging* 5, no. 2 (2018): 024501. On *Dota 2*, see Christopher Berner, Greg Brockman, Brooke Chan, Vicki Cheung, Przemysław Dębiak, Christy Dennison, David Farhi, et al.,

"Dota 2 with Large Scale Deep Reinforcement Learning," arXiv:1912.06680, 2019. On Atari games, see Adrià Puigdomènech Badia, Bilal Piot, Steven Kapturowski, Pablo Sprechmann, Alex Vitvitskyi, Daniel Guo, and Charles Blundell, "Agent57: Outperforming the Atari Human Benchmark," arXiv2003.13350, 2020.

6. David Silver, Julian Schrittwieser, Karen Simonyan, Ioannis Antonoglou, Aja Huang, Arthur Guez, Thomas Hubert, et al., "Mastering the Game of Go without Human Knowledge," *Nature* 550, no. 7676 (2017): 354–359.

7. Satinder Singh, Andy Okun, and Andrew Jackson, "Learning to Play Go from Scratch," *Nature* 550 (2017): 336–337.

8. For Sabeti's compositions, based on OpenAI's GPT-3, see arr.am.

9. Andrew Hodges, *Alan Turing: The Enigma* (Princeton, NJ: Princeton University Press, 2014), 652.

10. In 2014, chess grandmaster Magnus Carlsen had an Elo score of 2882. AlphaGo Zero has an Elo score of around 3600. David Silver, Thomas Hubert, Julian Schrittwieser, Ioannis Antonoglou, Matthew Lai, Arthur Guez, Marc Lanctot, et al., "Mastering Chess and shogi by Self-Play with a General Reinforcement Learning Algorithm," arXiv:1712.01815, 2017.

11. Shin Jinseo has an Elo score of 3745, according to goratings.org. AlphaGo Zero has an Elo score of 5185, according to Silver, David, Julian Schrittwieser, Karen Simonyan, Ioannis Antonoglou, Aja Huang, Arthur Guez, Thomas Hubert et al. "Mastering the Game of Go without Human Knowledge," *Nature* 550, no. 7676 (2017): 354–359.

12. Irving Good, "Speculations concerning the First Ultraintelligent Machine," in *Advances in Computers*, ed. Franz Alt and Morris Rubinoff (New York: Academic Press, 1965), 6:31–88.

13. Nick Bostrom, *Superintelligence: Paths, Dangers, Strategies* (Oxford: Oxford University Press, 2014), 123. By contrast, Joshua Gans has argued that a superintelligence may voluntarily subjugate its capabilities. See Joshua Gans, "Self-Regulating Artificial General Intelligence," NBER Working Paper 24352, National Bureau of Economic Research, Cambridge, MA, 2018.

14. Jack Clark and Dario Amodei, "Faulty Reward Functions in the Wild," *OpenAI* (blog), December 21, 2016.

15. Asimov originally proposed three laws and then subsequently added the "zeroth law." The laws have also provided plenty of fodder for others, such as Randall Munroe's cartoon, "Why Asimov Put the Three Laws of Robotics in the Order He Did," xkcd.com/1613.

16. David Kocieniewski, "Major Companies Push the Limits of a Tax Break," *New York Times*, January 7, 2013, A1.

17. Stephen M. Omohundro, "The Basic AI Drives," in *Artificial General Intelligence, 2008: Proceedings of the First AGI Conference*, ed. Pei Wang, Ben Goertzel, and Stan Franklin (Amsterdam: IOS Press, 2008), 171:483–492.

18. Thomas Murphy VII, "The First Level of Super Mario Bros. Is Easy with Lexicographic Orderings and Time Travel" (paper presented at SIGBOVIK, Carnegie Mellon University, Pittsburgh, 2013), 112–133.

19. Stuart Russell, *Human Compatible: Artificial Intelligence and the Problem of Control* (London: Allen Lane, 2019), 141.

20. Kurt Andersen, "Enthusiasts and Skeptics Debate Artificial Intelligence," *Vanity Fair*, November 26, 2014.

21. Jaron Lanier, "One-Half of a Manifesto," *Wired*, January 12, 2000.

22. Paul Allen and Mark Greaves, "Paul Allen: The Singularity Isn't Near," *MIT Technology Review*, October 12, 2011.

23. Alanna Petroff, "Elon Musk Says Mark Zuckerberg's Understanding of AI Is 'Limited,'" CNN Business, July 25, 2017.

24. IEEE Global Initiative on Ethics of Autonomous and Intelligent Systems, *Ethically Aligned Design: A Vision for Prioritizing Human Well-being with Autonomous and Intelligent Systems*, version 2 (Piscataway, NJ: Institute of Electrical and Electronics Engineers, 2017), 78.

25. Scott Alexander, "AI Researchers on AI Risk," *Slate Star Codex* (blog), May 22, 2015.

26. Russell, *Human Compatible*, 160.

27. For a data set of historical predictions, see "MIRI AI Predictions Dataset," aiimpacts.org.

28. Alexander, "AI Researchers on AI Risk."

29. Katja Grace, John Salvatier, Allan Dafoe, Baobao Zhang, and Owain Evans, "When Will AI Exceed Human Performance? Evidence from AI Experts," *Journal of Artificial Intelligence Research* 62 (2018): 729–754. See also AI Impacts. "2016 Expert Survey on Progress in AI," December 14, 2016, https://aiimpacts.org/2016 -expert-survey-on-progress-in-ai.

30. This estimate averages across the five probability bins (e.g., 0–20 percent, 21–40 percent, and so on), weighted by the midpoint of the bin (e.g., 10 percent, 30 percent, and so on).

31. Donald Michie, "Machines and the Theory of Intelligence," *Nature* 241, no. 5391 (1973): 507–512; L. Stephen Coles, Jay M. Tenenbaum, Oscar Firschein, and Martin A. Fischler, "Forecasting and Assessing the Impact of Artificial Intelligence on Society," in *Proceedings of the Third International Joint Conference on Artificial Intelligence* (Stanford, CA: Stanford University, 1973).

32. All statistics on artificial intelligence growth are from Raymond Perrault, Yoav Shoham, Erik Brynjolfsson, Jack Clark, John Etchemendy, Barbara Grosz, Terah Lyons, et al., *Artificial Intelligence Index 2019 Annual Report* (Stanford, CA: AI Index Steering Committee, Human-Centered AI Institute, Stanford University, December 2019), except conference attendance, which is from the spreadsheet at "AI Conference Attendance," aiimpacts.org.

33. Bostrom, *Superintelligence*, 248.

34. Alexander, "AI Researchers on AI Risk."

35. Russell, *Human Compatible*, 172–177. In a similar vein, see Geoffrey Irving, Paul Christiano, and Dario Amodei, "AI Safety via Debate," arXiv:1805.00899, 2018.

36. Tom Simonite, "The World Has a Plan to Rein in AI—But the US Doesn't Like It," *Wired*, January 6, 2020.

37. Anna Jobin, Marcello Ienca, and Effy Vayena, "The Global Landscape of AI Ethics Guidelines," *Nature Machine Intelligence* 1, no. 9 (2019): 389–399. See also Organisation for Economic Co-operation and Development, *Artificial Intelligence in Society* (Paris: OECD Publishing, 2019), 123.

38. Bostrom, *Superintelligence*, 253.

39. This approach has been effectively implemented in Singapore. See Danny Gilligan, *Global Data Wars: Building a Thriving Data Economy for Australia* (Sydney: Reinventure, 2016).

40. Toby Walsh, *Android Dreams: The Past, Present and Future of Artificial Intelligence* (Oxford: Oxford University Press, 2017).

Chapter 6

1. That year also saw the near-simultaneous release of *Antz* and *A Bug's Life*. It was a bad year for twin films.

2. The definitive study is Peter Schulte, Laia Alegret, Ignacio Arenillas, José A. Arz, Penny J. Barton, Paul R. Bown, Timothy J. Bralower, et al., "The Chicxulub Asteroid Impact and Mass Extinction at the Cretaceous-Paleogene Boundary," *Science* 327, no. 5970 (2010): 1214–1218.

3. For cumulative statistics, see cneos.jpl.nasa.gov.

4. Bryan Bender, "Trump versus the Killer Asteroids," *Politico*, September 27, 2018.

5. Casey Dreier, "How NASA's Planetary Defense Budget Grew by More Than 4000% in 10 Years," *Planetary Society* (blog), September 26, 2019.

6. Toby Ord, *The Precipice: Existential Risk and the Future of Humanity* (London: Bloomsbury, 2020), 167.

7. For example, people are more likely to support a policy when it is framed in terms of the employment rate than the unemployment rate. James N. Druckman, "Using Credible Advice to Overcome Framing Effects," *Journal of Law, Economics, and Organization* 17, no. 1 (2001): 62–82.

8. See, for example, Melissa L. Finucane, Paul Slovic, Chris K. Mertz, James Flynn, and Theresa A. Satterfield, "Gender, Race, and Perceived Risk: The 'White Male' Effect," *Health, Risk and Society* 2, no. 2 (2000): 159–172.

9. Robert Marcus, H. Jay Melosh, and Gareth Collins, "Earth Impact Effects Program," Imperial College London and Purdue University, 2010.

10. Ben G. Mason, David M. Pyle, and Clive Oppenheimer, "The Size and Frequency of the Largest Explosive Eruptions on Earth," *Bulletin of Volcanology* 66, no. 8 (2004): 735–748.

11. Clive Oppenheimer, "Climatic, Environmental and Human Consequences of the Largest Known Historic Eruption: Tambora Volcano (Indonesia) 1815," *Progress in Physical Geography* 27, no. 2 (2003): 230–259.

12. Clive Oppenheimer, "Limited Global Change due to the Largest Known Quaternary Eruption, Toba ≈ 74 kyr BP?," *Quaternary Science Reviews* 21, no. 14–15 (2002): 1593–1609.

13. On the racist origins of overpopulation claims, see Allan Chase, *The Social Costs of the New Scientific Racism* (New York: Alfred A. Knopf, 1977); Matto Mildenberger, "The Tragedy of the Tragedy of the Commons," *Scientific American*, April 23, 2019.

14. More precisely, Caplan places a 5 percent chance on this happening in the next thousand years, which is equivalent to a 0.5 percent risk in the next hundred years. Bryan Caplan, "The Totalitarian Threat," in *Global Catastrophic Risks*, ed. Nick Bostrom and Milan Ćirković (Oxford: Oxford University Press, 2008), 504–519.

15. Chris Phoenix and Mike Treder, "Nanotechnology as Global Catastrophic Risk," in *Global Catastrophic Risks*, ed. Nick Bostrom and Milan Ćirković (Oxford: Oxford University Press, 2008), 481–503.

16. Global Challenges Foundation, *Global Catastrophic Risks 2016* (Oxford: Centre for Effective Altruism, 2016), 58–62.

17. Martin Rees, *Our Final Hour, A Scientist's Warning: How Terror, Error, and Environmental Disaster Threaten Humankind's Future in This Century—on Earth and Beyond* (New York: Basic Books, 2003), 16.

18. Eric Schlosser, *Command and Control: Nuclear Weapons, the Damascus Incident, and the Illusion of Safety* (New York: Penguin Books, 2013), 36.

19. The phrase "radiance of a thousand suns" was used by Oppenheimer, quoting from the Hindu book the Bhagavad Gita.

20. Nick Bostrom, "The Vulnerable World Hypothesis," *Global Policy* 10, no. 4 (2019): 455–476.

21. The report was completed in June 2002 and published the following year. Jean-Paul Blaizot, Graham G. Ross, John Iliopoulos, J. Madsen, Peter Sonderegger, and Hans J. Specht, "Study of Potentially Dangerous Events during Heavy-Ion Collisions at the LHC: Report of the LHC Safety Study Group," No. CERN-2003–001, European Organization for Nuclear Research, Geneva, 2003.

22. More precisely, a 0.1 percent annual extinction risk translates to a 9.5 percent extinction risk over a century. For the relevant discussion, see Nicholas Stern, *The Economics of Climate Change* (London: HM Treasury, 2006), 47

23. Vicente Bayard, Paul T. Kitsutani, Eduardo O. Barria, Luis A. Ruedas, David S. Tinnin, Carlos Muñoz, Itza B. De Mosca, et al., "Outbreak of Hantavirus Pulmonary Syndrome, Los Santos, Panama, 1999–2000," *Emerging Infectious Diseases* 10, no. 9 (2004): 1635–1642. For other examples, see Abrahm Lustgarden, "How Climate Change Is Contributing to Skyrocketing Rates of Infectious Disease," *ProPublica*, May 7, 2020.

24. Former US deputy national security adviser Ben Rhodes, speaking on *Pod Save the World* (podcast), February 27, 2019.

Chapter 7

1. Richard Pipes, "Russian Marxism and Its Populist Background: The Late Nineteenth Century," *Russian Review* 19, no. 4 (1960): 316–337.

2. Vanessa Williamson, Theda Skocpol, and John Coggin, "The Tea Party and the Remaking of Republican Conservatism," *Perspectives on Politics* 9, no. 1 (2011): 25–43.

3. Eliana Plott, "Win or Lose, It's Donald Trump's Republican Party," *New York Times Magazine*, October 27, 2020.

4. Plott, "Win or Lose."

5. Jacob S. Hacker and Paul Pierson, *Let them Eat Tweets: How the Right Rules in an Age of Extreme Inequality* (New York: W. W. Norton, 2020).

6. Corbyn has a long Euroskeptic past. He supported Britain leaving the European Economic Community in 1975, opposed the 1993 Maastricht Treaty that created the European Union, and opposed the 2008 Lisbon Treaty, the current constitutional basis for the European Union. His advocacy for the "remain" case in 2016 lacked passion, but Corbyn did take a clear stance, stating in a speech on April 14, 2016, "The Labour Party is overwhelmingly for staying in," and summarizing the party's position as "remain and reform."

7. Jonathan Haidt, "When and Why Nationalism Beats Globalism," *American Interest* 12, no. 1 (2016); Sascha Becker, Thiemo Fetzer, and Dennis Novy, "Who Voted for Brexit? A Comprehensive District-Level Analysis," CESifo Working Paper No. 6438, April 2017.

8. Ginger Hervey and Mark Scott, "Inequality and Brexit," *Politico*, December 19, 2017.

9. On Trump's hostility to free trade, see Jacob Schlesinger, "Trump Forged His Ideas on Trade in the 1980s—and Never Deviated," *Wall Street Journal*, November 15, 2018.

10. On the accuracy of Johnson's columns, see Sonia Purnell, *Just Boris: The Irresistible Rise of a Political Celebrity* (London: Aurum Press, 2011), 121, 126. On how they laid the political groundwork for Brexit, see Martin Fletcher, "The Joke's Over—How Boris Johnson Is Damaging Britain's Global Stature," *New Statesman*, November 4, 2017.

11. Boris Johnson, "If Blair's So Good at Running the Congo, Let Him Stay There," *Daily Telegraph*, January 10, 2002; Boris Johnson, "Denmark Has Got It Wrong. Yes, the Burka Is Oppressive and Ridiculous—but That's Still No Reason to Ban It," *Daily Telegraph*, August 5, 2018.

12. "Trump? Don't Think I Know Him," *Economist*, January 16, 2021, 25.

13. Oliver Wright, "EU Referendum: Boris Johnson Is Like Donald Trump 'with a Thesaurus,' Claims Nick Clegg," *Independent*, June 2, 2016.

14. Dave Hill, *Zac versus Sadiq: The Fight to Become London Mayor* (London: Double Q, 2016), 31.

15. Walden Bello, "Hindutva and the Counter-Revolution in India," *New Frame*, October 8, 2018.

16. Sofia Ammassari, "Contemporary Populism in India: Assessing the Bharatiya Janata Party's Ideological Features," Student Paper 48, Institut Barcelona D'estudis Internacionals, Barcelona, 2018.

17. Pew Research Center, "A Closer Look at How Religious Restrictions Have Risen around the World," Pew Research Center, July 15, 2019.

18. Mujib Mashal and Sameer Yasir, "Modi's Response to Farmer Protests in India Stirs Fears of a Pattern," *New York Times*, February 3, 2021; Edmond Roy, "Crushing Dissent in a New Paranoid India," *Lowy Interpreter* (blog), February 10, 2021, https://www.lowyinstitute.org/the-interpreter/crushing-dissent-new-paranoid-india.

19. Thomas Pepinsky, "Indonesia's Upcoming Elections, Explained," Brookings Institution, Washington, DC, March 20, 2019. See also Marcus Mietzner, *Reinventing Asian Populism: Jokowi's Rise, Democracy, and Political Contestation in Indonesia*, Policy Studies 72 (Washington, DC: East-West Center, 2015).

20. On one view, the selection of Ma'ruf as vice president is indicative of President Widodo's accommodation of extreme Islamists, as demonstrated by his unwillingness to stand up publicly in favor of Basuki Tjahaja Purnama ("Ahok"), the Jakarta governor who was jailed for blasphemy in 2017. On another view, President Widodo chose Ma'ruf because he saw a leader from the moderate Nahdlatul Ulama Islamic organization as best able to confront a political threat from the more extreme Muhamadiyah Islamic organization.

21. Joshua Kurlantzick, "After Jokowi's Victory," *Council on Foreign Relations* (blog), May 28, 2019.

22. "Suharto with a Saw," *Economist*, October 17, 2020, 56.

23. Kurlantzick, "After Jokowi's Victory."

24. Thomas Power and Eve Warburton, eds., *Democracy in Indonesia: From Stagnation to Regression?* (Singapore: ISEAS—Yusof Ishak Institute, 2020); Edward Aspinall, "Twenty Years of Indonesian Democracy—How Many More?," *New Mandala*, May 24, 2018.

25. Matias Spektor, "It's Not Just the Right That's Voting for Bolsonaro. It's Everyone," *Foreign Policy*, October 26, 2018.

26. Jen Kirby, "Corruption, Fake News, and WhatsApp: How Bolsonaro Won Brazil," *Vox*, October 29, 2018.

27. Katy Watson, "Jair Bolsonaro: Who Supports Brazil's New President?," BBC News, October 29, 2018.

28. China and Pakistan have larger populations than Brazil, but the Economist Intelligence Unit classifies the former as authoritarian and the latter as a hybrid regime.

29. Marvin Barth, "'The Politics of Rage': What's Driving the Collapse of the Political Centre?," Barclays, March 9, 2017. Specifically, the analysis identifies a 12 percentage point fall in the combined vote share of center-left and center-right parties. Barth's analysis of the platforms of those parties that have benefited electorally (figure 6) shows them to be largely populist.

30. Max Roser and Hannah Ritchie, "Hunger and Undernourishment," Our World in Data, ourworldindata.org/hunger-and-undernourishment (it is possible that the global recession of 2020 caused this figure to worsen).

31. Facundo Alvaredo, Lucas Chancel, Thomas Piketty, Emmanuel Saez, and Gabriel Zucman, eds., *World Inequality Report 2018* (Paris: World Inequality Lab, 2018), 46.

32. Raj Chetty, David Grusky, Maximilian Hell, Nathaniel Hendren, Robert Manduca, and Jimmy Narang, "The Fading American Dream: Trends in Absolute Income Mobility since 1940," *Science* 356, no. 6336 (2017): 398–406.

33. "Jon Stewart Interviews Bruce Springsteen," *Rolling Stone*, March 14, 2012.

34. The precise figure is 63 percent. Daniel Alpert, Jeffrey Ferry, Robert C. Hockett, and Amir Khaleghi, "The U.S. Private Sector Job Quality Index," Cornell Legal Studies Research Paper No. 20-33, November 1, 2019, 8.

35. Eric Levitz, "Jobs, Jobs Everywhere, but Most of Them Kind of Suck," *New York Magazine*, December 6, 2019.

36. These comparisons cover the period from 1980 to 2015. Pew Research Center, "The State of American Jobs: How the Shifting Economic Landscape Is Reshaping Work and Society and Affecting the Way People Think about the Skills and Training They Need to Get Ahead," Pew Research Center, October 6, 2016.

37. David Autor, David Dorn, Gordon Hanson, and Kaveh Majlesi, "Importing Political Polarization? The Electoral Consequences of Rising Trade Exposure," *American Economic Review* 110, no. 10 (2020): 3139–3183.

38. Theodore Panagiotidis and Costas Roumanias, "Far Right, Extreme Left and Unemployment: A European Historical Perspective," Working Paper 20-11, Rimini Centre for Economic Analysis, 2020.

39. Manuel Funke, Moritz Schularick, and Christoph Trebesch, "Going to Extremes: Politics after Financial Crises, 1870–2014," *European Economic Review* 88 (2016): 227–260.

40. Maxwell Tani, "Nate Silver: 'Calm Down,' Donald Trump Won't Win the GOP Nomination," *Business Insider*, September 11, 2015.

41. Reid Wilson, "Final Newspaper Endorsement Count: Clinton 57, Trump 2," *Hill*, November 6, 2016.

42. Daniel Gross, "Here's Which American CEOs Are Supporting Hillary Clinton," *Fortune*, June 24, 2016.

43. Max Hastings, writing in the *Evening Standard*, July 14, 2000, quoted in Sonia Purnell, *Just Boris: The Irresistible Rise of a Political Celebrity* (London: Aurum Press, 2011), 318.

44. Purnell, *Just Boris*, 322.

45. Thomas Piketty, *Capital and Ideology* (Cambridge, MA: Harvard University Press, 2020).

46. Piketty, *Capital and Ideology*.

47. Raj Chetty, John Friedman, Emmanuel Saez, Nicholas Turner, and Danny Yagan, "Mobility Report Cards: The Role of Colleges in Intergenerational Mobility," NBER Working Paper 23618, National Bureau of Economic Research, Cambridge, MA, 2017.

48. Cécile Bonneau, "How Have Inequalities in Educational Spending in the United States Evolved over the Past Five Decades?," WID.world Issue Brief 2020/1, World Inequality Database, Paris, 2020.

49. Piketty, *Capital and Ideology*.

50. David Rueda, "Insider-Outsider Politics in Industrialized Democracies: The Challenge to Social Democratic Parties," *American Political Science Review* 99, no. 1 (2005): 61–74.

51. Brian Schaffner, "Follow the Racist? The Consequences of Trump's Expressions of Prejudice for Mass Rhetoric" (unpublished paper, Tufts University, Boston, 2018).

52. R. B. Ayal Feinberg, "Counties That Hosted a 2016 Trump Rally Saw a 226 Percent Increase in Hate Crimes," *Washington Post*, August 6, 2019.

53. Marc Hooghe and Ruth Dassonneville, "Explaining the Trump Vote: The Effect of Racist Resentment and Anti-Immigrant Sentiments," *PS: Political Science and Politics* 51, no. 3 (2018): 528–534; Brian F. Schaffner, Matthew Macwilliams, and Tatishe Nteta, "Understanding White Polarization in the 2016 Vote for President: The Sobering Role of Racism and Sexism," *Political Science Quarterly* 133, no. 1 (2018): 9–34. See also Vanessa Williamson and Isabella Gelfand, "Trump and Racism: What Do the Data Say?," Brookings Institution, August 14, 2019.

54. Jason L. Riley, "Blacks and Latinos for Trump," *Wall Street Journal*, November 10, 2020.

55. On the voting patterns of Black and Latino voters in past presidential elections, see Pew Research Center, *The Parties on the Eve of the 2016 Election: Two Coalitions, Moving Further Apart: Trends in Voter Party Identification 1992–2016* (Washington, DC: Pew Research Center, 2016).

56. Across the United States, residents of ethnically diverse neighborhoods tend to be less trusting, less altruistic, and have fewer friends. Robert D. Putnam, "E Pluribus Unum: Diversity and Community in the Twenty-First Century—the 2006 Johan Skytte Prize Lecture," *Scandinavian Political Studies* 30, no. 2 (2007): 137–174.

57. Edward L. Glaeser, "The Political Economy of Hatred," *Quarterly Journal of Economics* 120, no. 1 (2005): 45–86.

58. Public opinion on same-sex marriage is documented in Katherine Schaeffer, "U.S. Has Changed in Key Ways in the Past Decade, from Tech Use to Demographics," Pew Research Center, December 20, 2019.

59. Lydia Saad, "10 Major Social Changes in the 50 Years since Woodstock," *Gallup Blog*, August 16, 2019.

60. Felix Richter, "Landline Phones Are a Dying Breed," *Statistica*, June 15, 2020.

61. See, for example, Patrick Wagner, "Ride-Hailing Apps Surpass Regular Taxis in NYC," *Statistica*, April 10, 2018.

62. Walter Loeb, "More Than 14,000 Stores Are Closing in 2020 So Far—a Number That Will Surely Rise," *Forbes*, September 12, 2020.

63. Bret Kinsella, "Nearly 90 Million U.S. Adults Have Smart Speakers, Adoption Now Exceeds One-Third of Consumers," voicebot.ai, April 28, 2020; Fareeha Ali, "Amazon Prime has 112 Million Members in the US," digitalcommerce360.com, January 24, 2020.

64. Thomas L. Friedman, *Thank You for Being Late: An Optimist's Guide to Thriving in the Age of Accelerations* (New York: Farrar, Straus and Giroux, 2016)

65. Giray Gozgor, "The Role of Economic Uncertainty in Rising Populism in the EU," CESifo Working Paper No. 8499, CESifo, Munich, 2020.

66. In Wisconsin, Michigan, and Pennsylvania, Stein's vote exceeded the margin by which Trump beat Clinton.

67. The interview aired on April 25, 1988.

68. Under the principle of *foro privilegiado*, Brazil's politicians, judges, mayors, city councillors, and army officers can be tried only in the nation's higher courts. Because of delays, this can amount to immunity from crimes. See Joe Leahy and Andres Schipani, "Brazilian Politicians' Immunity Status Starts to Creak," *Financial Times*, December 23, 2017.

69. Flávio Bolsonaro, *Jair Messias Bolsonaro—Mito ou Verdade* (Rio de Janeiro: Altadena Editora, 2017), 77–79.

70. Yalçın Akdoğan, *Political Leadership and Erdoğan* (Newcastle upon Tyne: Cambridge Scholars Publishing, 2018).

71. On the demographics of asylum seekers, see Phillip Connor, "Number of Refugees to Europe Surges to Record 1.3 Million in 2015," Pew Research Center, August 2, 2016. On public attitudes to asylum seekers, see Richard Wike, Bruce Stokes, and

Katie Simmons, "Europeans Fear Wave of Refugees Will Mean More Terrorism, Fewer Jobs," Pew Research Center, July 11, 2016.

72. Margit Tavits and Joshua D. Potter, "The Effect of Inequality and Social Identity on Party Strategies," *American Journal of Political Science* 59, no. 3 (2015): 744–758.

73. A 2013 survey asked people estimate the current percentage of the US population that is composed of racial and ethnic minorities. The median response was 49 percent, considerably higher than the true figure at that time of 37 percent. See Ruy Teixeira and John Halpin with Matt Barreto and Adrian Pantoja, "Building an All-In Nation: A View from the American Public," Center for American Progress, October 22, 2013. For a good overview of the experiments that prime subjects' racial views, see Ezra Klein, *Why We're Polarized* (New York: Simon and Schuster, 2020), 107–109.

74. Klein, *Why We're Polarized*, 111–112.

75. Anita Desikan, "150 Attacks on Science and Counting: Trump Administration's Anti-Science Actions Hurt People and Communities Nationwide," *Union of Concerned Scientists* (blog), August 3, 2020.

76. Some exceptions are found in the United States, where even "never Trump" Republicans tend to oppose action on climate change. For a discussion of rising party polarization in US climate policy, see Cale Jaffe, "Melting the Polarization around Climate Change Politics," *Georgetown Environmental Law Review* 30, no. 3 (2018): 455–498.

77. Stella Schaller and Alexander Carius, *Convenient Truths: Mapping Climate Agendas of Right-Wing Populist Parties in Europe* (Berlin: Adelphi, 2019).

78. Robert A. Huber, "The Role of Populist Attitudes in Explaining Climate Change Skepticism and Support for Environmental Protection," *Environmental Politics* 29, no. 6 (2020): 959–982.

79. European Union, "Special Eurobarometer 488: Europeans' Attitudes towards Vaccination," EU Open Data Portal, 2019.

80. Author's analysis, based on monthly data reported in World Health Organization, "Measles and Rubella Surveillance Data," who.int.

81. Jonathan Kennedy, "Populist Politics and Vaccine Hesitancy in Western Europe: An Analysis of National-Level Data," *European Journal of Public Health* 29, no. 3 (2019): 512–516.

82. "Growing Anti-Vaccination Movement Linked to Rise of Populism," *Week*, February 26, 2019.

83. Jeffrey Sachs, "Why the US Has the World's Highest Number of COVID-19 Deaths," *CNN Opinion*, April 13, 2020.

84. "Trump: 'Even One Death That Makes Me Look Bad Is a Tragedy,'" *Onion*, May 26, 2020.

85. "Brazil's Losing Battle against COVID-19," *Economist*, May 28, 2020, 32–33.

86. For COVID-19 death rate statistics, see coronavirus.jhu.edu/data/mortality.

87. Ben Bland, "Jokowi Needs to Change Strategy," *Straits Times*, July 18, 2020.

88. Julio C. Teehankee, "Rodrigo Duterte's War on Many Fronts," *East Asia Forum*, August 9, 2020.

89. For COVID-19 death rate statistics, see coronavirus.jhu.edu/data/mortality.

90. Cary Funk, Meg Hefferon, Brian Kennedy, and Courtney Johnson, "Trust and Mistrust in Americans' Views of Scientific Experts," Pew Research Center, 2019.

91. Paul Lewis, Sarah Boseley, and Pamela Duncan, "Revealed: Populists Far More Likely to Believe in Conspiracy Theories," *Guardian*, May 2, 2019.

92. Eirikur Bergmann, *Conspiracy and Populism: The Politics of Misinformation* (London: Palgrave Macmillan, 2018); Matthew Rosenberg and Maggie Haberman, "The Republican Embrace of QAnon Goes Far beyond Trump," *New York Times*, August 20, 2020.

93. Matthew Rosenberg, "A QAnon Supporter Is Headed to Congress," *New York Times*, November 3, 2020.

94. Graeme Bruce, "Half of Trump's Supporters Think Top Democrats Are Involved in Child Sex-Trafficking," YouGov, October 21, 2020.

95. Susan Page and Sarah Elbeshbishi, "Defeated and Impeached, Trump Still Commands the Loyalty of the GOP's Voters," *USA Today*, February 21, 2021. See also Kathy Frankovic, "One Week Later, What Do Americans Make of the Capitol Attack?," YouGov.com, January 14, 2021.

96. Michael Lewis, "'This Guy Doesn't Know Anything': The Inside Story of Trump's Shambolic Transition Team," *Guardian*, September 27, 2018. This is an edited extract from Michael Lewis's *The Fifth Risk*, which makes the same points, but more expansively.

97. Kathryn Dunn Tenpas, "Tracking Turnover in the Trump Administration," Brookings Institution, Washington, DC, 2020. As with the White House staff, the ten departing cabinet members were subsequently replaced.

98. Jennifer Steinhauer and Zolan Kanno-Youngs, "Under Trump, Unfilled Posts Hinder Action," *New York Times*, March 27, 2020, A1.

99. Anna Grzymala-Busse, Didi Kuo, Francis Fukuyama, and Michael McFaul, *Global Populisms and Their Challenges* (Stanford, CA: Stanford Freeman Spogli Institute for International Studies, 2020).

100. Kenneth Roth, "The Dangerous Rise of Populism,' in *World Report 2017* (New York: Human Rights Watch, 2017), 1–14.

101. Kim Parker, "The Growing Partisan Divide in Views of Higher Education," Pew Research Center, August 19, 2019.

102. Quoted in Leonard Downie Jr., *The Trump Administration and the Media: Attacks on Press Credibility Endanger US Democracy and Global Press Freedom* (New York: Committee to Protect Journalists, 2020), 7.

103. The study surveyed people in Sweden, Spain, South Korea, and China: Malcolm Fairbrother, Gustaf Arrhenius, Krister Bykvist, and Tim Campbell, "How Much Do People Value Future Generations? Climate Change, Trust, and Public Support for Future-Oriented Policies," Working Paper, Institute for Futures Studies, Stockholm, 2020.

104. Vincent C. C. Cheng, Susanna K. P. Lau, Patrick C. Y. Woo, and Kwok Yung Yuen, "Severe Acute Respiratory Syndrome Coronavirus as an Agent of Emerging and Reemerging Infection," *Clinical Microbiology Reviews* 20, no. 4 (2007): 660–694.

105. The number of China-based CDC staff fell from forty-seven at the start of 2017 to fourteen in 2019. Christopher Sellers, Leif Fredrickson, Alissa Cordner, Kelsey Breseman, Eric Nost, Kelly Wilkins, and EDGI, "An Embattled Landscape Series, Part 2a: Coronavirus and the Three-Year Trump Quest to Slash Science at the CDC," Environmental Data and Governance Initiative, March 23, 2020.

106. "Handcuffing an Institution," *Economist*, May 23, 2020, 25–26; Sellers et al., "An Embattled Landscape."

107. The Trump administration also unsuccessfully proposed redirecting $252 million that had been appropriated to help African health care systems prevent future Ebola outbreaks. See Ed Yong, "Ebola Returns Just as Trump Asks to Rescind Ebola Funds," *Atlantic*, May 9, 2018.

108. Sellers et al., "An Embattled Landscape."

109. Michael Crowley, "Allies and Former U.S. Officials Fear Trump Could Seek NATO Exit in a Second Term," *New York Times*, September 3, 2020.

110. Bolsonaro's Facebook post was deleted, though not before it had been picked up by media outlets. See Tom Embury-Dennis, "Coronavirus: Bolsonaro Justifies Ignoring WHO with False Claim It Encourages Young Children to Masturbate," *Independent*, May 2, 2020.

111. David D. Kirkpatrick and José María León Cabrera, "How Trump and Bolsonaro Broke Latin America's Covid-19 Defenses," *New York Times*, October 27, 2020.

112. Richard E. Baldwin and Simon J. Evenett, eds., *COVID-19 and Trade Policy: Why Turning Inward Won't Work* (London: CEPR Press, 2020), 21.

113. "21st Century Tracking of Pandemic-Era Trade Policies in Food and Medical Products," EUI, GTA, and World Bank, May 4, 2020.

114. Office of Management and Budget, "Request for Comments on a Draft Memorandum to the Heads of Executive Departments and Agencies, 'Guidance for Regulation of Artificial Intelligence Applications': A Notice by the Management and Budget Office on 01/13/2020," Federal Document 2020–00261, *Federal Register* 85, no. 1825 (2020).

115. Michael Kratsios, "Why the US Needs a Strategy for AI," *Wired*, November 2, 2019.

116. Glenn Kessler, Meg Kelly, Salvador Rizzo, and Michelle Ye Hee Lee, "In 1,316 Days, President Trump Has Made 22,247 False or Misleading Claims," *Washington Post*, August 27, 2020.

117. Katie Rogers, "In Social Media Summit, Trump Praises Loyal Meme Makers," *New York Times*, July 12, 2019, A14.

118. According to the research director of the World Values Survey, "the existentially relieved state of mind is the source of tolerance and solidarity beyond one's in-group; the existentially stressed state of mind is the source of discrimination and hostility against out-groups." Christian Welzel, *Freedom Rising: Human Empowerment and the Quest for Emancipation* (New York: Cambridge University Press, 2013), xxiii.

119. The figures for Democratic voters are not much better. See Nathan P. Kalmoe and Lilliana Mason, "Lethal Mass Partisanship: Prevalence, Correlates, and Electoral Contingencies" (paper presented at the NCAPSA American Politics Meeting, Washington, DC, 2019).

120. Sendhil Mullainathan and Eldar Shafir, *Scarcity: Why Having Too Little Means So Much* (New York: Picador, 2013), 66.

121. Arjen Boin and Paul 't Hart, "Public Leadership in Times of Crisis: Mission Impossible?," *Public Administration Review* 63, no. 5 (2003): 544–553.

122. Quoted in "Science Scorned," *Nature* 467, no. 7312 (2010): 133.

Chapter 8

1. Richard Evans, *The Coming of the Third Reich* (New York: Penguin, 2003), 308. Levitsky and Ziblatt mistakenly report "squeak" as "squeal": Steven Levitsky and Daniel Ziblatt, *How Democracies Die* (New York: Crown, 2018), 15.

2. Evans, *The Coming of the Third Reich*, 314.

3. Ian Kershaw, *Hitler, 1889–1936: Hubris* (New York: W. W. Norton, 1999), 724.

4. Daniel Ziblatt, *Conservative Political Parties and the Birth of Modern Democracy in Europe* (Cambridge: Cambridge University Press, 2017), 332.

5. Louis Eltscher, *Traitors or Patriots?: A Story of the German Anti-Nazi Resistance* (Bloomington, IN: iUniverse, 2018), 14.

6. Levitsky and Ziblatt, *How Democracies Die*, 2.

7. The latest report is Economist Intelligence Unit, *Democracy Index 2020: In Sickness and in Health?* (London: Economist Intelligence Unit, 2021).

8. Levitsky and Ziblatt, *How Democracies Die*, 5.

9. Primitivo Mijares, *The Conjugal Dictatorship of Ferdinand and Imelda Marcos* (San Francisco: Union Square Publications, 1976), 113.

10. Alfred W. McCoy, *Policing America's Empire: The United States, the Philippines, and the Rise of the Surveillance State* (Madison: University of Wisconsin Press, 2009), 403.

11. Edsel Tupaz and Daniel Wagner, "The Missing Marcos Billions and the Demise of the Commission on Good Government," *Huffington Post*, October 13, 2014.

12. Levitsky and Ziblatt, *How Democracies Die*, 4.

13. Francis Fukuyama, *The End of History and the Last Man* (New York: Penguin, 1992), 211.

14. Ishaan Tharoor, "The Man Who Declared the 'End of History' Fears for Democracy's Future," *Washington Post*, February 9, 2017.

15. Francis Fukuyama, "America: The Failed State," *Prospect*, December 13, 2016.

16. Economist Intelligence Unit, *Democracy Index 2020*, 4.

17. Quoted in Economist Intelligence Unit, *Democracy Index 2019: A Year of Democratic Setbacks and Popular Protest* (London: Economist Intelligence Unit, 2020), 5.

18. Economist Intelligence Unit, *Democracy Index 2020, 21–25*.

19. Mila Versteeg, Timothy Horley, Anne Meng, Mauricio Guim, and Marilyn Guirguis, "The Law and Politics of Presidential Term Limit Evasion," *Columbia Law Review* 120, no. 1 (2020): 173–248.

20. Economist Intelligence Unit, *Democracy Index 2016: Revenge of the "Deplorables"* (London: Economist Intelligence Unit, 2017), 4.

21. Andrew Higgins, "Trump Borrows Election Tactics from Autocrats," *New York Times*, November 12, 2020, A1.

22. Anne Applebaum, *Twilight of Democracy: The Seductive Lure of Authoritarianism* (New York: Doubleday, 2020), 155.

23. Selam Gebrekidan, "Pandemic Temps Leaders to Seize Sweeping Powers," *New York Times*, March 31, 2020, A1.

24. Sunasir Dutta and Hayagreeva Rao, "Infectious Diseases, Contamination Rumors and Ethnic Violence: Regimental Mutinies in the Bengal Native Army in 1857 India," *Organizational Behavior and Human Decision Processes* 129 (2015): 36–47.

25. Jordan Kyle and Yascha Mounk, "The Populist Harm to Democracy: An Empirical Assessment," Tony Blair Institute for Global Change, 2018.

26. From 1998 to 2020, the share of people who agreed with the statement "Having a strong leader who does not have to bother with parliament and elections is good" grew by 4 percentage points in healthy democracies (from 29 to 33 percent), and by 18 percentage points in weak ones (from 44 to 62 percent): "Drifting Apart," *Economist*, August 22, 2020.

27. Larry Diamond, *Ill Winds: Saving Democracy from Russian Rage, Chinese Ambition, and American Complacency* (New York: Penguin, 2019), 64–65; Juan Linz, *The Breakdown of Democratic Regimes: Crisis, Breakdown and Reequilibration* (Baltimore: Johns Hopkins University Press, 1978), 29–30; Levitsky and Ziblatt, *How Democracies Die*, 23.

28. Zachary Fryer-Biggs, "Trump Reshaped the Courts. Now His Lawyers Want Them to Limit Voting," Center for Public Integrity, October 22, 2020.

29. "President Trump's 3,400 Conflicts of Interest," Citizens for Responsibility and Ethics in Washington, September 24, 2020.

30. Peter Baker, "Instead of Reconciliation, a Promise of Payback.," *New York Times*, February 7, 2020, A1.

31. Isaac Stanley-Becker, "Roger Stone Wanted WikiLeaks Dump to Distract from 'Access Hollywood' Tape, Mueller Witness Says," *Washington Post*, January 29, 2019; Stephan Lewandowsky, Michael Jetter, and Ullrich Ecker, "Donald Trump and Strategic Diversion in the Age of Twitter" (working paper, 2019).

32. Ipsos, *Perils of Perception 2016* (London: Ipsos, 2016).

33. Formally, Stenner's equation is *intolerance of difference = authoritarian predisposition × normative threat*: Karen Stenner, *The Authoritarian Dynamic* (Cambridge: Cambridge University Press, 2005). See also Karen Stenner and Jonathan Haidt, "Authoritarianism Is Not a Momentary Madness, but an Eternal Dynamic within Liberal Democracies," in *Can It Happen Here? Authoritarianism in America*, ed. Cass R. Sunstein in (New York: HarperCollins, 2018), 175–219.

34. Senator James Couzens, quoted in Levitsky and Ziblatt, *How Democracies Die*, 45.

35. We might see this as life imitating art, since Skynet was the name of the all-controlling artificial intelligence system first depicted in the 2009 film *Terminator Salvation*.

36. Robert Mickey, *Paths out of Dixie: The Democratization of Authoritarian Enclaves in America's Deep South, 1944–1972* (Princeton, NJ: Princeton University Press, 2015), 87.

37. Applebaum, *Twilight of Democracy*.

Chapter 9

1. This is based on country ratings in the widely used Polity V data set, which was first compiled by Ted Gurr in the 1960s, and has continued to be updated by Monty G. Marshall and the Center for Systemic Peace. In 1800, the Polity democracy score (which ranges from complete autocracy at minus ten to complete democracy at ten) for the United States was four. The next-closest countries were Korea (one) and the United Kingdom (minus two).

2. Kevin Narizny, "Anglo-American Primacy and the Global Spread of Democracy: An International Genealogy," *World Politics* 64, no. 2 (2012): 341–373.

3. Thomas Jefferson, "Letter to Samuel Kercheval," July 12, 1816 (Washington, DC: Library of Congress). See also Thomas Jefferson, "Letter to James Madison," September 6, 1789 (Washington, DC: Library of Congress).

4. These estimates are based on the Polity V database's Polity score for 2018. See Monty G. Marshall, *Polity5 Project* (Vienna, VA: Center for Systemic Peace, 2020), data set version p5v2018.

5. Figures on voter turnout by country are compiled by the International Institute for Democracy and Electoral Assistance, idea.int.

6. These figures are voters as a share of the voting eligible population, published by the University of Florida's Michael McDonald, electproject.org.

7. Richard Freeman, "What, Me Vote?," in *Social Inequality*, ed. Kathryn Neckerman (New York: Russell Sage Foundation, 2004), 1:703–728.

8. Nonetheless, one-fifth of states do not allow early in-person voting, while one-third of states require an excuse before issuing an absentee ballot. See "Voting Outside the Polling Place: Absentee, All-Mail and Other Voting at Home Options," ncsl.org.

9. Mark Hoekstra and Vijetha Koppa, "Strict Voter Identification Laws, Turnout, and Election Outcomes," NBER Working Paper No. 26206, National Bureau of Economic Research, Cambridge, MA, 2019.

10. Being too busy or having a conflicting schedule was the most common reason for not voting in presidential elections from 2000 to 2012, though dislike of candidates was the most common reason in 2016: Gustavo López and Antonio Flores, "Dislike of Candidates or Campaign Issues Was Most Common Reason for Not Voting in 2016," Pew Research Center, June 1, 2017.

11. South Korea and Israel also designate Election Day as a holiday.

12. Freeman, "What, Me Vote?"

13. Anthony Fowler, "Electoral and Policy Consequences of Voter Turnout: Evidence from Compulsory Voting in Australia," *Quarterly Journal of Political Science* 8, no. 2 (2013): 159–182.

14. This comparison between Vermont and Texas is based on ballots cast in the 2016 election. The democratic deficit is larger still if states are compared based on their populations (i.e., including children and noncitizens).

15. Ezra Klein, *Why We're Polarized* (New York: Simon and Schuster, 2020), 241–243; Andrew Gelman and Pierre-Antoine Kremp, "The Electoral College Magnifies the Power of White Voters," *Vox*, December 17, 2016.

16. See nationalpopularvote.com.

17. United Nations Development Programme, *Principles for Independent and Sustainable Electoral Management: International Standards for Electoral Management Bodies* (Cairo: UNDP Electoral Support Program, 2012).

18. See National Conference of State Legislators, "Redistricting Commissions: State Legislative Plans," January 9, 2020, ncsl.org.

19. Quoted in Jacob S. Hacker and Paul Pierson, *Let Them Eat Tweets: How the Right Rules in an Age of Extreme Inequality* (New York: W. W. Norton, 2020), 182.

20. Studying all national, provincial, and state elections since 1945 in Australia, Britain, Canada, and New Zealand, Jonathan Rodden finds that the party that won the most seats lost the popular vote thirty-six times, and that the Right benefited on twenty-eight of these occasions. Jonathan Rodden, *Why Cities Lose: The Deep Roots of the Urban-Rural Political Divide* (New York: Basic Books, 2019).

21. Nicolas Sauger and Bernard Grofman, "Partisan Bias and Redistricting in France," *Electoral Studies* 44 (2016): 388–396.

22. Alex Tausanovitch, *Voter-Determined Districts: Ending Gerrymandering and Ensuring Fair Representation* (Washington, DC: Center for American Progress, 2019).

23. John C. Moritz, "How Texas Became 'Ground Zero' for Gerrymandering, Voter Suppression," Caller Times, February 27, 2020. On a state level, the worst five states for partisan gerrymandering in the 2018 elections were Michigan, North Carolina,

Pennsylvania, Virginia, and Wisconsin. In all five cases, Republicans won a majority of lower house state seats, despite winning a minority of the popular vote. Christian Grose, Jordan Peterson, Matthew Nelson, and Sara Sadhwani, "The Worst Partisan Gerrymanders in U.S. State Legislatures," USC Schwarzenegger Institute, 2019.

24. The result would have been a Gore victory. See Michael Herron and Jeffrey Lewis, "Did Ralph Nader Spoil a Gore Presidency? A Ballot-Level Study of Green and Reform Party Voters in the 2000 Presidential Election," *Quarterly Journal of Political Science* 2, no. 3 (2007): 205–226.

25. David Daley, "An End to Spoiler Candidates," *Democracy*, November 1, 2018.

26. On the history of Australian democratic innovation, see Judith Brett, *From Secret Ballot to Democracy Sausage: How Australia Got Compulsory Voting* (Melbourne: Text, 2019). For a discussion of the many imperfections in Australian democracy, see Andrew Leigh and Nick Terrell, *Reconnected: A Community Builder's Handbook* (Melbourne: Black Inc., 2020), 22–27.

27. Andrea Kendall-Taylor, Erica Frantz, and Joseph Wright, "The Digital Dictators: How Technology Strengthens Autocracy," *Foreign Affairs* 99, no. 2 (2020): 103–115.

28. Alina Polyakova and Chris Meserole, "Exporting Digital Authoritarianism," Brookings Institution, Washington, DC, 2019.

29. Steven Levitsky and Daniel Ziblatt, *How Democracies Die* (New York: Crown, 2018), 25.

30. William N. Eskridge Jr., "Privacy Jurisprudence and the Apartheid of the Closet, 1946–1961," *Florida State University Law Review* 24, no. 4 (1997): 703–838.

31. U.S. Congress. Senate. *Executive Sessions of the Senate Permanent Subcommittee on Investigations of the Committee on Government Operations*, Public hearing, June 9, 1954. The army lawyer was Joseph Welch.

32. "The Fateful Vote to Impeach," *Time*, August 5, 1974, 10-18.

33. Michael Ignatieff, *Fire and Ashes: Success and Failure in Politics* (Cambridge, MA: Harvard University Press, 2013), 94.

34. Eitan Hersh, *Politics Is for Power: How to Move beyond Political Hobbyism, Take Action, and Make Real Change* (New York: Scribner, 2020).

35. National Assessment of Educational Programs, "The Nation's Report Card: 2018 Civics at Grade 8," National Center for Education Statistics, 2020.

36. Wolfram Schulz, John Ainley, Julian Fraillon, Bruno Losito, Gabriella Agrusti, and Tim Friedman, *Becoming Citizens in a Changing World: IEA International Civic and Citizenship Education Study 2016 International Report* (Amsterdam: IEA Secretariat, 2018).

37. Robert Pondiscio, "Seizing the Moment to Improve Civics Education," Fordham Institute, 2017.

38. Bruce Ackerman and James S. Fishkin, *Deliberation Day* (New Haven, CT: Yale University Press, 2004).

39. Daron Acemoglu, Suresh Naidu, Pascual Restrepo, and James A. Robinson, "Democracy Does Cause Growth," *Journal of Political Economy* 127, no. 1 (2019): 47–100.

40. Amartya Sen, *Poverty and Famines: An Essay on Entitlement and Deprivation* (Oxford: Oxford University Press, 1982).

41. Bryan Schonfeld, "Democracy Promotion as an EA Cause Area," July 1, 2020, forum.effectivealtruism.org.

42. Alice Duer Miller, *Are Women People? A Book of Rhymes for Suffrage Times* (New York: George H. Doran Company, 1915), 41.

43. E. M. Forster, *What I Believe* (London: Hogarth Press, 1939), 9.

Chapter 10

1. RadioLab, "The Cataclysm Sentence," WNYC Studios, April 18, 2020.

2. William MacAskill, "What We Owe the Future," Global Priorities Institute, April 2020, https://globalprioritiesinstitute.org/will-macaskill-what-we-owe-the-future/.

3. Adam Lee, "The New Ten Commandments," n.d., patheos.com.

4. Eliezer Yudkowsky, "Cognitive Biases Potentially Affecting Judgment of Global Risks," in *Global Catastrophic Risks*, ed. Nick Bostrom and Milan Ćirković (Oxford: Oxford University Press, 2008), 91–119.

5. Quoted in Leonard Lyons, "Loose-Leaf Notebook," *Washington Post*, January 30, 1947, 9.

6. Nick Bostrom, "Existential Risk Prevention as Global Priority," *Global Policy* 4, no. 1 (2013): 15–31.

7. Insurance Information Institute, "Facts + Statistics: Homeowners and Renters Insurance," Insurance Information Institute, iii.org.

8. "How Many Homes Are Insured? How Many Are Uninsured?," Insurance Information Institute, iii.org.

9. Michael Lewis, *The Fifth Risk: Undoing Democracy* (New York: W. W. Norton, 2018), 75, 77.

10. These cardinal virtues draw on Plato. See Plato, *The Republic*, circa 375 BCE, book 4, section 427e. They also appear in the writings of Aristotle and the Christian tradition.

11. Bryan Schonfeld and Sam Winter-Levy, "Factual or Moral Persuasion in the United States? Evidence from the Papal Encyclical on Climate Change" (working paper, Princeton University, Princeton, NJ, 2020).

12. Marcus Aurelius, circa AD 161 to 180, *Meditations*, book 11, section 18.5b.

13. Martha C. Nussbaum, *The Monarchy of Fear: A Philosopher Looks at Our Political Crisis* (New York: Simon and Schuster, 2018), 76, 226.

14. David McCullough, *The American Spirit: Who We Are and What We Stand For* (New York: Simon and Schuster, 2017), 108.

15. John Meacham, *The Soul of America: The Battle for Our Better Angels* (New York: Random House, 2018), 9.

16. John F. Kennedy, *State of the Union Address*, January 11, 1962.

17. This section draws on Paul I. Bernstein and Jason D. Wood, *The Origins of Nunn-Lugar and Cooperative Threat Reduction*, Center for the Study of Weapons of Mass Destruction Case Study 3 (Washington, DC: National Defense University Press, 2010).

18. *Congressional Record* 155, no. 194 (December 18, 2009), S13410.

19. The share of bills with bipartisan cosponsors has not fallen in recent years, but this may be due to the fact that around one-third of all congressional bills are ceremonial rather than substantive. Drew Desilver, "A Productivity Scorecard for the 115th Congress: More Laws than before, but Not More Substance," Pew Research Center, January 25, 2019.

Index

Abrams, Herbert L., 188n36
Acemoglu, Daron, 208n39
Acharya, Avidit, 61, 186n7
Ackerman, Bruce, 208n38
Adalja, Amesh, 177n47
Adams, Douglas, 5
Adger, W. Neil, 183n64
Affum-Baffoe, Kofi, 179n13
African Americans, 142, 145
Age of Surveillance Capitalism, The, 141
Agrusti, Gabriella, 207n36
Ainley, John, 207n36
Air-conditioning, 43
Air travel risk, 41–42
Akdoğan, Yalçin, 198n70
Albeck-Ripka, Livia, 184n74
Albright, David, 186n13
Alegret, Laia, 191n2
Alexander, Anneliese, 185n79
Alexander, Scott, 81, 84, 190n25,
   190n28, 191n34
Algohary, Ahmad, 188n5
Algorithmic generations, 77
Ali, Fareeha, 198n63
Alibek, Ken, 175nn29–30

Alilou, Mehdi, 188n5
Allen, Paul, 80, 190n22
Alley, Richard B., 182n44
Allison, Graham, 67, 187n20
Alpert, Daniel, 196n34
AlphaGo Zero, 74
Al Qaeda, 66
Alt, Franz, 189n12
Altruism, encoding, 78
Alvaredo, Facundo, 196n31
Amazon rainforest, 38–39, 53
American Lung Association, 180n29
American Type Culture Collection, 23
Amin, Ma'ruf, 107, 195n20
Ammassari, Sofia, 194n16
Amodei, Dario, 189n14
Ancestors, human, 5–6
Andersen, Kurt, 190n20
Anderson, Liana O., 184n75
Andino, Raul, 175n21
Andropov, Yuri, 59
Anger, 164–165
Animal viruses, 21
Antarctica, 38
Anthony, Simon J., 175n19

Anthrax, 18
Anthropocene, 37
Anthropogenic risks, 95–97, 99–100
Antimissile systems, 61
Anti-vaccination movement, 119–120
Antonoglou, Ioanis, 189n6, 189nn10–11
Applebaum, Anne, 135–136, 143,
    203n22, 205n37
Aragão, Luiz E. O. C., 184n75
Arctic, 39, 47
Arenillas, Ignacio, 191n2
Aristotle, 209n10
Arkhipov, Vasili, 58–59
ARkStorm, 46
Armageddon, 89
Armaments, spread of, 97
Arms race, 62
Arnold, Steve R., 179n11
Arnoud, Sacha, 188n5
Arrhenius, Gustaf, 201n103
Artaxo, Paulo, 184n75
Artificial intelligence, 13, 73–88
  algorithmic generations, 77
  alignment problem, 79, 84
  and atomic weapons, 101
  benefits, 83
  capability control, 79
  chess computers, 76
  and competitive development, 83–84
  control problem, 77–79
  encoding values, 78, 84–85, 164
  and extinction risk, 82
  global cooperation, 85–86
  government regulation, 86–87
  guidelines and principles, 85–86
  and human intelligence, 73, 81–82
  machine learning, 73–74
  mimicking styles, 74–76
  perverse instantiation, 78, 84
  recent progress, 83
  risks of, 79–84
  safety standards, 125–126
  tests of, 75–76, 81–82

Arz, José A., 191n2
Asimov, Isaac, 78
Aspinall, Edward, 195n24
Assail, Yannis M., 188n5
Asteroid strikes, 89–90
  deflecting, 90
  NASA tracking, 90
  risk of, 93
Astley, Rick, 63
Atmospheric carbon concentrations, 40
Atomic bombs, 65, 98–99
Atwood, Margaret, 140
Aum Shinrikyo cult, 24
Aurelius, Marcus, 209n12
Australia, 45, 147–148
  Black Saturday fires, 51
  democracy in, 151
  European diseases in, 19
  temperature measurement, 51
Austria, 147
Authoritarianism, 96–97, 131, 134
  and bioterrorism, 101
  and COVID-19 pandemic, 136
  and diversity, 140
  indicators of, 137–139
  and nativism, 139–140
  predisposition to, 140
Autism, 119
Autocracy, 14–15, 130–132. *See also*
    Authoritarianism
Autor, David, 173n22, 196n37
Availability bias, 9

B83 (nuclear weapon), 65
Badia, Adrià Puigdomènech, 189n5
Bailey, David A., 182n50
Baker, Nicholson, 157
Baker, Peter, 204n30
Baldwin, Richard E., 201n112
Barreto, Matt, 199n73
Barria, Eduardo O., 193n23
Barro, Robert J., 174n7
Barth, Martin, 195n29

Barton, Penny J., 191n2
Bat coronaviruses, 21
Battle, Katherine E., 176n45
Baudet, Thierry, 118
Bayard, Vicente, 193n23
Becker, Sascha, 194n7
Beig, Niha G., 188n5
Belarus, 63
Belgium, 147
Bello, Walden, 194n15
Bender, Bryan, 192n4
Benedict, Kennette, 171n2
Berenguer, Erika, 184n75
Bergmann, Eirikur, 200n92
Berlusconi, Silvio, 109
Berner, Christopher, 188n5
Bernstein, Paul I., 209n17
Bhatt, Samir, 176n45
Bias, availability, 9
Biden, Joe, 105
Biden administration, 55, 68
Bielecki, Coral R., 180n25
Bilir, T. Eren, 183nn56–58
Bill and Melinda Gates Foundation, 18
bin Laden, Osama, 66
Bindi, Marco, 182n43
Bioengineering, 28, 31
Biological weapons, 22–24, 30
Biological Weapons Convention, 23, 30,
    161
Bioterrorism, 12, 18, 24, 26
    and authoritarianism, 101
    reducing risk of, 30, 161
Bipartisanship, 127, 166–167
Bird flu (H5N1), 22
Black Brant, 58
Black death, 18–19
Black Lives Matter movement, 117
Black Saturday fires, 51
Black swan events, 99
Black swan storm, 51
Blair, Bruce, 70, 185n5, 187n28
Blaizot, Jean-Paul, 193n21

Bland, Ben, 200n87
Blastland, Michael, 93, 180n21
Block, Steven, 175n31
Blockley, Ed, 182n50
BloombergNEF, 185n85
Blue Ribbon Study Panel on Biodefense,
    177n48
Blundell, Charles, 189n5
Boccaccio, Giovanni, 18, 173n2
Body temperatures, 35–36
Boer, Matthias M., 181n38
Boin, Arjen, 202n121
Boivin, Nicole, 171n1
Bolotin, Shelly, 174n12, 176n46
Bolsonaro, Flávio, 198n69
Bolsonaro, Jair, 53, 108–109, 115–116,
    118, 120, 124, 201n110
Bondanella, Peter, 173n2
Bonneau, Cécile, 197n48
Borup, Birthe, 173n3, 174n8
Boseley, Sarah, 200n91
Bostrom, Nick, 77, 83, 86, 98–99,
    172nn13–14, 189n13, 191n33,
    191n38, 192nn14–15, 193n20,
    208n4, 208n6
Bown, Paul R., 191n2
Boxall, Bettina, 180n32
Brackney, Doug E., 177n50
Bradstock, Ross A., 181n38
Brahmin Left, 112
Bralower, Timothy J., 191n2
Brazil, 53, 108, 120, 122
Breseman, Kelsey, 201n105
Brett, Judith, 207n26
Brexit, 105–106
Brigham Young University Global Popu-
    lism Database, 173n18
Broad, William, 175n28, 176n38, 187n27
Brockman, Greg, 188n5
Brookhaven Relativistic Heavy Ion Col-
    lider, 99
Brooks, Rodney, 76
Brown, Noam, 188n4

Brown, Sally, 182n43
Brownstein, John S., 176n45
Bruce, Graeme, 200n94
Brynjolfsson, Erik, 191n32
Buchanan, Pat, 116
Buhaug, Halvard, 183n64
Bulatov, Yaroslav, 188n5
Bunn, Matthew, 186n16, 187n19
Bureau of Arms Control, Verification and
    Compliance, 176n33
Burke, Edmund, 6, 172n7
Burke, Marshall, 183n64
Burke, Paul J., 173n21
Burkhard, Sarah, 186n13
Burt, Christopher C., 178n1
Bush, George W., 11
Bush, George W. H., 56, 111, 166
Bush, Jeb, 104
Bushuk, Mitchell, 182n50
Butler, James H., 179n17
Bykvist, Krister, 201n103

Cabrera, José María León, 201n111
Caldwell, Iain R., 180n25
California, 44
Cambodia, 134
Cameron, David, 105
Camilloni, Ines, 182n43
Campbell, Tim, 201n103
Camp Fire, 44
Cane, Mark A., 183n62
Capitalism, 108
Caplan, Bryan, 97, 192n14
Carbon bomb, 39
Carbon concentrations, atmospheric, 40
Carbon cycle, 50
Carbon emissions, 42, 47, 161
    and crop yields, 48
    and extinction risk, 50
    and global warming, 55
    and government policies, 52
    offset markets/pricing schemes, 52
    reducing, 55–56

and renewable energy, 54
and temperatures, 37, 39–40, 55
Carey, John, 176n32
Carius, Alexander, 199n77
Carlsen, Magnus, 189n10
Carlsen, Magnus, 189n10
Carter, Ash, 166
Carter, Sarah R., 178n63
Casanovas-Massana, Arnau, 177n50
Castilho, Carolina, 179n13
Cataclysm Sentence, The, 157
Catastrophic risks, 2–4, 158. See also Arti-
    ficial intelligence; Climate change;
    Existential risks; Long-term risks;
    Nuclear weapons; Pandemics
    and anthropogenic risks, 100
    and everyday risks, 4, 100
    increase over time, 4–5
    insuring against, 160
    and politics, 14, 101–102, 160
    and populism, 128
    reducing, 12
Catastrophic weather, 44
Center for Systemic Peace, 205n1
Centers for Disease Control and Preven-
    tion (CDC), 28, 123
Challinor, Andrew J., 183nn56–58
Chan, Brooke, 188n5
Chan, Minnie, 187n29
Chancel, Lucas, 196n31
Chandler, Mark A., 184n66
Chase, Allan, 192n13
Chatterjee, Monalisa, 183nn56–58
Chávez, Hugo, 131, 133, 139
Che, Xiaoyu, 175n19
Chen, Jing M., 184n75
Cheney, Dick, 166
Cheng, Vincent C. C., 201n104
Chess computers, 76
Chetty, Raj, 196n32, 197n47
Cheung, Vicki, 188n5
Chhetri, Netra, 183n57
China, 22, 70, 124–125, 141
Chou, Jimmy, 73

Christensen, Jens Hesselbjerg, 182n43
Christensen, Peter, 180n24
Christidis, Nikolaos, 181n33
Christie, Chris, 104
Churchill, Winston, 154
Cicero, Anita, 177n47
Ćirković, Milan, 172nn13–14, 192nn14–15, 208n4
Citizenship, 154
Civics education, 154
Civil conflict, 49
Clack, Christopher T. M., 185n79
Clade X, 17
Clark, Jack, 189n14, 191n32
Clarke, Arthur C., 79
Climate Action Tracker, 184n73
Climate change, 12–13, 36–56. *See also* Carbon emissions; Global warming
    Amazon rainforest, 38–39, 53
    Arctic peat fires, 39
    and average temperatures, 37, 42–43
    and catastrophic risk, 39–40, 49
    and civil conflict, 49
    climatic zones, 36–37
    and crime, 48
    extreme weather, 43–46
    greenhouse effect, 37, 50–51
    ice sheet melting, 38, 46–47
    impacts of, 53–54
    international agreements, 52, 56
    and migration, 43
    modeling, 42
    and nuclear war, 101
    and pandemics, 101
    and populists, 118
    probabilities, 40–41
    reducing risk of, 161
    sea levels, 47–48
    skeptics, 51–52
    and weather, 51
    wildfires, 44–45
Climate sensitivity factor, 40
Climate Shock, 38

Clinton, Bill, 25
Clinton, Hillary, 105, 111, 115, 198n66
Coal power, 54
CoastRunners, 78
Coats, Daniel R., 176n43
Cobra Event, The, 25
Cochrane, Kevern, 183nn56–58
Cockell, Charles S., 172n6
Coffel, Ethan, 180n26
Coggin, John, 193n2
Cohen, William, 152
Coles, L. Stephen, 191n31
Collins, Gareth, 192n9
Columbian Exchange, 19
Columbus, Christopher, 19
Combat death, 95, 97
Command-destruct mechanisms, 71
Common colds, 20
Common good principle, 86
Communism, 108
Compassion for suffering, 9
Compulsory voting, 147–148
Computer learning, 73–74. *See also* Artificial intelligence
Connor, Phillip, 198n71
Conspiracy theories, 120–121
Contagion, 22
Contagiousness, 26–28
Corbyn, Jeremy, 105–106, 194n6
Cordner, Alissa, 201n105
Coronaviruses, 20–21
Cosmopolitanism, 15–16
Costa, Flávia, 179n13
Cotton-Barratt, Owen, 171n3
Coughlin, Charles, 104
Counsell, Chelsie W. W., 180n25
Coups, 131
Courage, 163
Coutinho, Alexandra, 171n5
Couzens, James, 204n34
COVID-19 pandemic, 18, 20, 167
    and authoritarianism, 136
    death toll, 21

COVID-19 pandemic (cont.)
  economic cost of, 21
  and export controls, 125
  and health care system, 29, 124
  and social change, 11–12
  spread of, 21–22
  and technology, 12
  tracking, 28–29
  and Trump administration, 123
  vaccine opposition, 119–120
  warnings of, 123
C programming language, 80
Cretaceous-Paleogene extinction, 50
Crime, 48–49
Crimmins, Allison, 185n78
Crop failures, 48, 65
Crowcroft, Natasha S., 174n12, 176n46
Crowley, Michael, 201n109
Cruz, Ted, 90, 104
Cuba, 131
Cuban missile crisis of 1962, 58
Culture wars, 126, 138–139

da Silva, Luiz Inácio (Lula), 108
Daesh (ISIS), 66
Dafoe, Allan, 190n29
Daley, David, 150, 207n25
Dark Winter scenario, 17–18
Dassonneville, Ruth, 197n53
Daszak, Peter, 175n20, 175n22, 175n25
Day After, The, 13
Dead Hand, 70–71
DeAngelo, Benjamin, 181n35
Death Valley, 35
Debernard, Jens Boldingh, 182n50
Debiak, Przemyslaw, 188n5
De Dios, Víctor Resco, 181n38
Deeks, Shelley L., 174n12, 176n46
Deep Impact, 89
Deforestation, 39, 53
De Freitas, Nando, 188n5
Dekker, Evelien, 182n50
Deliberation Day, 154

Democracies, 14–15, 129–143
  and authoritarian indicators, 137–139
  coups, 131
  and cynicism, 135–136
  and education, 154
  erosion of, 131–134, 142–143
  and fascism, 130
  flawed, 135
  hybrid regimes, 131, 134
  international cooperation, 150–151
  merits of, 154–156
  and nativism, 139–140
  and Nazism, 129–130
  and party outsiders, 141
  and party protections, 151–152
  and populism, 134–137
  strengthening, 162–163
  and technology, 141
  and voting rights, 142
  weak/healthy, 137
Democracy Index, 131, 134
Democratic Party, 111–112
Demographics, 117
De Mosca, Itza B., 193n23
Dennison, Christy, 188n5
De Oliveira, Gabriel, 184n75
Desikan, Anita, 199n75
Desilver, Drew, 209n19
De Villers, J. W., 187n22
Devonian extinction, 50
Diamond, Larry, 134, 137, 204n27
Diedhiou, Arona, 182n43
DiEuliis, Dianne, 178n63
Dimson, Elroy, 172n8
Disaster films, 2–3
Disasters
  cost of, 45
  and social change, 11
Discount rates, 7–8
Diseases. See Infectious diseases
Ditlevsen, Peter, 182n43
Diversity, 140

DNA synthesis, 31–32
Dr. Strangelove, 60
Doherty, Sarah, 181n35
Dokken, David J., 181n39, 183nn56–58
Doomsday Clock, 2
Doomsday scenarios, 14
Dorn, David, 196n37
Dörr, Jakob, 182n50
Doughty, Caitlin, 157
Dousset, Bénédicte, 180n25
Downie, Leonard Jr, 201n102
Dreier, Casey, 192n5
Drexler, K. Eric, 97
Driverless cars, 75
Droppo, Jasha, 188n5
Druckenmiller, Matthew L., 179n14
Druckman, James N., 192n7
Dual use research, 26, 32
Dubner, Rachel S., 176n41
Dunbar, Adam, 185n79
Duncan, Pamela, 200n91
Duterte, Rodrigo, 109, 120, 136
Dutta, Sunasir, 204n24
Dwyer, Gary S., 184n66

Ebola, 23, 27
Ecker, Ullrich, 204n31
Economist Intelligence Unit, 203n7, 203n20, 203nn16–18
Ecosystem failures, 95
Edlund, Hanna, 171n5
Educational spending, 112
Egalitarianism, 155
Elbeshbishi, Sarah, 200n95
Elections, constitutional, 137–138, 146–147. See also Democracies
Electoral college, 148
Electricity sector, 54
Electric vehicles, 55
Elites, 10, 103, 117–118
Ellsberg, Daniel, 67, 187n21
Elo scale, 76
Eltscher, Louis, 203n5

Emanuel, Kerry A., 182n44
Embury-Dennis, Tom, 201n110
Emissions. See Carbon emissions
Emmett, Ed, 45
Engelberg, Stephen, 175n28, 176n38
Environmental Data and Governance Initiative, 201n105
Environmental risks, 95–96
Epictetus, 163
Equine encephalitis, 23
Erdoğan, Recep Tayyip, 109, 116, 139
Eskridge, William N. Jr, 207n30
Esvelt, Kevin M., 32, 178n64
Etchemendy, John, 191n32
Ethics violations, 139
Eugenics, 95
Europe
  anti-vaccination sentiment, 119
  black death in, 18–19
  right-wing parties in, 110
European Union (EU)
  Brexit, 105–106
  climate change measures, 52–53, 118
  and populism, 124
Evans, Owain, 190n29
Evans, Richard, 202n1–2
Evenett, Simon J., 201n112
Event 201, 18
Everyday risks, 4, 91–95, 100
Ewango, Corneille E. N., 179n13
Existential risks, 159, 167. See also Catastrophic risks; Long-term risks; Populism
  anthropogenic, 95–97, 99–100
  asteroids, 90
  compounding, 100–101
  and everyday risks, 91–95
  fifth risk, 162
  natural hazards, 93–95
  Ord's probabilities, 91, 95–96, 100
  superintelligence, 96
Experts, 167
Extinction, species, 43, 50, 157, 167

Extinction risks, 3–4, 8, 49, 53. *See also* Existential risks
   and artificial intelligence, 82
   and carbon emissions, 50
   climate change, 95
   and environmental damage, 96
   nuclear war, 95
   Ord's estimate, 100
   pandemics, 96
Extreme weather, 43–46

Facial recognition technology, 151
Fahey, David W., 181n35, 181n39
Fairbrother, Malcolm, 201n103
Farhi, David, 188n5
Farquhar, Sebastian, 171n3
Fascism, 130
Fear, 165
Fearnley, Lyle, 175n24
Fearon, James D., 183n64
Fein, Steven, 183n61
Feinberg, R. B. Ayal, 197n52
Fermi, Enrico, 98
Fernandez, Elizabeth, 178n1
Ferry, Jeffrey, 196n34
Fertility rates, 95
Fetzer, Thiemo, 194n7
Fichera, Angelo, 173n1
Field, Christopher B., 183nn56–58, 183n64
Fifteenth Amendment of 1870, 145
Fifth risk, 162
Finucane, Melissa L., 192n8
Fire insurance, 159–160
Firschein, Oscar, 191n31
Fischler, Martin A., 191n31
Fisher, Erich M., 184n70
Fishkin, James S., 208n38
Fitbit, 29
Fitzgerald, Jennifer, 173n23
Five Cs Pentathlon, 76
Five Star Movement, 119
Fletcher, Martin, 194n10

Flooding, 46
Flores, Antonio, 206n10
Flu, seasonal, 20
Flynn, James, 192n8
Forbrook, Jason, 176n41
Ford, Henry, 141
Forest, James, J.F., 174n3
Formula One car racing, 100
Forster, E. M., 155, 208n43
Fossil fuel shortages, 95
Foust, Dean, 176n32
Fowler, Anthony, 206n13
Fraillon, Julian, 207n36
France, 119
Francis, Pope, 164
Frank, Peggy, 35
Franklin, Benjamin, 160
Franklin, Stan, 190n17
Frankovic, Kathy, 200n95
Frantz, Erica, 207n27
Frazer, Ian, 174n11
Fredrickson, Leif, 201n105
Freedom of press, 138
Freeman, Richard, 205n7
Friedman, John, 197n47
Friedman, Susan Hatters, 188n35
Friedman, Thomas L., 114, 198n64
Friedman, Tim, 207n36
Fryer-Biggs, Zachary, 204n28
Fuglestvedt, Jan S., 185n83
Fukuyama, Francis, 134, 200n99, 203n13, 203n15
Fuller, Dorian, 171n1
Funk, Cary, 200n90
Funke, Manuel, 196n39
Future generations, 6–9

G20 Human-Centered AI Principles, 85–86
Gaddhafi, Mu'ammar, 63
Gaffney, Owen, 179n10, 179n12
Gain-of-function research, 30
Galloway, Scott, 28, 177n49

Game theory, 60
Gamma rays, 94
Gandhi, Indira, 107
Gans, Joshua, 83, 189n13
Garner, Andra J., 182n44
Gates, Bill, 18, 84
Gatze, Michael G., 175n21
Gauthier, Nicolas, 171n1
Gayle, Albert A., 174n13
Gebrekidan, Selam, 204n23
Gelfand, Isabella, 197n53
Gelman, Andrew, 206n15
Gene editing, 25–26
Genetic evolution, 77
Genome sequencing, 25
Gent, Edd, 176n40
Geoengineering, 97
Geo Risks Research, 181n34
Germany, 145
Germ games, 17
Germ warfare, 24
Geronimo, Rollan C., 180n25
Gerrymandering, 149–150
Ghose, Soumya, 188n5
Gilligan, Danny, 191n39
Gillingham, Kenneth, 180n24
Glaeser, Edward L., 114, 198n57
Gleick, James, 157
Glikson, Andrew, 179n14, 184n68
Global Challenges Foundation, 192n16
Global climate modeling, 42
Global Partnership on Artificial Intelligence, 85
Global warming, 37, 56. *See also* Climate change; Temperatures
  and average temperature increase, 37, 42
  and carbon emissions, 55
  and climate volatility, 44
  and crop failures, 48
  probabilities, 40–41
  and sea levels, 47, 49–50
  storms and floods, 45–46
  and uncertainty, 38

  and violence, 49
Go (game), 74, 76
Goertzel, Ben, 76, 190n17
Gohlke, Julia M., 183n60
Golden Rule, 158–159
Good, Irving, 77, 189n12
Goodell, Jeff, 47, 182n53
Goodfellow, Ian J., 188n5
Google, 74–75
Gopinath, Gita, 174n14
Gopnik, Alison, 157
Gore, Al, 207n24
Gowtage-Sequeria, Sonya, 175n17
Gozgor, Giray, 198n65
Grace, Katja, 190n29
Gray goo scenario, 97
Great Migration, 45
Greaves, Jane S., 172n6
Greaves, Mark, 190n22
Greene, Jeremy A., 174n9
Greene, Marjorie Taylor, 121
Greenhouse effect, 37, 50–51
Greenhouse gases, 39, 50, 55
Greig, Denise J., 175n19
Gribble, James N., 174n10
Grillo, Edoardo, 61, 186n7
Grinsted, Aslak, 182n43
Grofman, Bernard, 206n21
Gronvall, Gigi Kwik, 176n35, 177n47, 178n63
Grose, Christian, 207n23
Gross, Daniel, 196n42
Grosz, Barbara, 191n32
Grubaugh, Nathan D., 177n50
Grusky, David, 196n32
Grzymala-Busse, Anna, 200n99
Guerra, Fiona M., 174n12, 176n46
Guez, Arthur, 189n6, 189nn10–11
Guim, Mauricio, 203n19
Guirguis, Marilyn, 203n19
Günther, Torsten, 171n5
Guo, Daniel, 189n5
Gurr, Ted, 205n1

Haberman, Maggie, 200n92
Hacker, Jacob S., 105, 193n5, 206n19
Haidt, Jonathan, 194n7, 204n33
Hall, Timothy, 181n39
Hallinan, Conn, 187n34
Halpin, John, 199n73
Halstead, John, 171n3
Handfield, Toby, 172n13
Handmaid's Tale, The, 140
Hanley, Brian, 173n3, 174n8
Hansen, James, 37, 184n69
Hanson, Gordon, 196n37
Hantavirus pulmonary syndrome, 101
Harmon, Katherine, 177n47
Harris, John, 174n6
Hart, Paul 't, 202n121
Hastie, Trevor, 178n2
Hastings, Max, 196n43
Hate crimes, 113
Hauer, Mathew E., 181n40
Haverinen-Shaughnessy, Ulla, 183n61
Hay, Simon I., 176n45
Hayhoe, Katharine, 51, 181n35, 184n71
Health care reserves, 29
Heat index, 42–43
Heatstroke, 36
Heat waves, 36
Heffernan, Jane, 174n12, 176n46
Hefferon, Meg, 200n90
Hell, Maximilian, 196n32
Hendren, Nathaniel, 196n32
Hendrix, Cullen, 184n64
Heneghan, Conor, 177n52
Herring, Stephanie C., 181n33
Herron, Michael, 207n24
Hersh, Eitan, 153, 207n34
Hervey, Ginger, 194n8
Hessler, Peter, 175n20
Hibbard, Kathy A., 181n35, 181n39
Hicks, Allison L., 175n19
Higgins, Andrew, 203n21
Hill, Dave, 194n14
Hindu nationalism, 107

Hiroshima, 65
Hitler, Adolf, 129–130, 133, 151
HIV/AIDS, 24
Hockett, Robert C., 196n34
Hodges, Andrew, 189n9
Hoegh-Guldberg, Ove, 182n43
Hoekstra, Mark, 205n9
Hoell, Andrew, 181n33
Hoerling, Martin P., 181n33
Hofeller, Thomas, 149
Hogan, William W., 179n19
Home insurance, 159–160
Homo sapiens, 5–6, 114. *See also* Human species
Honeybees, 95–96
Hooghe, Marc, 197n53
Hopkins, Claire, 177n51
Horley, Timothy, 203n19
Horsepox, 26
Horton, Benjamin P., 182n44
Horton, Radley M., 180n26, 180n28, 181n35
Howard, Philip N., 173n17
Howard, Richard, 186n6
How Democracies Die, 131
Howden, S. Mark, 183nn56–58
Hoy, Chris, 174n15
Hsiang, Solomon M., 183n62
Hsu, Karen J., 176n41
Huang, Aja, 11, 189n6
Huang, Ally, 176n41
Huang, Kristin, 187n29
Huang, Xuedong, 188n5
Huber, Robert A., 199n78
Hubert, Thomas, 10–11, 189n6
Hugenberg, Alfred, 129
Human Genome Project Information Archive, 176n39
Human life, value of, 8
Human species
   ancestors, 5–6
   destruction of, 3
   future generations, 6–9

genetic evolution, 77
lifespan, 5–6
Humidity, 36
Hungary, 122, 135–136, 139
Hunger, 109
Hurricane Harvey, 45, 51
Hurricane Isaiah (fictional model), 46
Hurricane Katrina, 45
Hurricane Maria, 45
Hurricane Michael, 45
Hurricanes, 45–46, 51
Hussein, Saddam, 23
Hydrogen bombs, 65
Hypercanes, 46

Ibarz, Julian, 188n5
Icebergs, 46–47
Iceland, 19
Ice sheet melting, 38
IEEE Global Initiative on Ethics of
    Autonomous and Intelligent Systems,
    190n24
Ienca, Marcello, 191n37
Ignatieff, Michael, 152, 207n33
Iliopoulos, John, 193n21
Improvisation, 165
India
  Modi government, 106–107, 136
  nuclear weapons, 70, 101
  and Pakistan, 62
Indonesia, 107–108, 120
Inequality, 105, 116
Infectious diseases, 11, 17–34. *See also*
    COVID-19 pandemic
  animal viruses, 21
  and bioengineering, 28, 31
  and biological weapons, 22–24
  and bioterrorism, 18, 24, 26, 30
  coronaviruses, 20–21
  deadliness and contagiousness, 26–28
  detection and control of, 28–29
  and DNA synthesis, 31–32
  and dual use research, 26, 32

and gene editing, 25–26
historical treatments, 32
and laboratory safety, 30–31
mortality from, 19–20
new, 22
and pathogen screening, 31–32
and permafrost, 101
rhinoviruses, 20
and surge capacity, 29
and synthetic biology, 25
Influenza, 19–20
Influenza pandemic of 1918, 19
Innovation + Equality, 83
Institute for Science and International
    Security, 186n17
Insurance, 159–160
Insurance Information Institute,
    208nn7–8
Intergovernmental Panel on Climate
    Change (IPCC), 37, 85
Internationalist Egalitarians, 105, 112
Internationalist Libertarians, 105,
    111–112
International Panel on Artificial Intel-
    ligence, 85
International trade, 125
Ipsos, 204n32
Iqbal, Muhammad Mohsin, 183nn56–58
Iran, 64, 68
Iraqi germ weapons, 23
Ireland, 112
Irenic striving, 117, 126
ISIS, 66
Israel, 62, 151
Italy, 119

Jackson, Andrew, 189n7
Jacob, Daniela, 182n43
Jaffe, Cale, 199n76
Jambor, Ivan, 188n5
Japan, 145
Jardine, Roger, 187n22
Jefferson, Cord, 157

Jefferson, Thomas, 145–146, 205n3
Jeffries, Martin O., 179n14
Jetter, Michael, 204n31
Jinseo, Shin, 189n11
Jobin, Anna, 191n37
Jobs, 109–110, 117
Johns Hopkins Center for Health Security, 17–18, 177n47
Johnson, Boris, 105–106, 109, 111, 116, 120, 194nn10–11
Johnson, Christine K., 175n19
Johnson, Courtney, 200n90
Johnson, Lyndon, 132
Jokowi, 107
Jones, David S., 174n9
Journalism, 123
Junk news, 10
Jupiter, 89
Justice, 163

Kaczyński, Lech, 109
Kalmoe, Nathan P., 202n119
Kaltwasser, Christóbel Rovira, 173n18
Kanno-Youngs, Zolan, 122, 200n98
Kaplan, Edward H., 177n50
Kapor, Mitch, 79
Kapturowski, Steven, 189n5
Kardashian, Kim, 44
Kasparov, Garry, 76
Kaul, Susanne, 173n15
Kay, Andrea, 171n1
Kazakhstan, 63
Kelly, Meg, 202n116
Kendall-Taylor, Andrea, 207n27
Kenedi, Christopher, 188n35
Kenna, Maryn, 177n53
Kennedy, Brian, 185n86, 200n90
Kennedy, John F., 165, 209n16
Kennedy, Jonathan, 199n81
Kenrick, Douglas T., 183n61
Kershaw, Ian, 202n3
Kessler, Glenn, 202n116
Khaleghi, Amir, 196n34

Khan, A. Q., 63, 66
Khan, Jo, 174n11
Khorrami, Mohammadhadi, 188n5
Kim, David, 173n15
Kim, Dong, 73
Kim Jong-un, 63
Kimmelman, Michael, 181n39
King Midas problem, 77–78, 84
Kinney, Patrick L., 180n28
Kinsella, Bret, 198n63
Kirby, Jen, 195n26
Kirchner, Cristina Fernández de, 109
Kirkpatrick, David D., 201n111
Kissinger, Henry, 69
Kitsutani, Paul T., 193n23
Klein, Ezra, 117, 199nn73–74, 206n15
Klotz, Lynn, 178n57, 178n60
Knutson, Thomas, 181n39
Knutti, Reto, 184n70
Ko, Albert I., 177n50
Kocieniewski, David, 190n16
Kohler, Timothy A., 179n5
Kolesnikov, Mikhail, 57
Kopp, Robert E., 182n44
Koppa, Vijetha, 205n9
Korth, Marcus J., 175n21
Kossin, James P., 181n39
Kraan, Caroline M., 183n64
Kramer, Sarah, 175n19
Kratsios, Michael, 126, 202n115
Kremp, Pierre-Antoine, 206n15
Ku Klux Klan, 142
Kunkel, Kenneth E., 181n39
Kuo, Didi, 200n99
Kupferschmidt, Kai, 176n44
Kurlantzick, Joshua, 195n21, 195n23
Kyle, Jordan, 136–137, 204n25
Kyoto Protocol of 1997, 52

Lab-bred pandemics, 96
Laboratory safety, 30–31
Lai, Matthew, 189n10
Lamothe, Dan, 186n5

Lanctot, Marc, 189n10
Langsdorf, Martyl, 171n2
Lanier, Jaron, 80, 190n21
Lankester, Joanna, 178n2
Large Hadron Collider, 13–14, 99
Larrick, Richard P., 183n61
Latin America, 103
Lau, Susanna K. P., 201n104
Launch on warning policy, 71
Laurance, William F., 184n75
Law, G. Lynn, 175n21
Lazar, Seth, 172n12
Leahy, Joe, 198n68
Lederberg, Joshua, 22
Lee, Adam, 208n3
Lee, Michelle Ye Hee, 202n116
Lee-Taylor, Julia, 186n15
Left-wing political parties, 103–104, 110,
    112, 117
Lehrer, Tom, 62, 186n8
Leigh, Andrew, 173n21, 207n26
Lenin, Vladimir, 103
Lenton, Timothy M., 179n5, 179n10,
    179n12
Le Pen, Jean-Marie, 116
Levermann, Anders, 182n47
Levitsky, Steven, 131–132, 134, 137, 141,
    151, 202n1, 203n6, 203n8, 203n12,
    204n27, 204n34, 207n29
Levitz, Eric, 196n35
Lewandowsky, Stephan, 204n31
Lewis, Gregory, 32, 177n56, 177n65,
    178n65
Lewis, Jeffrey, 207n24
Lewis, Michael, 121, 162, 200n96, 208n9
Lewis, Paul, 200n91
Lewis, Simon L., 179n13
Ley, Catherine, 178n2
Li, Tiantian, 180n28
Li, Ye, 174n12, 176n46
Libratus, 73
Liebreich, Michael, 185n80
Lightning strikes, 95

Lim, Gillian, 174n12, 176n46
Limbaugh, Rush, 128
Lin, Ning, 182n44
Lindbergh, Charles, 141
Linz, Juan, 137, 204n27
Littell, Jeremy S., 181n37
Liu, Ying, 174n13
Lobell, David B., 183nn56–58
Loeb, Walter, 198n62
Loebner Prize, 75
Long-term risks, 167. *See also* Cata-
    strophic risks; Existential risks
    and coronavirus pandemic, 12
    insuring against, 15
    and populism, 10, 14, 117–118, 123,
    127
López, Gustavo, 206n10
Losito, Bruno, 207n36
Lugar, Richard, 127, 166
Lukashenko, Alexander, 109
Lula, 108
Lund, Marianne T., 185n83
Luntz, Frank, 111
Lustgarden, Abrahm, 175n18, 181n41,
    193n23
Lynas, Mark, 42, 51, 180n22, 183n55,
    184n69
Lynteris, Christos, 175n24
Lyons, Leonard, 208n5
Lyons, Linda, 171n4
Lyons, Terah, 191n32

MacAskill, William, 8, 158, 172n11,
    208n2
MacDonald, Alexander E., 185n79
MacFarlane, Steven W., 183n61
Mach, Katharine J., 183nn56–58, 183n64
Machine learning, 73–74
MacKinnon, Linda C., 177n54
Macron, Emmanuel, 85
Macwilliams, Matthew, 197n53
Madsen, J., 193n21
Maduro, Nicolás, 109, 131

Mahan, Erin R., 177n55
Mainstream political parties, 111–112
Majlesi, Kaveh, 196n37
Malaysia, 125
Maldives, 47
Mallonee, Laura, 182n49
Malmendier, Ulrike, 173n20
Malmström, Helena, 171n5
Manduca, Robert, 196n32
Manhattan Project, 67
Manhattan Project II, 67, 72, 161
Mann, Michael E., 182n44
Mann, Thomas, 129
Manning, Preston, 116
Marcos, Ferdinand, 132–133, 139
Marcos, Imelda, 133
Marcus, Robert, 192n9
Marcus Aurelius, 163–164
Mares, Dennis M., 183n59
Marital fidelity, 97
Market strategies, 160
Marsh, Paul, 172n8
Marshall, Monty G., 205n1, 205n4
Marshalla, Suzanne, 176n41
Marston, Robert Q., 188n36
Martinich, Jeremy, 185n78
Marwick, Ben, 171n1
Mashal, Mujib, 195n18
Mason, Ben G., 192n10
Mason, Lilliana, 202n119
Masson-Delmotte, Valérie, 182n43,
    182n46, 182n52, 182n54
Masters, Jeff, 51
Mastrandrea, Michael D., 183nn56–58
Maycock, Thomas K., 181n39
McCain, John, 11
McCandless, David, 27
McCarthy, Joseph, 151–152
McCoy, Alfred W., 203n10
McCullough, David, 165, 209n14
McDonald, Michael, 205n6
McFaul, Michael, 135, 200n99
McNamara, Robert, 60

Meacham, David, 209n15
Meacham, Jon, 165
Measles, 27
Media cycle, 9
Medical exports, 125
Meinshausen, Nicolai, 184n70
Melosh, H. Jay, 192n9
Meng, Anne, 203n19
Meng, Kyle C., 183n62
Merchant Right, 112
Merkel, Angela, 121
MERS, 20
Mertz, Chris K., 192n8
Meserole, Chris, 207n28
Meteorological events. See Weather
Metz, Cade, 188n2
Meyer, Diane, 177n47
Michie, Donald, 191n31
Mickey, Robert, 205n36
Mietzner, Marcus, 195n19
Migration, 43, 45
Mijares, Primitivo, 203n9
Mildenberger, Matto, 192n13
Miller, Alice Duer, 155, 208n42
Miller, James, 187n31
Miller, Judith, 175n28, 176n38
Miller, Peter, 182n45
Mills, Michael J., 186n15
Mintenbeck, Katja, 52, 54, 182n46
Missile interceptor systems, 61
Mississippi, 142
Moderation, 163–164
Modi, Narendra, 106–107, 109, 136
Moffett, Kenneth W., 183n59
Montzka, Stephen A., 179n17
Mora, Camilo, 180n25
Morales, Evo, 109
Morens, David M., 175n22, 175n25
"More Who Die, the Less We Care,
    The," 9
Moritz, John C., 206n23
Morozov, Yuri, 187n19
Morrison, Scott, 111

Moses, Daniel, 188n5
Motorcycle riders, 95
Motor vehicle accidents, 95
Mounk, Yascha, 136–137, 204n25
Moutinho, Paulo, 184n75
Mowatt-Larssen, Rolf, 187n19
Moyes, Catherine L., 176n45
Mozambique, 134
Mudde, Cas, 173n18
Mullainathan, Sendhil, 127, 202n120
Mumps, 27
Munich Re, 181n34
Muñoz, Carlos, 193n23
Munroe, Randall, 189n15
Munters, Arielle R., 171n5
Murdoch, Rupert, 44
Muro, Mark, 185n78
Murphy, Thomas, VII, 79, 190n18
Musa, Mark, 173n2
Musk, Elon, 84, 158
Muslims, 106–107, 139–140
Mutually assured destruction (MAD),
    60–62, 64
Myre, Greg, 186n9

Nagasaki, 65
Nagel, Stefan, 173n20
Naidu, Suresh, 208n39
Nanotechnology, 97
Narang, Jimmy, 196n32
Narizny, Kevin, 205n2
NASA Planetary Defense Coordination
    Office, 90
Nashville, 46
Natarajan, Aravind, 177n52
NatCatSERVICE, 181n34
Nathanson, Neal, 175n21
National Academies of Sciences, Engi-
    neering, and Medicine, 185n84
National Assessment of Educational
    Progress, 207n35
National Centre for Health Statistics,
    171n3

National Conference of State Legislators,
    205n8, 206n18
National Popular Vote Interstate Com-
    pact, 148–149
National Rally party, 119
National Research Council, 178n59
Native Americans, 19
NATO (North Atlantic Treaty Organiza-
    tion), 63, 124
Natural hazards, 93–94
Nazareno, Alison G., 184n75
Nazism, 130
Nelson, Cassidy, 28
Nelson, Matthew, 207n23
Nepotism, 138
Netanyahu, Benjamin, 68, 109
"Never Gonna Give You Up," 63
News stories, 9–10
New York City, 46
Ng, Andrew, 79
Nicaragua, 131, 134
Nilsson, Nils John, 76
1984, 141, 161
Nineteenth Amendment of 1920, 145
Nixon, Richard, 70, 114, 152
Nixon administration, 30
No lone zones, 72
Nordhaus, William, 179–180n20, 180n24
Norm Chronicles, The, 93
North Korea, 63
North Pole sea ice, 46–47
Norwegian rocket launch, 58
Nost, Eric, 201n105
Notz, Dirk, 182nn50–51
Novel coronavirus simulation, 18
Novy, Dennis, 194n7
Nozick, Robert, 163
Nteta, Tatishe, 197n53
Nuclear deterrence, 60
Nuclear proliferation, 62–68
Nuclear war, 13, 101. *See also* Nuclear
    weapons
    and conventional war, 70

Nuclear war (cont.)
  and global temperatures, 65
  risks, 67, 72, 95
Nuclear weapons, 57–72, 161, 166
  and artificial intelligence, 101
  atomic/hydrogen bombs, 65, 98–99
  and civilian facilities, 64–65
  distribution of, 63–64
  first strike, 70
  giving up, 67–68
  launch authority, 69–72
  and mental illness, 71–72
  mutually assured destruction (MAD),
    60–62, 64
  proliferation of, 62–68
  protocols, 70–71
  reducing stockpiles, 68–69
  and terrorists, 66–67, 69
Nuclear winter, 65
Nunn, Nathan, 174n4
Nunn, Sam, 69, 127, 166
Nunn-Lugar Cooperative Threat Reduc-
    tion Program, 166–167
Nussbaum, Martha C. 15, 165, 173n24,
    209n13
Nuzzo, Jennifer B., 177n47

Obama, Barack, 66, 113, 187n18
Obersteiner, Michael, 184n76, 184n77
Ocean warming, 46
Odell, Jenny, 157
Office of Management and Budget,
    202n114
Okun, Andy, 189n7
O'Loughlin, John, 183n64
O'Malley-James, Jack, T., 172n6
Oman, Luke, 186n14
Omohundro, Stephen M., 78, 190n17
OpenAI's GPT-3, 74
Oppenheimer, Clive, 192nn10–12
Oppenheimer, Robert, 65
Orbán, Viktor, 109, 136, 139

Ord, Toby, 3, 25, 91, 95–96, 100, 172n10,
    177n56, 192n6
Ordovician-Silurian extinction, 50
Orenstein, Ronald, 175n23
Organisation for Economic Co-operation
    and Development, 85, 191n37
Orooji, Mahdi, 188n5
Ortega, Daniel, 109
Ortiz-Juarez, Eduardo, 174n15
Orwell, George, 15, 141, 161, 173n25
Overpopulation, 95
Ozone pollution, 43

Pace of change, 114–115, 117
Page, Susan, 200n95
Pahwa, Shivani, 188n5
Pakistan, 62–63, 66, 101
Palin, Sarah, 122
Panagiotidis, Theodore, 196n38
Panama, 101
Pan-American Health Organization, 124
Pandemics, 12, 96, 101, 123, 161. *See also*
    COVID-19 pandemic
Pantoja, Adrian, 199n73
Papen, Franz von, 129
Paradise, CA, 44
Paris Agreement of 2015, 52
Parker, Janet, 178n58
Parker, Kim, 201n101
Parsonnet, Julie, 178n2
Particle colliders, 13–14, 99
Patel-Weynand, Toral, 181n37
Pathogen screening, 31–32
Patriotism, 125, 138
Peccia, Jordan, 177n50
Pedestrian accidents, 100
People vs Tech, The, 141
Pepinsky, Thomas, 195n19
Perfect world, 1–2
Permafrost releases, 101
Permian-Triassic extinction, 50
Permissive Action Links, 60

Perrault, Raymond, 191n32
Perry, William, 69
Perverse instantiation, 78, 84
Peterson, David L., 181n37
Peterson, Jordan, 207n23
Petroff, Alanna, 190n23
Petrov, Stanislav, 59
Pew Research Center, 194n17, 196n36, 197n55
Philippines, 120, 122, 132–133, 136, 139
Phoenix, Chris, 192n15
Photovoltaic cells, 54–55
Pierre-Louis, Kendra, 180n27, 184n74
Pierson, Paul, 105, 193n5, 206n19
Pigott, David M., 176n45
Piketty, Thomas, 112, 196n31, 197nn45–46, 197n49
Piot, Bilal, 189n5
Piper, Kelsey, 178nn61–62
Pipes, Richard, 193n1
Pirani, Anna, 182n43
Plato, 209n10
Pliocene epoch, 49–50
Plott, Eliana, 193nn3–4
Plot against America, The, 141
Plumer, Brad, 185n81
Podesta, John, 115
Podolsky, Scott H., 174n9
Poker, 73
Poland, 122
Polasky, Stephen, 184n76, 184n77
Political activism, 153–154
Politics. *See also* Democracies; Populism
    and anger, 164–165
    bipartisanship, 127, 166–167
    and catastrophic risks, 14, 101–102, 160
    centrists, 111–112
    of division, 126–127, 153
    and education, 154
    left-wing, 103–104, 110, 112, 117
    local, 153
    quadrants of, 105

    and racism, 114
    right-wing, 103–104, 110, 115–117
    stoic approach to, 164
    and "today" issues, 10
Poloczanska, Elvira, 182n46, 182n52, 182n54
Polyakova, Alina, 207n28
Pondiscio, Robert, 208n37
Popova, Maria, 158
Popper, Ben, 188n1
Populism, 10–11, 14–15, 103–128
    anti-intellectualism, 118
    Brazil, 108
    causes of, 109
    and centrists, 111
    and climate denial, 118
    and conspiracy theories, 120–121
    and constitutional elections, 137–138
    crisis response, 127–128
    and cultural offense, 117
    defining characteristic of, 103
    and democracy, 134–137
    and elites, 103, 117–118
    India, 106–107
    Indonesia, 107–108
    and institutions, 121–122
    and internationalism, 105, 124–125
    and jobs, 109–110, 117
    leaders of, 109
    left-wing, 103–104, 110
    and long-term threats, 10, 14, 117–118, 123, 127
    and luck, 115–116
    and mainstream media, 122–123
    plutocratic, 105
    and political quadrants, 105
    and racism, 113–114, 116, 125
    and Republican Party, 104–105
    right-wing, 103–104, 110, 115
    rise of, 108–109
    risks of, 142, 162
    and scientists, 118

Populism (cont.)
  slogans, 124
  stability of, 127
  technical and social change, 114–115, 117
  UK, 105–106, 111
  and universities, 122
  US, 104–106, 109, 111–112
  vaccine opposition, 119
  voter support for, 109, 111–112, 118, 120
Populist Egalitarians, 105
Populist Libertarians, 105, 111
Popvich, Nadja, 184n74
Porter, John Roy, 183nn56–58
Pörtner, Hans-Otto, 182n43, 182n46, 182n52, 182n54
Portney, Paul, 172n12
Posner, Richard, 172n13
Potter, Joshua D., 199n72
Powell, Enoch, 116
Powell, Farrah E., 180n25
Power, Thomas, 195n24
Prayut Chan-o-cha, 136
Precipice, The, 3
Precipitation, 38–39, 43–44
Preitner, Claud, 188n35
Presentism, 8
Presidential election of 2016, 115
Press, freedom of, 138
Preston, Richard, 25
Preston, Samuel H., 174n10
Program for Monitoring Emerging Diseases (ProMED), 29
Protsiv, Myroslava, 178n2
Proud Boys, 113
Prudence, 163
Pry, Peter Vincent, 185n1
Public health, 20
Puerto Rico, 147
Purnell, Sonia, 194n10, 196n43, 197n44
Putin, Vladimir, 109
Putnam, Robert D., 197n56

Pyle, David, M., 192n10
Pyroconvective events, 45

QAnon theory, 121
Qian, Nancy, 174n4
Quammen, David, 175n16

Racism, 113–114, 116, 125
RadioLab, 208n1
Ragsdale, Amy, 178n3
Rahmstorf, Stefan, 179n10, 179n12
Rainfall, 38–39, 43–44, 51
Rainforest, 38–39, 53
Rajiah, Prabhakar, 188n5
Rajneesh, Bhagwan Shree, 24
Rakshit, Sagar, 188n5
Ramos, Fernando M., 184n76, 184n77
Ranked-choice voting, 150
Rao, Hayagreeva, 204n24
Rat-transmitted disease, 101
Raven, John A., 172n6
Rawls, John, 163
Raymond, Colin, 180n26
RCP 8.5 scenario, 42
Reagan, Ronald, 61, 136
Recombinant biotechnology, 25
Redistricting, 149–150
Rees, Martin, 193n17
Reifman, Alan S., 183n61
Religious morality, 159
Renewable energy, 54–55
Reproduction ratio (R_0), 20
Republican Party, 10–11
  attitudes to political opponents, 126
  Trumpification of, 104–105, 117
  and university research, 122
Restaurant at the End of the Universe, The, 5
Restrepo, Pascual, 208n39
Retributive anger, 164
Revenge of the "Deplorables," 135
Reynolds, Elisabeth, 173n22
Rhinoviruses, 20
Rhodes, Ben, 193n24

Rhodes, Keith, 178n59
Richardson, Katherine, 179n10, 179n12
Richter, Felix, 198n60
Richter-Menge, Jacqueline, 179n14
Rick, Torben, 171n1
Riedel, Stefan, 175n27
Riess, Mitchell, 187n22
Right-wing political parties, 103–104,
    110, 115–117
Riley, Jason L., 197n54
Rio Earth Summit of 1992, 56
Risks. *See also* Catastrophic risks; Extinc-
    tion risks; Long-term risks
    air travel, 41–42
    anthropogenic, 95–97, 99–100
    artificial intelligence, 79–84
    asteroid strikes, 93
    environmental, 95–96
    everyday, 4, 91–95, 100
    gene editing, 26
    loss of wallet vs. burglary, 3
    nuclear war, 67, 72, 95
    of populism, 142
    reducing, 159–161
    and technology, 3
    world catastrophe, 2–4
Ritchie, Hannah, 195n30
Rizzo, Salvador, 202n116
Roberts, Debra C., 182n43, 182n46,
    182n52, 182n54
Robinson, Brent, 35
Robinson, James A., 208n39
Robock, Alan, 186nn14–15
Robots, laws for, 78
Rocklöv, Joacim, 174n13
Rockström, Johan, 179n10, 179n12
Rodden, Jonathan, 206n20
Rodriguez, Faith, 176n41
Rogers, Katie, 202n117
Romney, Mitt, 11
Roosevelt, Franklin D., 141
Rosenberg, Matthew, 200nn92–93
Roser, Max, 196n30

Ross, Graham, 193n21
Roston, Eric, 179n7
Roth, Kenneth, 122, 201n100
Roth, Philip, 141
Rothman, Daniel, 184n68
Rothman, David, 50
Roumanias, Costas, 196n38
Roy, Edmond, 195n18
Rubinoff, Morris, 189n12
Rubio, Marco, 104
Rueda, David, 197n50
Ruedas, Luis A., 193n23
Ruggiero, Greg, 187n21
Rumsfeld, Donald, 97
Russell, Stuart, 79, 84, 190n19, 190n26,
    191n35
Russia
    authoritarianism, 134
    nuclear weapons, 65, 69
Russian Revolution of 1917, 103
Russian roulette, 3, 100

Saad, Lydia, 198n59
Sabeti, Arram, 74
Sachs, Jeffrey, 199n83
Sadhwani, Sara, 207n23
Saez, Emmanuel, 196n31, 197n47
Sahulka, Stuart, 187n21
Salmonella, 24
Salvatier, John, 190n29
Samset, Bjørn H., 185n83
Sanchez, Aida Cuni, 179n13
Sanders, Bernie, 105
Sandholm, Tuomas, 188n4
Sanger, David, 187n27
Saradzhyan, Simon, 187n19
Sarin gas, 24
SARS, 20, 22
Satterfield, Theresa A., 192n8
Sauger, Nicolas, 206n21
Schaefer, K. E., 188n36
Schaeffer, Katherine, 198n58
Schaffner, Brian F., 197n51, 197n53

Schaller, Stella, 199n77
Scheffer, Marten, 37, 179n5
Schelling, Thomas, 172n12
Schellnhuber, Hans Joachim, 179n10, 179n12
Scherer, Glenn, 179n9
Schipani, Andres, 198n68
Schlebusch, Carina M., 171n5
Schlesinger, Jacob, 194n9
Schlosser, Eric, 71, 185nn3–4, 187n33, 193n18
Schoch-Spana, Monica, 177n47
Schonfeld, Bryan, 208n41, 209n11
Schrittwieser, Julian, 189n6, 189n10
Schubert, Stefan, 171n3
Schularick, Moritz, 196n39
Schulte, Peter, 191n2
Schulz, Wolfram, 207n36
Schwarzenegger, Arnold, 127
Scott, Mark, 194n8
Scranton, Roy, 182n48
Sea-based missiles, 60
Sea levels, 47–50
Seasonal flu, 20
Seide, Frank, 188n5
Sell, Tara Kirk, 177n47
Sellers, Christopher, 201n105, 201n108
Seltzer, Mike, 188n5
Sen, Amartya, 208n40
Seneca, 163
Shafir, Eldar, 127, 202n120
Sharpiegate, 118
Shaughnessy, Richard J., 183n61
Shet, Vinay, 188n5
Shillingford, Brendan, 188n5
Shinawatra, Thaksin and Yingluck, 109
Shiradkar, Rakesh, 188n5
Shoemaker-Levy 9 comet, 89
Shoham, Yoav, 191n32
Short selling, 160
Shukla, Priyadarshi R., 182n43
Shultz, George, 69
Siberian wildfires, 44

Sicknick, Brian, 139
Silver, David, 189n6, 189n10–11
Silver, Nate, 111
Simmons, Katie, 199n71
Simonite, Tom, 191n36
Simonyan, Karen, 189n6
Sinn Féin Party, 112
Sippel, Sebastian, 184n70
Six Degrees, 42
Sjödin, Per, 171n5
Skea, Jim, 182n43
Skocpol, Theda, 193n2
Skydiving, 96
Skynet, 141
Slovic, Paul, 9, 173n15, 192n8
Smallpox, 19, 23, 26
Smith, David L., 176n45
Smith, Margaret Chase, 152
Smoking, 96
Snyder-Beattie, Andrew, 171n3
Social democratic parties, 112
Social disruption, 114–115
Social media, 10
Solar photovoltaic power, 54–55
Solomon, Fred, 188n36
Sonderegger, Peter, 193n21
Sopoaga, Enele, 47
Soterroni, Aline C., 184n76, 184n77
South Africa, 63, 67
South America, 19
South Korea, 63, 125
Soviet Union, 23, 63
    Dead Hand, 70–71
    dissolution of, 166
    missile simulation of 1983, 59–60
    submarine incident of 1962, 58–59
Space exploration, 97
Specht, Hans J., 193n21
Species extinction, 43
Spektor, Mathias, 195n25
Spiegelhalter, David, 93, 180n21
Spielberg, Steven, 89
Spracklen, Dominick V., 179n11

Sprechmann, Pablo, 189n5
Springsteen, Bruce, 110
Stalin, Joseph, 159
Stanley-Becker, Isaac, 204n31
Stark, Jessica C., 176n41
Stark, Peter, 178n3
Stark, Scott C., 184n75
Stars, energy of, 94–95
Star Wars, 61
Staunton, Mike, 172n8
Steffen, Will, 179n10, 179n12
Stein, Jill, 115, 198n66
Steinhauer, Jennifer, 122, 200n98
Stellar explosions, 94–95
Stenchikov, Georgiy L., 186n14
Stenner, Karen, 140, 204n33
Stephens, Lucas, 171n1
Stern, Adi, 175n21
Stern, Nicholas, 100, 193n22
Stewart, Brooke C., 181n39
Stockholm International Peace Research
    Institute, 186n12
Stock market returns, 7–8
Stoicism, 15, 163–164
Stokes, Bruce, 198n71
Stolcke, Andreas, 188n5
Storms, 45–46
Stott, Peter A., 181n33
Strangelets, 99
Strategic Defense Initiative, 61
Stricker, Andrea, 186n13
Stroeve, Julienne, 182n51
Su, Hao-Wei, 177n52
Subianto, Prabowo, 107
Submarines, nuclear, 58–60, 72
Suffering, response to, 9
Sullivan, Martin J. P., 179n13
Sullivan, Patricia, 177n54
Summers, Anthony, 187n26
Sumner, Andy, 174n15
Superbugs, 25
Superintelligence, 13, 78–79, 96, 101,
    161. See also Artificial intelligence

Supervolcanoes, 93–94
Surda, Pavol, 177n51
Surge capacity, 29
Surveillance technologies, 141, 151,
    161–162
Survival of future generations, 9
Svenning, Jens-Christian, 179n5
Sweden, 151
Switzerland, 125
Synthetic biology, 25
Syria, 64
Székely, Enikőo, 184n70

Tallinn, Jaan, 84
Tambora volcano, 94
Tancer, Bill, 171n4
Tani, Maxwell, 196n40
Tansey, W. A., 188n36
Taubenberger, Jeffrey K., 175n22,
    175n25
Tausanovitch, Alex, 206n22
Tavits, Margit, 199n72
Tax code, 78
Taylor, C. M., 179n11
Taylor, Michael, 182n43
Tea Party, 104
Technology
    and catastrophic risk, 3
    and coronavirus pandemic, 12
    and democracy, 141
    surveillance, 141, 151, 161–162
Teehankee, Julio C., 200n88
Teixeira, Ruy, 199n73
Teller, Edward, 98
Temperatures. See also Climate change
    body, 35–36
    and carbon emissions, 37, 39–40, 55
    highest, 35
    increase in average, 37, 42–43
    niches, 36–37
    and nuclear war, 65
    and ozone pollution, 43
    and uncertainty, 38

Tenenbaum, Jay M., 191n31

Tenpas, Kathryn Dunn, 200n97

Terrell, Nick, 207n26

Terrorist groups, 66–67, 69

Tetris, 79

Thailand, 136

Tharoor, Ishaan, 203n14

Thawani, Rajat, 188n5

Thiel, Peter, 74

Thompson, Nicholas, 187n32

Thurmond, Strom, 104

Tierney, Dominic, 187n30

Tignor, Melinda, 52, 54, 182n46

Tinnin, David S., 193n23

Tobey, William H., 187n19

Toon, Owen B., 186n15

Totalitarianism, 96–97, 101, 130, 161. *See also* Authoritarianism

Total Perspective Vortex machine, 5

Townshend, Charles, 176n37

Trade, international, 125

Trapp, Robert J., 181n39

Travasso, Maria Isabel, 183nn56–58

Trebesch, Christoph, 196n39

Treder, Mike, 192n15

Triassic-Jurassic extinction, 50

Tropical cyclones, 45

Trudeau, Justin, 85

Trump, Donald, 10–11, 52–53, 68, 104–106, 109, 111–113, 115, 118–126, 135–136, 139

Trump administration, 121–123

Tsunamis, 94

Tucker, Jonathan B., 177n55

Tupaz, Edsel, 203n11

Turco, Richard, 65

Turing, Alan, 75–76

Turkey, 135, 139

Turner, Nicholas, 197n47

Tuvalu, 47

Two-person rule, 72

Tyson, Alec, 185n86

Ukraine, 63

Unborn, prejudice against, 8

Uncertainty, 38

Unemployment, 110

Union of Concerned Scientists, 187nn24–25

United Kingdom, 105–106, 111, 116, 145

United Nations Development Programme, 206n17

United States
and AI, 85
and authoritarian governments, 151
and biological weapons, 23, 30
climate change measures, 52–53
democracy in, 135, 142, 145–146
earnings in, 110
economic growth in, 109–110
educational spending, 112
health care, 123
infectious diseases in, 19
job growth, 110
laboratory safety, 30–31
medical instruments, 125
migration from coastlines, 45
nuclear stockpiles, 69
pace of change, 114–115
populism in, 104–106, 109, 111–112
rainfall measurement, 51
redistricting in, 149–150
suicide in, 110
war game alarm of 1979, 59
in WWII, 145

Unknown unknowns, 13–14, 97–99

Urban, Mark C., 180n31

Ursúa, José F., 174n7

US Army, 175n28

US Congress, 207n31, 209n19

USS *Randolph,* 59

Vaccines, 20, 119–120

Valdivia, Asuncion, 35

Vanunu, Mordechai, 62

Varros, Vicente R., 183nn56–58
Vasey, Daniel E., 174n5
Västfjäll, Daniel, 9, 173n15
Vayena, Effy, 191n37
Venezuela, 131–132, 135, 139
Venter, Craig, 25
Venus, 50–51
Verne, Jules, 60, 186n6
Versteeg, Mila, 203n19
Victor, David G., 185n78
Violence, political, 138
Virtues, Stoic, 163–164
Viruses, 20–22. See also Infectious diseases
Viswanath, Satish, 188n5
Vitvitskyi, Alex, 189n5
Vose, James M., 181n37
Voter identification laws, 146–147
Voting
  African Americans, 142, 145
  age, 146
  compulsory, 147–148
  and election day, 147
  electoral college, 148–149
  left-wing, 112
  participation, 146–147
  populist, 109, 111–112, 118, 120
  and racism, 113
  ranked-choice, 150
  and redistricting, 149–150
  women, 145
Voting Rights Act of 1965, 142, 145

Wagner, Daniel, 203n11
Wagner, Gernot, 38, 40, 42, 55, 179n8, 179n15, 179n19, 180n23, 183n61
Wagner, Patrick, 198n61
Waliser, Duane E., 181n39
Walker, Abigail, 177n51
Wallace, Chris, 123
Wallace, George, 104
Wallace-Wells, David, 44, 49, 54, 184n65, 184n67, 185n82

Walsh, Toby, 87, 191n40
Wang, Pei, 190n17
Warburton, Eve, 195n24
"War with Crazy Types," 61
Water conflicts, 49
Watergate, 152
Water Will Come, The, 47
Watson, Dougal, 188n35
Watson, Katy, 195n27
Watters, Kyle, 176n42
Watts, Jonathan, 179n6, 182n47
Wearables, 29
Weather, 43–46, 51
Wehner, Michael F., 181n39
Weisskopf, Victor, 98
Weitzman, Martin, 38–40, 42, 55, 179n8, 179nn15–16, 179n18, 180n23
Welch, Joseph, 207n31
Wells, Heather, 175n19
Wells, H. G., 97–98
Welzel, Christian, 202n118
Weng, Joanna, 174n7
Wenig, Erica, 186n13
West Antarctica ice sheet, 38
Wet markets, 21–22
Weyant, John, 172n12
Whiteson, Shimon, 188n5
Whiton, Jacob, 185n78
"Who's Next?," 62
Wiblin, Rob, 172n10
Widodo, Joko, 107, 109, 120, 195n20
Wier, Anthony, 186n16
Wike, Richard, 198n71
Wiki Government, 141
Wilczak, James, 185n79
Wilder-Smith, Annelies, 174n13
Wildfires, 44–45, 53
Wilkins, Kelly, 201n105
Williamson, Vanessa, 193n2, 197n53
Willis, Bruce, 89
Wilson, Edward, 185n2
Wilson, Judy M., 188n36

Wilson, Reid, 196n41
Wind and solar power, 54
Winter-Levy, Sam, 209n11
Women
  exclusion of, 164
  voters, 145
Woo, Patrick C. Y., 201n104
Wood, Jason D., 209n17
Woolhouse, Mark E. J., 175n17
"A World Free of Nuclear Weapons," 69
World Health Organization, 124, 174n10
Wozniak, Steve, 76, 84
Wright, Joseph, 207n27
Wright, Lawrence, 173n19
Wright, Oliver, 194n13
Wu, Connor Y. H., 183n60
Wuebbles, Donald J., 181n35, 181n39
Wuhan, 18

Xie, Liyong, 183nn56–58
Xie, Yuanfu, 185n79
Xiong, Wayne, 188n5
Xu, Chi, 179n5

Yagan, Danny, 197n47
Yasir, Sameer, 195n18
Yeltsin, Boris, 57–58
Yesin, Viktor I., 187n19
Yong, Ed, 201n107
Yu, Dong, 188n5
Yucatán Peninsula, 89
Yudkowsky, Eliezer, 9, 159, 172n14,
    173n16, 208n4
Yuen, Kwok Yung, 201n104

Zaitchik, Benjamin F., 183n60
Zhai, Panmao, 46, 52, 54, 182n43
Zhang, Baobao, 190n29
Zhuang, Juzhong, 172n9
Ziblatt, Daniel, 131–132, 134, 137, 141,
    151, 202n1, 203n4, 203n6, 203n8,
    203n12, 204n27, 204n34, 207n29

Zolotarev, Pavel S., 187n19
Zuckerberg, Mark, 80
Zucman, Gabriel, 196n31
Zulli, Alessandro, 177n50
Zuma, Jacob, 109
Zweig, Geoffrey, 188n5